The Churchill coalition and wartime politics

For S.M.J.

Kevin Jefferys

The Churchill coalition and wartime politics, 1940–1945

Manchester University Press

Manchester and New York

Distributed exclusively in the USA and Canada by St. Martin's Press

Copyright © Kevin Jefferys 1991, 1995

Published by Manchester University Press
Oxford Road, Manchester M13 9PL, UK
and Room 400, 175 Fifth Avenue,
New York, NY 10010, USA

*Distributed exclusively in the USA and Canada
by* St. Martin's Press, Inc.,
175 Fifth Avenue, New York, NY 10010, USA

British Library cataloguing in publication data
Jefferys, Kevin
   The Churchill coalition and wartime politics, 1940–1945.
   I. Title
   320.9

Library of Congress cataloging in publication data
Jefferys, Kevin.
   The Churchill coalition and wartime politics, 1940–1945/Kevin
Jefferys.
      p. cm.
   Includes bibliographical references (p.   ) and index.
   ISBN 0-7190-2559-1
   1. World War, 1939–1945 — Great Britain. 2. Churchill,
Winston, Sir, 1874–1965. 3. Great Britain — Politics and
government — 1936–1945. I. Title.
   D759.J44 1980
   940.53'41 — dc20

Paperback edition published 1995

ISBN 0 7190 2560 5 *paperback*

Typeset in Hong Kong by Best-set Typesetter Ltd.
Printed in Great Britain
by Biddles Limited, Guildford and King's Lynn

Contents

List of illustrations

Acknowledgements

I am very grateful to a variety of individuals and institutions for the help they have provided in the preparation of this study. Amongst those I should particularly like to mention, for help ranging from finding source material to reading draft chapters, are Stuart Ball, Stephen Brooke, Richard Cockett, John Grigg, Helen Jones, Rodney Lowe, John Ramsden, Andrew Thorpe, and John Turner.

I should like to thank the following both for their invaluable guidance and for allowing me to quote from copyright material in their possession: the Bodleian Library, Oxford (Simon papers, Selborne papers; Stokes papers – courtesy of Mr John Hull); Birmingham University Library (Neville Chamberlain papers); British Library of Political and Economic Science (Dalton diary); the Master, Fellows and Scholars of Churchill College in the University of Cambridge (Hankey papers); Durham Record Office (Headlam diaries); the trustees of the Beaverbrook Foundation and of the Clerk of the Records at the House of Lords (Beaverbrook and Lloyd George papers); Mass-Observation material reproduced by permission of the Trustees of the Mass-Observation Archive, University of Sussex; Reading University Library (Astor papers); the Master and Fellows of Trinity College, Cambridge (Butler papers); and the National Library of Wales (Griffiths papers).

I am also grateful to the Twenty-Seven Foundation for generously granting an award to meet the cost of reproducing the illustrations.

Needless to say, I alone remain ultimately responsible for the views expressed in what follows.

Preface to paperback edition

Few subjects have generated more controversy among contemporary historians than that of Britain's 'post-war consensus'. Did such a consensus really exist? If so, how might it be characterised? Did it represent a genuine convergence of opinion about the need for welfare reform and full employment? Or was it an artificial compromise dictated mainly by electoral calculation? When did the new dispensation first come into being? And why did the attachment to consensus apparently break down in the 1970s?

This book was first published in 1991 as a contribution to the debate about the origins of consensus politics during and after the Second World War. Two changes have been made in this new paperback edition. In the first place, the notes accompanying the introduction have been amended to take account of writings published since 1991. Secondly, a bibliographical update has been added to inform readers of recent developments in other aspects of wartime historiography, notably the 1945 general election.

In addition to those whose help has been recognised in the acknowledgements, I should like to thank Vanessa Graham at Manchester University Press for her assistance and timely encouragement.

K.J.
June 1995

Introduction

'The differences of opinion which separate us in this country, whether political or religious', said the Labour leader, Clement Attlee, in 1940, 'are like ditches when compared with the great gulf which separates us from Hitler and Mussolini.'[1] Attlee's comment upon the instinctive unity of the British nation in its struggle against the fascist powers has coloured many subsequent accounts of the Second World War, and helps to explain a certain neglect of the period by historians of British politics. Developments in British politics in those dramatic years between 1939 and 1945 have tended to be overshadowed, both by the military and diplomatic events that determined the outcome of the war, and by the striking social changes associated with the experience of a 'people's war'.[2] In addition, moreover, because the nation was led from 1940 onwards by a coalition government which brought together the major political parties, it has been easy to assume that party politics were suspended and effectively put on ice for the duration. Nor have the political consequences of the war occasioned much dispute. Whereas the first European war of 1914–18 has raised major questions of historical interpretation — above all on the issue of Liberal decline at the expense of the Labour party — the results of the Second World War appear much more clear-cut. In the first place, the war shattered a long spell of Conservative ascendancy. Neville Chamberlain, who led Britain into war as head of the Tory-dominated National government, was forced to give way in May 1940 to Winston Churchill's more broadly based coalition of Conservative and Labour forces. Churchill, of course, was to achieve lasting fame for his inspirational war leadership, but he was powerless to prevent an inexorable swing to the left in public opinion, the most tangible result of which was Labour's landslide victory at the 1945 general election. Simultaneously, the impact of 'total war' served to create an entirely new political agenda: by the time Attlee became Prime Minister, the stage had been set for the introduction of Britain's welfare state and mixed economy.

These themes lay at the heart of the only comprehensive study of wartime politics to date, Paul Addison's *The Road to 1945*, first published, thirty years after the cessation of hostilities, in 1975. For Addison, the influence of Labour ministers in the coalition made the government the most radical since Asquith's Liberal administration in the Edwardian period. The war, he argues, had a decisive effect on official opinion and clearly placed on the agenda the major items of the post-war welfare state: social security for all, a national health service, full employment policies, improved educational opportunities and a new system of family allowances. *The Road to 1945* also considers the impact of wartime changes on political opinion generally. In looking beyond the official world of Whitehall, Paul Addison claims that the war had equally important implications for the major political parties. At the hustings in the 1945 election, he notes, Conservative and Labour supporters alike committed themselves to the principles of social and economic reconstruction endorsed by their leaders as members of the wartime coalition. The circumstances of the war had thus produced a new middle ground upon which the parties would henceforth compete for political power. In contrast to the negative hostility of the inter-war years, there was now emerging between Conservative and Labour forces a common approach to welfare reform, a new and positive social policy 'consensus'. The war, in short, had in-augurated a distinct new era in British politics: the era of 'Attlee's consensus', later sustained by growing economic prosperity in the 1950s and popularly known as 'Butskellism'.[3] In his more recent writing, Paul Addison has qualified his use of the term 'consensus', preferring instead to speak of a 'postwar settlement'. At the same time, he has reinforced the idea of the war as a catalyst for change, extending his argument beyond high political agreement to claim that the years after 1940 provided an administrative framework for reform by transforming the civil service, while also initiating a trend towards 'corporatism' in the British economy.[4]

The performance of the British economy has latterly become prominent in the historiography of the war years in its own right. Keith Middlemas, for example, in his wide-ranging study of modern industrial politics, traces the origins of corporatism to

wartime circumstances; the product, he claims, of an alliance
between government, employers and trade unions, forged initially
to counter the Nazi menace but subsequently enshrined in the 1944
commitment to tackling unemployment.[5] This reading of the war
years also underpins Corelli Barnett's forceful polemic against
consensus and corporatism, *The Audit of War*. Britain's post-war
industrial decline, Barnett maintains, was rooted in the period
when Churchill's coalition, instead of giving priority to much-
needed economic regeneration, chose to focus on the creation of a
social miracle, a 'New Jerusalem', evangelised by a so-called motley
collection of misguided 'do-gooders'.[6] Butskellism — for better or
worse — has thus become a central theme in contemporary history,
though in more recent writing the whole notion of consensus as a
guiding principle in post-war politics has begun to be called into
question. In seeking to explain what looked like the breakdown of
Keynesian social democracy in the 1960s and 1970s, political
scientists have placed much emphasis on the persistence of class
antagonisms and the failure of government to establish satisfactory
working relations with organised producer groups.[7] This has left
them open to the charge that consensus itself is a misleading
concept; that the post-war settlement was always superficial and
vulnerable, a temporary compromise between hostile groups
rather than a genuine agreement about fundamentals. 'The British
post-war consensus', writes Ben Pimlott, 'could be defined, not
entirely flippantly, as the product of a consensus among historians
about those political ideas that should be regarded as important,
and hence to be used as touchstones of the consensus.'[8]

The aim of this study is to re-examine British politics during the
Second World War, and in the process to contribute to the debate
about the origins and significance of the post-war settlement. In
seeking to explain the major changes in the decade after
Chamberlain became Prime Minister, it has to be recognised that
concern with long-term domestic policy formed only one of several
threads in British politics. Until the end of 1942 the primary
concern of the political nation was with matters military; indeed, in
the desperate summer of 1940 simply resisting invasion was the
sole preoccupation. Hence, what follows falls into two distinct
halves. The early chapters focus mainly on developments in the
period when Britain remained militarily on the defensive: the events
that led to Chamberlain's downfall and the establishment of

coalition; Churchill's consolidation of power during the months of imminent invasion in 1940; the government's efforts to improve the effectiveness of the war economy; and the renewed criticism of the Prime Minister when British forces suffered a series of humiliating defeats in 1942. The 'turn of the tide' at the end of the year was to coincide with a sudden upsurge of interest in post-war reconstruction, stimulated above all by the publication of the Beveridge Report. Following this pattern of wartime developments, the second half of the book therefore switches to concentrate on post-war problems, dealing separately with the formulation of the government's reconstruction programme; the breakdown of co-operation in local politics; and the retreat from coalition after the D-Day landings of 1944. The final chapters go on to reconsider the significance of, and reasons for, Labour's victory in the 1945 election, and look forward to the reforms initiated by the post-war Attlee government.

What, then, are the major themes in what follows? In the first place, it will be suggested that the wartime swing to the left in political opinion was a complex, uneven process: the 'road to 1945' took many twists and turns. Labour's progress, culminating in the 1945 victory, clearly owed something to the prestige associated with participation in government after 1940. And in Ernest Bevin, who served at the Ministry of Labour, the party had found a figure of considerable force on the home front; by the end of the war he was in many respects second only in authority to Churchill himself. But other Labour leaders made much less of an impression on the public, and, like Bevin, found themselves continually beset by internal party wrangling. In particular, the desire of Labour activists for tangible evidence of the government's commitment to reconstruction placed constant pressure on ministers, and on occasions posed a serious threat to the unity of the coalition. If, as seemed possible at times during 1942–43, the coalition had broken up prematurely, then it was widely believed that Churchill's popularity, combined with the urgency of the military situation, would have ensured a repeat of Labour's 1931 humiliation. In the event, Labour's improved fortunes owed much to the fortuitous weakness of wartime Conservatism. The Tory party, as it turned out, proved unable to recover from the manner of Chamberlain's removal in May 1940. Many rank-and-file Conservatives found it difficult to reconcile themselves to their new leader, the arch antiappeaser of the 1930s; in turn, Churchill was disdainful both of the old Chamberlainite faction and of party matters in general. More important still, the Prime Minister — unlike the Labour party — missed the opportunity open to him after 1942 to forge a popular domestic political position, thereby helping to secure his own electoral fate. After the breakup of the coalition, Churchill made matters worse: his violent anti-socialist language during the 1945 campaign further alienated voters, and did nothing to convince the electorate that they were being asked to choose between agreed, consensual party programmes.

This leads directly to another central concern of this study, which is to challenge the notion of wartime consensus. The years after 1939, without doubt, created unprecedented demands for the creation of a new social order. Pressure for change emanated from a variety of sources: away from Westminster, the lead was taken by writers and intellectuals, by much of the national press and by specialist pressure groups. But such widespread pressure did not imply, and should not be confused with, the emergence of a new consensus between the political parties. Consensus — defined here as a historically unusual degree of agreement over a broad range of economic and social policies — did not, it will be argued, embrace the opposing front-bench teams by 1945, still less party stalwarts on the back-benches and in the constituencies.[9] The idea of the coalition as a radical, reforming ministry will be challenged by suggesting that the maintenance of agreement between Tory and Labour leaders was contingent upon agreeing to disagree. The government deliberately limited its areas of domestic activity, and on crucial issues where controversy threatened to erupt — such as over the future ownership of industry — conflict was avoided simply by postponing the matter under consideration. The coalition programme for reconstruction, moreover, remained very much at the planning stage. In spite of all the sound and fury, the Beveridge Report was not acted upon before 1945, and, apart from the 1944 Education Act and the introduction of family allowances, no major items of social legislation reached the statute book before the end of the war. The reason for this was clear-cut: it reflected, at base, intractable differences between the major coalition partners. The government, to a large extent, was incapable of proceeding beyond promises of reform. The white papers it produced were not intended as an inviolable guide to post-war policy, and were sufficiently ambiguous to allow of very different interpretations by opposing political leaders, as was evident in the run-up to the 1945 election. Britain's welfare state and mixed economy, in other words, were not cast in tablets of stone by the end of the war.

The Churchill coalition will thus be presented here as an administration with a dual identity. As Attlee implied in his comment early on in the war, political opinion on the left and right was unanimous in its desire to see Hitler defeated. But this did not mean that domestic differences ceased to exist; indeed, such disagreements soon began to resurface once the crisis of 1940–41 had passed. Some policy options were inevitably narrowed by wartime experience. But in practical, as well as ideological, terms, differences between the parties remained profound. Indeed, although the arguments had moved on, party activists were still in many ways as far apart as they had been before 1939. The Labour party, as we shall see, was able to sharpen its commitment to economic planning and welfare reform as the political tide ran in its direction. By contrast, mainstream Conservative opinion had grave doubts about both the feasibility and desirability of the New Jerusalem. Churchill's 'caretaker' government, which would have shaped post-war policy had it been elected in 1945, as many commentators expected, was ambiguous about many coalition proposals. For senior Tories, wartime proclamations were not seen as entailing binding commitments for the future. In the meantime, progressive elements in the parliamentary party were still in a minority. For the majority of Conservative opinion — anticipating electoral victory under a revered war leader — there was simply no need to contemplate anything more than a superficial revision of domestic policy. The incentive to consider a more far-reaching revision of the party programme came not during the war years: it was provided only after the shock of a crushing defeat at the polls in the summer of 1945.

Nineteen forty-five therefore stands out as a key turning point in modern British history. On the evidence presented here, there can be little doubt that a post-war administration led by Churchill would have pursued a very different course from that chosen by Attlee. It follows that the creation of the mixed economy and the welfare state — a system of universal benefits and services designed to provide security 'from the cradle to the grave' — cannot be seen simply as the working out of agreed wartime reforms; these developments were ultimately dependent upon the distinctive approach and aspirations of Attlee's government. Much of Labour's programme after 1945, it must be remembered, was fiercely contested at the time. The Conservative party was to vote against the introduction of the National Health Service in 1946, for example, and Tory MPs were hostile both to nationalisation and to the progressive, egalitarian taxation policies pursued immediately after the war. Hence, it would be mistaken to regard the British welfare state as the product of a consistent, linear process, stretching back through the war to the 'middle opinion' of the 1930s. The post-war settlement, the dispensation that was to preside for a generation to come, was the particular product of the 1940s, and its central features were forged after — and not before — the election of 1945. What the Second World War did was something rather different: it moved the electorate to the left in a manner unprecedented in twentieth-century politics, and it provided a theoretical basis for welfare reform of a sort that had been unimaginable when Neville Chamberlain became Prime Minister. The war, in short, made possible the creation of a brave new world; it did not make it certain.

Notes

1 The *Daily Herald*, 17 February 1940, cited in K. Harris, *Attlee*, London, 1982, pp. 181–2.
2 H. Pelling, *Britain and the Second World War*, London, 1970; A. Calder, *The People's War: Britain 1939–45*, London, 1969.
3 P. Addison, *The Road to 1945: British Politics and the Second World War*, London, 1975. Addison's work was the first to highlight some of the major arguments that raged between coalition ministers — for example, over the Beveridge Report and employment policy. This evidence does not, however, alter the central thesis of 'consensus', elaborated upon particularly in the conclusion of *The Road to 1945*.
4 P. Addison, 'The road from 1945', in P. Hennessy and A. Seldon (eds), *Ruling Performance: British Governments from Attlee to Thatcher*, London, 1987.
5 K. Middlemas, *Power, Competition and the State*, Vol. I: *Britain in Search of Balance, 1940–1961*, London, 1986.
6 C. Barnett, *The Audit of War: the Illusion and Reality of Britain as a Great Nation*, London, 1986. There are some significant differences of emphasis and tone in the work of Addison, Middlemas and Barnet, but they arguably share an implicit assumption that consensual, rather than

adversarial, politics were a central feature of the war years.

7 D. Marquand, *The Unprincipled Society: New Demands and Old Politics*, London, 1988.

8 B. Pimlott, 'The myth of consensus', in L. M. Smith (ed.), *The Making of Britain: Echoes of Greatness*, London, 1988. Pimlott's view is challenged in D. Kavanagh and P. Morris, *Consensus Politics from Attlee to Thatcher*, Oxford, 1989.

9 This definition is taken from a forthcoming article by Rodney Lowe, 'The Second World War, consensus and the foundation of the welfare state', in which the case for an 'elite consensus' developing after 1943 is argued. I am grateful to Dr Lowe for allowing me to see an advance copy.

1

The road to 1940

Why and how was the Churchill coalition formed? The outbreak of the Second World War in September 1939 dealt a severe blow to Neville Chamberlain, head of the National government, who had staked his reputation on concerted efforts to preserve European peace. When the so-called 'phoney war' came to an end in the spring of 1940, British military failure in Scandinavia provoked a domestic revolt. After the celebrated 'Norway debate' in the House of Commons, Chamberlain was forced to resign. In his stead, Winston Churchill formed a new coalition, a symbol of national unity, combining Conservative and Labour forces; this was to last for five years, until Britian finally secured victory over Nazi Germany. The change of government was to influence profoundly the whole course of wartime politics: providing an opportunity for Churchill to establish himself as the nation's great war hero; undermining the pre-war Tory domination of British politics; and marking a vital breakthrough for the Labour party, foreshadowing the election landslide of 1945. None of these consequences, though, was inevitable or easy to predict on the day that Churchill entered Downing Street, the same day that Hitler launched his blitzkrieg attack on Belgium and France. It was only much later, with the benefit of hindsight, that the importance of May 1940 as a turning point in the pattern of modern British politics could be fully appreciated.

And yet the historiography of this aspect of the war has always tended to treat the downfall of Chamberlain, and his replacement by Churchill, as unavoidable — a logical product of Britian's wartime experience. As the leader who fell from power, Chamberlain has often been presented unkindly: he was, according to one writer, by 1940 'an anachronism, an exhausted old man whose day had passed',[1] Churchill, conversely, has been seen as a man 'walking with destiny'; this, in fact, was a notion he himself originated in his influential memoirs on the war, though it has always retained a powerful appeal, not least in Churchill's official biography.[2] This chapter sets out to get behind these established viewpoints and to present the events of May 1940 in a fresh light. Here it will be argued that there was nothing inevitable about Chamberlain's fall from power, and that with slightly different handling he may well have survived the military failure in Norway. Similarly, it will be suggested that Churchill came to power not as the 'man of destiny', but rather because he proved most adept at exploiting what was an unexpected political crisis. The formation of Churchill's government, as we shall see, was the product of Chamberlain's specific failings during the phoney war, and came about in circumstances that were to leave a lasting legacy for coalition politics. In order to appreciate this, we must first look briefly at British politics before the war.

The Conservative party dominated British politics between the wars. With the exception of two minority Labour governments, which occupied a total of only three years, the Conservatives were continually in office — whether in their own right or as the dominant partner in a coalition — from the armistice in 1918 through to the outbreak of the Second World War. Tory electoral domination was based on an image of 'safety first': in the period of economic dislocation that followed the First World War, the party of Baldwin and Chamberlain offered a combination of sound financial methods and cautious social progress. The inter-war years were by no means barren of domestic reform: between periodic bouts of retrenchment, the state was increasingly driven to intervene in economic and social policy, and expenditure on the social services as a proportion of the gross domestic product continued to increase. But successive Conservative administrations showed little of the urgency associated with pre-1914 Liberalism. Above all, it was the persistence of mass unemployment that necessitated government intervention, primarily through a variety of insurance and assistance schemes. For the most part, though, orthodox Conservatism was resolutely opposed to major extensions of state power, and had little sympathy with the advocates of far-reaching change. As Jose Harris has observed:

Pressure for a comprehensive social welfare scheme — together with a full employment programme and corporatist planning — had begun in the early 1930s: but these demands had foundered not merely on practical grounds but on the much more philosophical ground that they would require central government to play a new and constitutionally illegitimate role in the direction of national life.[3]

Neville Chamberlain was the leading architect of domestic Tory policy before 1939. Contrary to the popular stereotype of an ineffectual old man with an umbrella, he was one of the most forceful Prime Ministers in modern British history. Chamberlain's authority stemmed in part from the circumstances he inherited from his predecessor, Stanley Baldwin, in May 1937. The Conservative-dominated National government had been re-elected in 1935 with a formidable majority, in excess of 200 parliamentary seats. In such circumstances, the government had to pay little heed to the concerns of the opposition Labour party, whose leader, Clement Attlee, was still regarded by many as a weak, transitional figure. Equally important to Chamberlain's domination, however, was his personal political style. By the time he became Prime Minister, Chamberlain had built up a considerable personal following among Tory loyalists. This was due not only to his widely acclaimed administrative ability, displayed in various high offices of state since the early 1920s, but also to his determination to lead from the front. Chamberlain set out to dictate government policy in a manner alien to Baldwin's more diffident style. Both in domestic and foreign affairs, Chamberlain provided a strong lead, enabling him in the process to establish personal ascendancy over the cabinet, the parliamentary party and local Conservative associations. The regard of rank-and-file Tories for their leader was further enhanced by his tough brand of partisan politics, which delighted in scoring points off the opposition. If Chamberlain never suffered fools gladly, then his greatest contempt had always been reserved for Labour MPs; they in return detested him with an intensity that was to continue until his death, in 1940.

This points us towards an important but neglected theme of British politics in the 1930s: the intensification of party hostilities during Chamberlain's premiership. In writings on the emergence of the post-war welfare state, much has been made of 'middle opinion' between the wars — progressive intellectuals, pressure groups and 'centre' politicians, it is often stressed, were already gaining ground with ideas that led inexorably to wholesale reform after the Second World War. But a brief survey of the political landscape after 1937 indicates, conversely, that 'middle opinion' was marginalised between two entrenched and polarised political viewpoints. Chamberlain was fond of proclaiming his commitment to welfare reform, though his approach as party leader suggests a vision of social change that had not progressed beyond the caution of the 1920s. The Prime Minister was determined to hold down the cost of unemployment benefit so as not to discourage the incentive to work; his emphasis on private sector house building precluded any large-scale construction of council housing for the poor; and raising the school-leaving age to fifteen was undermined by the provision of 'beneficial exemption' for those able to find suitable employment. Underpinning these reforms were the assumptions that welfare reform was primarily a matter of administrative logic — tackling issues only where obvious need arose — and that state interference should not be contemplated wherever it posed a threat to individual enterprise. In consequence, Chamberlain and his party were resolutely opposed to the reforms advocated in *Labour's Immediate Programme* of 1937. These included a national health service, a co-ordinated system of social insurance benefits and secondary education for all; the latter idea had been urged by the influential Spens Report of 1938, but was deliberately cold-shouldered by the government.[4]

Nor should the economic policies of the National government be seen simply as a series of *ad hoc* responses to the depression of the early 1930s. As Chancellor of the Exchequer since 1931, it was Chamberlain, in fact, who modified the Treasury's hitherto deflationary approach in order to allow a degree of positive intervention in the economy. This was aimed at improving not only the budgetary position but also the competitive power of British industry, with measures designed to increase profitability being central in the latter context. Such priorities help to explain why unemployment remained persistently high after Chamberlain became Prime Minister. He agreed with officials at the Treasury — the most powerful department in Whitehall — that greater profitability would be endangered by alternatives designed to reduce unemployment, which remained above 1.25 million in spite of Britian's rearmament programme.[5] The Treasury's whole strategy, moreover, militated against a more interventionist industrial policy to 'plan' the economy, and against the Keynesian concept of boosting demand by deficit-finance. 'Planning' was rejected not only on practical grounds but above all for ideological reasons: mainstream Conservative thinking in the 1930s remained resolutely committed to the free market economy. Chamberlain and his associates had little sympathy for 'middle opinion', which was itself less radical in many respects than Labour's economic thinking, as reshaped after the debacle of 1931 by Hugh Dalton and his colleagues.[6] The idea of a straightforward line of development from 'middle opinion' between the wars to acceptance of the mixed economy after 1945 must, therefore, be treated with caution. Chamberlain's domestic ambitions were not in the direction of what became known as the welfare state; he was an advocate of piecemeal, evolutionary reform, but he regarded any major extension of state power as both undesirable and unnecessary.

Domestic policy after 1937 was overshadowed, of course, by the prospect of war. Chamberlain's policy towards the European dictators has been the subject of intense scrutiny and controversy; here the intention is not to reconsider his whole foreign policy but rather to concentrate simply on showing that the origins of his fall and replacement by Churchill should not be sought in the pursuit of appeasement before 1939.[7] His domination of overseas policy before the outbreak of war was, in fact, as complete as his control of domestic affairs. The idea of combining increased rearmament with a search for general European peace — though shaped by Chamberlain and his senior cabinet colleagues, Lord Halifax, Samuel Hoare and Sir John Simon — met with widespread approval in party ranks. In spite of the controversy about the Munich settlement of September 1938, no local association registered any public protest against the concessions granted to Hitler in Czechoslovakia; indeed, several constituency parties were still expressing their approval of appeasement in the summer of 1939.[8] There were, naturally enough, sceptics in the Tory ranks. But such critics did not constitute a group of principled anti-appeasers, and their influence on policy remained negligible, at least until the beginning of the war.

Prominent among the critics was Anthony Eden, Chamberlain's initial choice as Foreign Secretary in 1937. Eden's resignation in early 1938, ostensibly over differences with Chamberlain about how far to conciliate Mussolini, was soon forgotten, however, after his replacement by a more senior party figure in Lord Halifax. As tensions increased with Hitler's support for the Sudeten Germans in Czechoslovakia, Eden was careful not to be seen openly criticising his former colleagues. In practice, he proved something of a disappointment even to the small band of Tory MPS whose private deliberations in 1938 earned them the name the 'Eden group'. These twenty or so 'glamour boys', as the party whips dubbed them, had growing doubts about the wisdom of Chamberlain's foreign policy. But open rebellion was never seriously considered. In the first place, Conservative Central Office, tacitly backed by the Prime Minister, clearly encouraged local associations to put pressure on Tory critics to come into line, or else face the consequences. The younger critics in particular were thus torn between dissent and a desire not to jeopardise their own political futures. Duff Cooper, for example, the only minister to resign over Munich, was within weeks seeking a return to office by clumsy assurances to Chamberlain of continued goodwill; at the time, the Prime Minister saw no reason to forgive and forget.[9] The Eden group, in other words, offered no concerted opposition to the government either before or after Munich. Eden himself, half promised a return to office, remained non-committal in his public statements, and indeed the moderation of his reaction to Hitler's take-over of Prague in the spring of 1939 removed any doubt about his desire for a recall.[10]

Eden's motives were equally apparent in his dealings with the Prime Minister's leading Tory critic — Winston Churchill. Out of office in the 1930s, Churchill had not been as consistent in his anti-appeasement as his memoirs later suggested. His personal antipathy towards Baldwin had been expressed mainly in criticisms about air parity, and his concern about Chamberlain's policy only became vociferous during and after Munich. The prospect of Churchill being invited to join the government was so remote that he was less constrained in his views than many of the younger critics, though he, too, faced considerable pressure from his Epping constituency to toe the party line. Throughout this period, moreover, Eden's followers were determined that Churchill and his few associates, notably Brendan Bracken and Robert Boothby, should not be brought into their deliberations. The coolness between Eden and Churchill was partly personal. Before the outbreak of war they remained equals and rivals; the idea of Eden as Churchill's protégé and successor emerged only after 1940. For the Eden group as a whole there was a wider consideration: association with Churchill was certain to bring with it charges of disloyalty to the party leadership.[11] Churchill had made so many enemies that he was widely regarded in the party as an isolated demagogue, motivated above all by bitterness at his exclusion from office. Divisions between the Tory critics clearly made the Prime Minister's task easier. Although Churchill began to attract a measure of press support after Munich, Chamberlain as yet had no reason to feel unduly threatened.

The Prime Minister therefore remained firmly in control in the pre-war period. Germany's entry into Prague naturally dented his public popularity, and led to growing demands from all quarters — including Tory back-benchers — for the reshaping of the government. Britain's guarantees to protect Poland, however, helped to take the wind out of the sails of party critics. The Eden and Churchill groups were still reluctant to co-operate either with each other or with the Labour opposition, which had gradually abandoned its neo-pacifism of the early 1930s to demand a tough stand against the dictators. Attempts to create a '1931 in reverse' — an alliance between Labour and the Tory rebels — had come to nothing, and increasing frustration among Labour activists was seen in calls for a broad 'popular front' to oppose government policy.[12] Nor was there much evidence that public opinion had turned decisively against the Prime Minister. The success of an anti-appeasement candidate at the Bridgwater by-election in late 1938 was countered when a Tory critic, the Duchess of Atholl, was defeated after resigning her seat to fight in opposition to Chamberlain's foreign policy. Though public opinion had become increasingly polarised, the best Labour could hope for in the general election scheduled for 1940 was modest inroads into the National majority.[13] The Prime Minister's tight and unprecedented control of the lobby system, in addition, ensured that he continued to receive a favourable press from most of the national newspapers.[14] In the summer of 1939, with the prospect of war impending, there was no question that if and when hostilities began, Neville Chamberlain would be the man at the helm.

The origins of Chamberlain's downfall lay in September 1939. It was not simply that the outbreak of hostilities marked the clear failure of his foreign policy; the Prime Minister's reticence in declaring war also caused profound unease. After Hitler's invasion of Poland on 1 September, MPs gathered at Westminster in anticipation of an immediate announcement. But Chamberlain held back, ostensibly because of difficulties in co-ordinating an Anglo-French ultimatum. This hesitation caused grave disquiet in the Commons. Leo Amery could not resist an interjection calling on Arthur Greenwood — replying for Labour in the absence of Attlee — to 'speak for England'. Certainly, Greenwood was alarmed by reactions in the House, and afterwards told Chamberlain in private that without immediate action 'neither you nor I nor anyone else will be able to hold the House of Commons'.[15] That same night Churchill was urged by some of his supporters to go to the House and break the Prime Minister's hold on the Tory party. Churchill decided, after some thought, to ignore this advice, in part because he was now almost certain to return to high office.[16]

By the time Chamberlain made his famous radio broadcast declaring war on the morning of 3 September, the damage had been done. For many back-benchers, the Prime Minister's behaviour had sown the seeds of doubt about his suitability as a war leader. One illustration of this was the formation soon afterwards of an All-Party Parliamentary Action Group, chaired by the hitherto loyal Liberal MP Clement Davies. Initially, the Action Group's aim was simply to help ginger up the war effort, but as membership steadily increased to include over sixty back-benchers, it soon became a focus for anti-government feeling, and provided an outlet for discontent that could not easily be expressed on the floor of the House.[17] In the short term, though, the Action Group posed little discernible threat to the Prime Minister, who showed great resilience in setting out to re-establish his authority. The damage caused on 2 September, as we shall see, was by no means irreversible, and, indeed, the recovery of Chamberlain's prestige was a central political theme of the early weeks of the so-called 'phoney war'.

The Prime Minister's handling of his erstwhile opponents was clearly crucial in this context. Chamberlain considered the idea of creating a small War Cabinet on the 1916 model, but eventually settled on a nine-strong team, none of whom was entirely free from departmental duties. The composition and size of the cabinet had a particular advantage for the Premier: it allowed him scope to control the most important addition to the government, Churchill, who was invited to become First Lord of the Admiralty. While Churchill was euphoric at his sudden change of fortune, the same could not be said of Anthony Eden, who reluctantly accepted a post outside the War Cabinet as Dominions Secretary.[18] These appointments had a dual importance. They not only silenced the most potentially dangerous sources of party opposition but also left effective power in the hands of Chamberlain and his coterie of senior advisers. The Prime Minister could thus confidently exclude other leading critics from his re-formed administration. When the idea was raised of including Amery and Duff Cooper, Chamberlain dismissed it 'with an irritated snort'.[19] In all, more than two-thirds of ministers kept their places from the peacetime government.

Nor was the Prime Minister much concerned by the Labour party's rejection of his offer to join a wartime coalition. Labour's hostility to Chamberlain was so deep-seated that they preferred to opt for 'patriotic opposition': support for the war against Hitler, while reserving the right to criticise. This approach, however, brought its own problems. By refusing to serve, Labour remained powerless to influence any aspect of government policy. Labour leaders such as Hugh Dalton were inclined to make a virtue out of necessity, noting that the '1916 situation developed as a result of serious reverses in the field'; the government should, therefore, be allowed to create its own unpopularity.[20] But, in the meantime, the opposition was left with the worst of all worlds. On the one hand, direct attacks on the government left Labour open to the charge of disloyalty in wartime. On the other hand, when party leaders adopted patriotic measures, such as an electoral truce which forbade by-election contests between the major parties for the duration, they were heavily criticised by constituency activists, who, until recently, were preparing for a general election. Labour, in short, had backed itself into something of a corner, and as the weeks passed signs multiplied of growing party restlessness.[21]

In the early weeks of the war, therefore, the Prime Minister continued to look unassailable. The nature of the phoney war clearly eased pressures on the government. After the defeat of Poland, there were few signs of British forces becoming involved in any large-scale military engagements in the near future; indeed, it was still widely assumed that Hitler was incapable of waging a long war, and that the French army would prevent any further Nazi

advance on the continent. Measures affecting the civilian population, such as evacuation and the black-out, did inevitably provoke
some disquiet, especially as the reduced level of government activity
left back-benchers with more time free to criticise in the House.
But, as Sam Hoare noted in November 1939, once the public had
come to terms with irritating restrictions on everyday life, Chamberlain was well placed to contain his critics.[22] Political opponents
of the war itself, such as the Independent Labour Party (ILP) and
the Fascists, were small in number and provided no co-ordinated
opposition; they fared poorly in by-election contests, which they
remained free to contest against official Conservative or Labour
nominees.[23] And, with the exception of Lloyd George, whose
scepticism contained a strong hint of personal bitterness, pessimists
about the war effort found little publicity for their views in the
national press.[24] The majority of proprietors decided that, in spite
of their misplaced trust in appeasement, it was now their patriotic
duty loyally to support the government. Opinion polls in November showed that Chamberlain had reached a new peak in public
popularity.[25]

But if the Prime Minister was in a commanding position in late
1939, over the next few months a gradual ebbing of confidence was
to take place among even his own supporters; a process so
imperceptible that government whips were to be caught completely
off guard by the strength of feeling that came to the surface in May
1940. In so far as this movement of opinion derived from perceived
failures in policy, two issues stand out. In the first place,
Chamberlain's handling of personnel was the subject of much
criticism. The inclusion of Churchill and Eden only temporarily
silenced those who had long argued that the nation's best talent
remained untapped. In practice, many of the new appointments
made after September 1939 were taken as further evidence of the
undue influence wielded by Chamberlain's closest advisers, Horace
Wilson and David Margesson, the Chief Whip. Although there was
little personal sympathy for the controversial Secretary of State for
War, Leslie Hore-Belisha, when he was dismissed in January 1940,
unease surfaced because the Prime Minister again rejected demands
for the creation of a smaller, non-departmental War Cabinet.[26]
During the spring, the fall of the Daladier government in France
created renewed pressure for the introduction of new blood. But the
major feature of Chamberlain's response, a reshuffle carried out in

April 1940, turned out to be a simple exchange of posts between two leading ministers, Sam Hoare and Kingsley Wood. This move caused dismay among press commentators, and by now loyal Conservatives were conceding in private that the Prime Minister must somehow be moved to consider more sweeping changes.[27]

The second major area of criticism focused on the handling of the war economy. The Chamberlain government did, of course, recognise · its major task in this context: the need to maximise war production on the home front in a manner consistent with providing adequate manpower for the armed forces. To this end, production targets were set in key industries; plans were introduced to raise an army of fifty-five divisions; and new ministries were established in Whitehall with wide-ranging powers.[28] For the critics, though, the government remained far too committed to pre-war orthodoxies. Relations with the trade union movement showed only partial improvement, and the Labour opposition was able to make a series of telling attacks in this area: on the reticence of the Chancellor's first war budget; on the persistence of high unemployment, still standing at over 1 million in April 1940; and on the administrative failings of departments such as the Ministry of Supply. Nor was criticism confined to the Labour benches. A vigorous campaign was soon underway amongst those whose collective experience went back to the innovative days of the Lloyd George coalition during the Great War. The likes of Keynes and Beveridge, backed by sections of the press, began arguing that state control of the war economy needed to be drastically extended. Above all, the idea of appointing a powerful Minister for Economic Co-ordination found widespread support. But the Prime Minister remained unmoved. When the suggestion was proposed in the Commons in February 1940, Chamberlain refused to take the idea seriously, candidly admitting that such an appointment would undermine his own authority and that of the Treasury.[29]

These criticisms, however, were not in themselves directly responsible for the fall of Chamberlain. Similar complaints, as we shall see, were to persist at least until 'the turn of the tide' in late 1942. For many at Westminster, urging personnel changes and bemoaning production levels represented the best of limited opportunities available to bolster the war effort. What mattered, as the demand for an economic overlord demonstrated, was the inflexibility of the Prime Minister's response. Chamberlain in wartime had become increasingly intolerant of criticism, dismissing the 'opposition riff-raff', and confident that his own party's support would remain solid.[30] 'The House of Commons', Brendan Bracken lamented, 'was no good, the Tory Party were tame yes-men of Chamberlain. 170 had their election expenses paid by Tory Central Office and 100 hoped for jobs.'[31] But by the spring of 1940 Chamberlain's refusal to yield any ground to his critics was causing a hardening of feeling. Under the guidance of Leo Amery, the Eden group of Tory critics moved to a more overtly hostile position. More important, discontent was extending beyond the ranks of the long-established critics. The All-Party Action Group was now in touch both with Labour leaders and Tory dissidents, and in a new development during April the senior Conservative peer Lord Salisbury formed what became known as the 'Watching Committee'. This group included government loyalists as well as critics, and for Salisbury its initial purpose was to employ private persuasion in moving ministers to greater urgency, in preference to damaging public dissension. But the committee soon found Chamberlain immune to its constructive criticism; within weeks, Salisbury's group was also becoming more openly critical.[32]

Hence, by April 1940, the Prime Minister was faced with considerable, if understated, parliamentary opposition. The new mood of back-benchers crystallised, above all, around the ending of the phoney war. As Hitler's forces swept into Scandinavia, British troops became involved in a hastily conceived and ultimately unsuccessful effort to defend Norway. Early signs that the campaign was having mixed fortunes inevitably heightened tension at Westminster. The Labour party's National Executive Committee (NEC) met to reaffirm that it would not join any new coalition led by Chamberlain, a development the Prime Minister increasingly came to favour as the war intensified. Rumours began to proliferate. There was talk of an open political clash between loyal Chamberlainites and the 'glamour boys', and even of Lloyd George seeking to form a new alliance with Labour.[33] More important, there was intense speculation about the first signs of disunity inside the cabinet. Since Hore-Belisha's sacking in January, Kingsley Wood for one had been concerned that he might be sacrificed in order to save Chamberlain. It was no coincidence that Wood was soon to ally himself with Churchill — the first senior minister to begin distancing himself from the Prime Minister.

In recent writing on the relationship between Churchill and Chamberlain during the phoney war, the emphasis has been placed on their mutual respect and concurrence on nearly all aspects of policy and strategy.[34] But this view arguably understates the extent to which the two men needed each other at the outbreak of war. The Prime Minister was grateful for the support of a genuinely popular national figure, one who would clearly be a rallying point for opposition if still excluded from office. Churchill, for his part, conscious that he had no party base, was thankful to be rescued from the political wildnerness, and indeed made clumsy attempts to ensure that his gratitude was known. By the spring of 1940, however, the relationship was changing. Chamberlain had hitherto been successful in resisting Churchill's desire to have overriding responsibility for the conduct of the war. As the Scandinavian campaign for which he had pushed so hard began to go wrong, Churchill renewed his demands to be made Minister of Defence or to be given greater control over the powerful Military Co-ordination Committee. After a poor performance in the Commons, which renewed doubts about Churchill's leadership qualities and left him open to charges of prime responsibility for failures now becoming evident in Norway, Churchill began to dissociate himself from the cabinet.[35] The Chamberlainite MP and diarist Sir Henry ('Chips') Channon reported that Churchill, though hitherto loyal, was now being tempted to lead a revolt against the Prime Minister; he was seen associating in the smoking room with the likes of Labour's A. V. Alexander and the opposition Liberal Archie Sinclair, 'the new Shadow Cabinet'.[36] It was against this troubled background that the crucial Norway debate of May 1940 was to take place.

The Allied Supreme War Command conceded at the end of April that, having been outflanked by the speed of Hitler's assault on Norway, British forces would have to be evacuated. At Westminster the natural response — after months of military inactivity — was an outburst of criticism. Harold Nicolson, visiting the Watching Committee, reflected that

Black Week in the Boer War can hardly have been more depressing. They think that this will mean the fall of Chamberlain and Lloyd George as Prime Minister. The Whips are putting it about that it is

all the fault of Winston who has made another forlorn failure. . . .
Eden is out of it. Churchill is undermined by the Conservative
caucus. Halifax is believed . . . to be a tired man.[37]

If the Prime Minister did consider making Churchill a scapegoat,
then he quickly changed course. By the time he announced the
evacuation of Allied forces south of Trondheim on 2 May, and
made arrangements for an adjournment debate the following week,
the sense of impending crisis was such that the government had
decided the best course was to 'shelter' behind the First Lord.[38]

In the days before the debate, parliamentary critics marshalled
their forces. The Watching Committee had become convinced that
a new coalition, to include Labour, was now essential; this view
was leaked to the press in order to increase pressure on the
government.[39] But there was little support for the idea, put to the
All-Party Action Group by Clement Davies, that the debate should
be turned into a vote of no confidence in the Prime Minister.
Labour leaders in particular feared this would rally Tory support
behind Chamberlain and so strengthen his government.[40] The
Prime Minister was, in fact, not unduly worried by the prospect of
an inquest into the Norwegian campaign, and remained confident
that his critics would be no more effective than in the past. Most of
the doubters, he told his sister, were enemies of the government
who would try to exploit every setback; others who attacked to
gratify their partisanship 'are really traitors just as much as
Quisling'. The Chief Whip, Margesson, was also confident of
success: on the eve of the debate he suggested that the government
should itself consider introducing a motion of confidence in order
to isolate the critics if circumstances seemed propitious.[41]

The drama of the two-day Norway debate has, of course, been
frequently recalled. What though, in view of its unforeseen
outcome and legacy for the Churchill coalition, were the decisive
moments of this unique parliamentary occasion? With the House in
a volatile mood, the Prime Minister in opening for the government
deliberately set out to lower the temperature. He refused to be
knocked out of his stride by constant Labour interruptions —
mocking his earlier claims that Hitler had 'missed the bus' — and
was ineffective only in failing to give assurances that the position in
Norway would improve.[42] The first influential attack on the
government came from Admiral Sir Roger Keyes, who was listened
to in 'breathless silence' as — bedecked in full military uniform —

he lambasted the Naval General Staff.[43] The most notable criticism on the first day, however, and indeed in many ways the key contribution of the whole debate, came from the Tory critic Leo Amery, who was almost prevented from rising by the partiality of the Speaker. Amery was not noted as a compelling parliamentary performer, but his carefully prepared critique of his former associate Chamberlain precisely evoked the misgivings of the House. 'I found myself', he recorded that night in his diary, 'going on to an increasing crescendo of applause. So evident was the whole feeling on our side, as well as on the opposition, ready for a change that I cast prudence to the winds and ended full out with my Cromwellian injunction to the Government to go in God's name.'[44] This speech, in retrospect, was 'the dagger in the heart'.[45]

Amery's assault was critical in two ways: it articulated and strengthened the widespread dissatisfaction of back-benchers, and it encouraged critics to force a division in the Commons. On the morning of 8 May, Labour's NEC agreed by a narrow majority that the opportunity to discredit Chamberlain could not now be missed, notwithstanding the danger of rallying support behind the government.[46] In announcing his party's intention to force a division, Herbert Morrison for Labour opened the second day of the debate with a forceful and partisan speech, cleverly designed to rile the Prime Minister. The effect was as intended, noted Hugh Dalton; visibly angered, 'up jumped Chamberlain, showing his teeth like a rat in a corner'.[47] In practice, the Prime Minister had no alternative other than to meet his opponents head on, but by making the issue at stake personal — in calling on his 'friends' to support him in the vote — he clearly shocked the sensibilities of the House. In many ways Chamberlain's short intervention was the most vital factor on the second day; the outcome of the debate was not subsequently influenced to any great degree either by the few loyalists who rallied to the government or by critics such as Duff Cooper and Lloyd George. The latter's vitriolic language was regarded primarily as an attempt to repay bitter personal scores against Chamberlain, though he did enliven proceedings with his injunction to Churchill not 'to allow himself to be converted into an air-raid shelter to keep the splinters from hitting his colleagues'.[48] The First Lord certainly took this message to heart. In winding up the debate, Churchill's chief preoccupation, according to one observer, was to guard against accusations of treachery. This he did with what

Channon called a 'magnificent piece of oratory. . . . How much of the fire was real . . . we shall never know, but he amused and dazzled everyone with his virtuosity.'[49]

Churchill's triumph — in defending the government while distancing himself from responsibility — came too late to prevent a serious anti-government revolt. Earlier in the evening, before he spoke, Clement Davies had presided over a meeting of the All-Party Group, now joined by the Tory critics. With over a hundred MPs present, the decision was taken to vote *en masse* against the government. Chamberlain's Parliamentary Private Secretary (PPS), who approached some of the critics with an offer drastically to reconstruct the government in return for continued support, was firmly told that things had gone too far; and members of the Watching Committee agreed to ignore Lord Salisbury's advice to abstain rather than vote against the party leader.[50] Tensions were naturally running high as the debate came to a close. Chips Channon vividly described the scene:

At last the Speaker called a division, which Winston nearly talked out. I went into the Aye Lobby . . . and we watched the insurgents file out of the Opposition Lobby. . . . 'Quislings', we shouted at them . . . 'Yes-men', they replied. 'We are all right', I heard someone say, and so it seemed as David Margesson came in and went to the right, the winning side of the table. . . . '281 to 200' he read, and the Speaker repeated the figures. There were shouts of 'Resign-Resign' . . . and that old ape Josh Wedgwood began to wave his arms about and sing 'Rule Britannia'. Harold Macmillan, next to him joined in, but they were howled down. Neville appeared bowled over by the ominous figures, and was the first to rise.[51]

Chamberlain had every reason to feel crushed by the figures. None of his party had voted against the government after Munich, but forty National MPs had now registered a vote of no confidence, and at least thirty more had deliberately abstained, in spite of intense pressure from the whips.

The Prime Minister's initial reaction was to consider resignation. But as the dust settled overnight, he decided to seek means of continuing in office. He was fortified in this resolve by supporters and sympathisers, and by early signs of contrition among those who had voted against the government. Inside the cabinet, Chamberlain found backing especially from Lord Hankey, who hoped 'that you will not let the Labour Party and the "Fifth Column" bomb you out of it'.[52] More important, the chairman of the back-bench 1922 Committee, Sir Patrick Spens, reassured Chamberlain that he alone had the confidence of 'the great mass of moderate Conservative opinion, in the House, in the Party & in the country', and that his removal would lead within weeks to 'a grand National disaster'.[53] This coded attack on the claims of the Prime Minister's main rivals, especially Churchill, tipped the balance, and for thirty-six hours after the Norway debate Chamberlain desperately sought ways of reconstructing his government in order to remain in office.

The first avenue explored by the Prime Minister on the morning of 9 May was the renewal of attempts to win over some of the Tory rebels by promises of preferment. Amery in particular was approached, but the possibility of detaching him from other critics was forestalled when he was pointedly asked to chair a meeting which repeated calls for a new government.[54] This left no option but to make a further appeal for the Labour party to form a coalition. At a private meeting in the afternoon, however, Attlee and Greenwood made it plain that the party would not accept Chamberlain's leadership.[55] In a decisive move, the Labour leaders

Fig 1 One position that isn't going to be evacuated

then left London to consult the party conference at that moment gathering in Bournemouth, thereby preventing further talks or the possibility of a counter-attack in a reconvened House. News of the German invasion of the Low Countries on the morning of 10 May opened up one final possibility. The Prime Minister now began to claim that any government reconstruction should be postponed in order to meet this new intensification of the war in Europe. Rumours about Chamberlain's intentions led Brendan Bracken to despair that removing the Prime Minister was like 'trying to get a limpet off a corpse'.[56] But the Labour leadership remained steadfast, and by late afternoon on 10 May Attlee had confirmed by telephone from Bournemouth that the party would serve only under another Prime Minister. Within an hour Chamberlain had resigned.

The succession had already been arranged. Political and public opinion was divided between Churchill and Lord Halifax, but could only await the outcome of discussions among senior ministers, notably at a crucial meeting on 9 May. Churchill's prolonged silence on this occasion, which led Halifax to volunteer that he could not lead a government from the upper chamber, has established the conventional wisdom that Halifax effectively ruled himself out, in spite of being Chamberlain's chosen successor and enjoying cross-party support.[57] This begs the question, though, of why Chamberlain — never an indecisive leader — called such a meeting, rather than simply advising the King of his successor. On this point, it may have been that the Prime Minister privately preferred Churchill, but did not wish this to be publicly known. Chamberlain certainly harboured some thoughts of returning to national leadership after the war; with this in mind, Churchill's unpopularity within the Tory party and his age would make him preferable to Halifax. This may also help to explain the behaviour of the other senior minister who helped to determine the succession, Kingsley Wood. It was Wood who counselled Churchill to remain silent at the meeting on 9 May, and he later claimed to have started negotiations around the turn of the year to ensure such an outcome.[58] There was, of course, the additional advantage for Wood that by swapping horses in midstream he secured high office for himself after Chamberlain's removal. Whatever the reality, it was clear that a remarkable political transformation had taken place: far from letting 'events unfold' in May 1940, as he later claimed in his memoirs, Winston Churchill had, to all intents and purposes, seized the Premiership of wartime Britain.

Chamberlain's downfall was the product of what turned out to be, in retrospect, Britain's major wartime political crisis. Though matters came to a head only in May 1940, the crisis clearly had its roots in developments since the outbreak of war, with the final outcome being determined by a wide variety of groups and individuals. The Labour party, for instance, played a critical role, both in forcing a division on 8 May and in standing firm against the Prime Minister as the military situation deteriorated. As Hugh Dalton put it, 'the last blow which dislodged the old limpet was struck by us at Bournemouth'.[59] But Labour's role must be kept in perspective: the party was able to act decisively only *after* it became clear that a sea-change had taken place on the Conservative benches. The lead in shifting Tory opinion had, over a long period, been taken by the so-called Eden group; from this quarter during the Norway debate came not only Amery's devastating speech but also nearly half of the forty National MPs to vote with the opposition. The established Tory critics, however, had themselves been easily contained by the government until the last moment. What this meant was that they in turn were dependent for effectiveness on a more general hardening of party feeling against the Prime Minister. A sizeable revolt took place, for example, among back-benchers serving in the armed forces. Although twice as many service MPs voted with the government as against it when the crunch came, the sight of sixteen uniformed officers declaring their lack of confidence left a profound impression.[60] Equally important, a significant number of hitherto loyal MPs refused to respond when Chamberlain appealed to his friends. A few of these — including the likes of Nancy Astor — actually voted against the government, while a larger group totalling more than thirty decided instead to abstain, thereby helping to make the difference between a comfortable victory and the halving of the Prime Minister's majority. A pivotal role in the fall of Neville Chamberlain, it must be concluded, was played by the abstentionists, an anonymous group of whom no one thought to make a record at the time.[61]

Why, though, had Conservative opinion turned so dramatically against the Prime Minister? In contrast to the respect and admiration he commanded during the 1930s, the belief inexorably gained ground after September 1939 that he was temperamentally unsuited to war leadership. He was especially vulnerable to the charge of complacency, and indeed any intensification of the war was bound to provoke searching questions about the government's organisation of war production and relationship with organised labour. But this does not in itself explain Chamberlain's fall. Churchill, as we shall see, was himself to survive a protracted series of military reversals during 1941–42, many of them with strategic consequences at least as serious as those of the Scandinavian campaign. Rather, in explaining the impact of the Norway episode, we must ultimately go back to Chamberlain's political style. Unlike Baldwin, Chamberlain had never taken the trouble to consult party opinion, either at Westminster or in the constituencies. Under the pressure of war, he became increasingly remote even from the constructive criticism of respected Tory loyalists led by Lord Salisbury.[62] To a considerable extent, therefore, the Prime Minster brought his fate upon himself by personal failings of man-management. With greater awareness and flexibility, there was no reason why he might not have survived in May 1940, just as Asquith had survived his first wartime crisis in 1915 even if he, too, was likely to fall at a subsequent fence. Instead, Chamberlain failed to realise that the loyalty of those around him had to be earned, and not simply demanded as of right. His own assessment of why he was forced out characteristically placed the blame on an 'accumul-ated mass of grievances', and hostility towards colleagues such as Simon and Hoare.[63] A more accurate conclusion was reached by the Tory politician who wrote on the evening of 10 May: 'One is sorry for Neville, but I should imagine that he has only himself . . . to blame.'[64]

Chamberlain's demise was thus by no means inevitable, at least in the short term, and the same must be said for the succession of Churchill, which few were predicting at the start of the Norway debate. Though closely connected, this was in some ways a discrete event, engineered by only a small group of senior ministers. Churchill's role since returning to office was certainly more ambiguous than his memoirs later suggested. He had been loyal to the Prime Minister in the early months of the war in part because he had no choice; to have stepped out of line would simply have alienated him further from mainstream Conservative opinion. As the phoney war came to an end, the First Lord faced new dangers and sensed new possibilities, and was well aware that he was now playing for high stakes. He was letting it be known via Bracken that he was unlikely to serve under Halifax even before the Norway vote had been taken; and the following day reassurances from Boothby about likely support in both main parties enabled him to force Halifax's hand with confidence at the crucial ministerial meeting.[65] Churchill did not come to power, in other words, as the 'man of destiny' or as the saviour of the nation. Before the collapse of France, the main demand of the dissaffected was not for a saviour but rather for a leader who would accept advice where necessary and bring greater urgency to Britain's military and economic war effort. In the event, it was Churchill who came to the forefront when the opportunity presented itself because his instinct and urge for power greatly outweighed that of his major rival. This is not to ascribe to him purely personal motives; Churchill was, of course, more so than most, desperately anxious to see the Nazi menace defeated. But the political context in which he operated must not be ignored; the idea of Churchill as 'national saviour' can be judged only in the light of what he did after entering Downing Street.

In reassessing the events of May 1940, we must also recognise the impossibility of predicting at the time just how profound the consequences would be for British politics in the long term. The coalition that Churchill now formed between Conservative and Labour forces was, after five hard years, to result in military victory abroad and a landslide towards Labour at home. Chamberlain's downfall was a vital moment in the wartime swing to the left because it undermined at a stroke the easy Tory dominance of the inter-war period. Thereafter, Conservatives were obliged to follow a Prime Minister who many continued to distrust; in spite of the reputation that Churchill established as an indispensable war leader, party stalwarts remained particularly concerned about his contempt for 'appeasers' and his neglect of policy and organisation. The discomfiture of many Tories was compounded by the knowledge that Chamberlain's resignation marked a major political breaktrough for the Labour party. In the long run, Labour was to have the best of all worlds: gaining both from the radical expectations raised by wartime social change, and from the aura of responsibility and competence that stemmed from participation in government. But such an outcome seemed remote in May 1940. Aside from the overriding question of how the war would unfold, there was no guarantee that Labour would prove able to exploit its sudden change of fortune; and indeed, as we shall see, for many months Labour ministers struggled to make a positive impression. As Churchill went to Buckingham Palace, where he accepted the King's invitation to form a government, the full impact of the Norway episode could only be a matter for wild speculation. During the desperate months that followed, in fact, the coalition, and the nation at large, had in any case only one real priority — survival.

Notes

1 L. W. Fuchser, *Neville Chamberlain and Appeasement*, New York, 1982, pp. 190–1. For a detailed assessment of the fall of Chamberlain, see Addison, *The Road to 1945*, pp. 53–102.

2 W. S. Churchill, *The Second World War*, Vol. I, *The Gathering Storm*, London, 1948, p. 601; M. Gilbert, *Winston S. Churchill*, Vol. VI, *Finest Hour 1939–1941*, London, 1983, pp. 285–318.

3 J. Harris, 'Political ideas and the debate on State welfare, 1940–45', in H. L. Smith (ed.), *War and Social Change: British Society in the Second World War*, Manchester, 1986, p. 236.

4 D. Howell, *British Social Democracy*, London, 1976, pp. 94–7; K. Jefferys, 'The educational policies of the Conservative party, 1918–44', unpublished Ph.D. thesis, University of London, 1984, pp. 136–7. The case for 'middle opinion', which has remained strong in subsequent historiography, was first made by A. Marwick, 'Middle opinion in the thirties: planning, progress and political "agreement"', *English Historical Review*, LXXIX, 1964, pp. 285–98.

5 A. Booth, 'Britain in the 1930s: a managed economy?', *Economic History Review*, XL, 4, 1987, pp. 499–522.

6 The distinctions between middle opionion and socialist thinking are outlined in D. Ritschel, 'Non-socialist planning in the interwar period', unpublished D.Phil. thesis, University of Oxford, 1987. See also B. Pimlott, *Hugh Dalton*, London, 1985, pp. 212–24.

7 For an overview of the whole appeasement controversy, see K. Robbins, *Appeasement*. Oxford, 1988. The most strident recent defence of appeasement is J. Charmley, *Chamberlain and the Lost Peace*, London, 1989.

8 J. A. Ramsden, *The Age of Balfour and Baldwin 1902–1940*, London, 1978, p. 366.

9 J. Charmley, *Duff Cooper: the Authorised Biography*, London, 1986, pp. 132–3.

10 D. Carlton, *Anthony Eden: a Biography*, London, 1981, pp. 145–6.

11 P. Emrys Evans to L. S. Amery, 1 July 1954, Emrys Evans papers,

British Library, (BL), Add. Mss. 58247, ff. 22–3. Emrys Evans, a prominent member of the Eden group, added that the coolness of the Edenites was something which Churchill never forgave.

12 B. Pimlott, *Labour and the Left in the 1930s*, Cambridge, 1977, pp. 162–9.

13 M. Pugh, *The Making of Modern British Politics 1867–1939*, Oxford, 1982, pp. 292–3.

14 R. B. Cockett, 'The Government, the press and politics in Britain 1937 to 1945', unpublished Ph.D. thesis, University of London, 1988, pp. 66–99, illustrates the role of Chamberlain's associate, Sir Joseph Ball, in orchestrating violently worded attacks on Churchill in a widely circulated Whitehall newsletter. See also Chapter 3 of Richard Cockett's *Twilight of Truth: Chamberlain, Appeasement and the Manipulation of the Press*, London, 1989.

15 Cited in M. Cowling, *The Impact of Hitler: British Politics and British Policy 1933–1940*, Cambridge, 1975, p. 345.

16 Duff Cooper, *Old Men Forget*, London, 1953, pp. 259–60.

17 D. M. Roberts, 'Clement Davies and the fall of Neville Chamberlain, 1939–40', *Welsh History Review*, VIII, 2, 1976, pp. 198–9: the first meeting of the group took place on 13 September, when it was agreed to establish sub-committees to deal with foreign policy and war strategy, home defence and economic planning.

18 Carlton, op. cit., pp. 157–8: Eden's disappointment was compounded by the recognition that Churchill had now clearly superseded him in public recognition and esteem.

19 R. J. Minney, *The Private Papers of Hore-Belisha*, London, 1960, p. 230.

20 Pimlott, *Hugh Dalton*, p. 272.

21 P. Addison, 'Political change in Britain, September 1939 to December 1940', unpublished D.Phil. thesis, University of Oxford, 1971, pp. 410–2; T. D. Burridge, *British Labour and Hitler's War*, London, 1976, pp. 25–45.

22 Sam Hoare to Lord Lothian, 11 November 1939, cited in Viscount Templewood, *Nine Troubled Years*, London, 1954, p. 409.

23 On wartime by-elections and the electoral truce, see below, Chapter 6.

24 C. Cross (ed.), *Life with Lloyd George: the Diary of A. J. Sylvester 1931–45*, London, 1975, p. 238: in October 1939, Lloyd George was busy creating the impression 'that we had damned well lost and that we should come to terms. . . . '

25 Cockett, 'Government, press and politics', pp. 112–14.

26 A. J. P. Taylor (ed.), *Off the Record: W. P. Crozier, Political Interviews 1933–1944*, London, 1973, pp. 128–31: Hore-Belisha told Crozier of the *Manchester Guardian* that Chamberlain had told him out of the blue that he was being moved because of military opinion. Churchill had angrily refused a request to intervene on Hore-Belisha's behalf; Lloyd George surmised that Churchill would not be sorry to see Hore-Belisha out of the way 'on the road to the Premiership'.

27 See, for example, the reaction of the Tory MP Euan Wallace in his

diary entry for 4 April 1940: Wallace diary, Bodleian Library, Oxford, Ms. Eng. Hist. c. 496.

28 Addison, *Road to 1945*, pp. 56–60.

29 V[olume] 356 H[ouse] [of] C[ommons] Deb[ates] 5th s[eries], c[olumn] 1336, 1 February 1940.

30 Neville to Ida Chamberlain, 20 January 1940, cited in Lord Butler (ed.), *The Conservatives*, London, 1977, p. 395.

31 Bracken interview with Crozier, 29 March 1940: Taylor (ed.), op. cit., p. 156.

32 Minutes of the Watching Committee, 16–29 April 1940, Emrys Evans papers, BL Add. Mss. 58270.

33 Labour Party, *National Executive Committee [NEC] Minutes*, 3 April 1940; R. Rhodes James (ed.), *Chips: the Diaries of Sir Henry Channon*, London, 1967: diary entry for 26 April 1940, p. 243.

34 E.g. D. Dilks, 'The twilight war and the fall of France: Chamberlain and Churchill in 1940', in D. Dilks (ed.), *Retreat from Power*, Vol. II, *After 1939*, London, 1981, pp. 38–57.

35 Cowling, op. cit., pp. 368–72.

36 *Channon Diary*, 1 May 1940, p. 244.

37 N. Nicolson (ed.), *Harold Nicolson: Diaries and Letters 1939–1945*, London, 1967: diary entry for 30 April 1940, p.74.

38 Emrys Evans diary, 1 May 1940, BL Add. Mss. 58245, ff. 123–5.

39 *Evening Standard*, 6 May 1940: this reported that the Salisbury group favoured Lord Halifax as the head of a new National coalition.

40 Roberts, op. cit., p. 205; Pimlott, op. cit., p. 273 — Dalton feared Chamberlain might call an election which would wipe Labour 'further out than in 1931'. This defensiveness was shared on the left by Aneurin Bevan, who thought there was 'not a hope' of Chamberlain being beaten — J. Campbell, *Nye Bevan and the Mirage of Socialism*, London 1987, p. 95.

41 Neville to Hilda Chamberlain, 4 May 1940; Margesson note to the Prime Minister, 6 May 1940: Chamberlain papers, Birmingham University Library, NC8/35/47.

42 Tory critics were divided in their impressions. Amery thought the speech was a flop and 'the flop could be heard in Birmingham' — J. Barnes and D. Nicholson (eds), *The Empire at Bay: the Leo Amery Diaries 1929–1945*, London, 1988: entry for 7 May 1940, p. 592. Harold Macmillan, *The Blast of War 1939–1945*, London, 1967, p. 68, was more generous in his assessment.

43 *Nicolson Diary*, 7 May 1940, pp. 76–7.

44 *Amery Diary*, 7 May 1940, p. 592. Amery's exact words were: 'This is what Cromwell said to the Long Parliament when he thought it was no longer fit to conduct the affairs of the nation: "You have sat too long here for any good you have been doing. Depart, I say, and let us have done with you. In the name of God, go"' — 360 H. C. Deb., 5 s., c. 1150, 7 May 1940.

45 Lord Home (Alec Dunglass, Chamberlain's PPS), *The Way the Wind*

Blows, London, 1976, p. 74.
46 B. Pimlott (ed.), *The Political Diary of Hugh Dalton 1918–40, 1945–60*, London, 1986: entry for 8 May 1940, p. 340.
47 Hugh Dalton, *The Fateful Years: Memoirs 1931–1945*, London, 1957, p. 305.
48 360 H. C. Deb., 5 s., c. 1283, 8 May 1940. See also Leo Amery, *My Political Life*, Vol. III, *The Unforgivingg Years 1929–1940*, London, 1955, p. 367.
49 'Memorandum on events leading to the downfall of Neville Chamberlain', n.d., written anonymously: Clement Davies papers, National Library of Wales, Aberystwyth, 1/2/8; *Channon Diary*, 8 May 1940, p. 246.
50 Emrys Evans diary, 8 May 1940, ff. 125–6.
51 *Channon Diary*, 8 May 1940, pp. 246–7.
52 Hankey to Chamberlain, 9 May 1940, cited in S. Roskill, *Hankey: Man of Secrets*, Vol. III, *1931–1963*, London, 1974, p. 463.
53 P. Spens to Chamberlain, 9 May 1940, Chamberlain papers, NC7/11/33/162.
54 *Amery Diary*, 9 May 1940, pp. 611–12. See also *Dalton Diary*, 9 May 1940, p. 343: 'The Old Man was telephoning from 8.00 onwards, trying to conciliate opponents of yesterday. He seems determined himself to stick on — like a dirty old piece of chewing gum on the leg of a chair.'
55 Harris, *Attlee*, pp. 174–5.
56 Cited in C. E. Lysaght, *Brendan Bracken*, London, 1979, p. 174.
57 E.g. Earl of Birkenhead, *Halifax: the Life of Lord Halifax*, London, 1965, pp. 453–4.
58 See Carlton, op. cit., pp. 161–2, and references cited there.
59 *Dalton Diary 1918–40*, 10 May 1940, p. 345.
60 B. Pimlott (ed.), *The Second World War Diary of Hugh Dalton 1940–45*, London, 1986: diary entry for 16 May 1940, p. 9 — Harold Macmillan explained the action of the service MPs on the grounds that 'in the Army their loyalty to the King overcame their loyalty to the Old Man and Margesson. When they saw the mess in Norway, some at first hand, they made up their minds.'
61 J. S. Rasmussen, 'Party discipline in war-time; the downfall of the Chamberlain government', *Journal of Politics*, XXXII, 1970, pp. 380–2.
62 On the second day of the Norway debate the Tory critic Richard Law complained that a divisive vote was unavoidable as this was the only way the government's supporters with reservations about the war effort could express themselves — 360 H. C. Deb., 5s., c. 1486, 8 May 1940.
63 Chamberlain diary, 11 May 1940, cited in K. Feiling, *The Life of Neville Chamberlain*, London, 1947, p. 440.
64 Diary of Cuthbert Headlam, MP, Durham Record Office: entry for 10 May 1940, D/He 36. I am grateful to Dr Stuart Ball of the University of

Leicester for pointing out the importance of this source.

65 Emrys Evans diary, 8 May 1940, f. 126; Boothby to Churchill, 9 May 1940, cited in Gilbert, op. cit., p. 303 — 'I find a gathering consensus of opinion in all quarters that you are the necessary and inevitable Prime Minister . . .'.

2

'All behind you, Winston'

The year 1940 will always be remembered as Britain's 'finest hour'. The fall of Chamberlain coincided with a sudden intensification of the war in Europe; during the desperate months that followed, Churchill's magnificently inspired leadership proved to be critical. After the defeat of the French army in June, Britain was left to stand alone against the might of Nazi Germany, and with the prospect of invasion now imminent, the new Prime Minister played a vital role in stirring the nation to resist. Over the long summer of 1940 the RAF denied Goering's Luftwaffe aerial supremacy in the Battle of Britain, and by the autumn Churchill was confident that Britain had survived its sternest test. Although the civilian population faced untold new horrors in the Blitz, the prospect of invasion had receded — for good, as it turned out — and the government could begin considering ways of striking back at the enemy. Inevitably, the coalition which Churchill formed in May 1940 had to devote its entire energies to the war effort. 'The situation which faced the members of the new Government', writes Alan Bullock, 'left them no time to think about the future: they needed all their resolution to believe there was going to be a future at all.'[1]

British politics in the summer and autumn of 1940 thus had an air of unreality. But it would be wrong to assume that the nation's finest hour did not produce any political devolpments of significance. This chapter sets out to demonstrate that the early months of coalition had important implications for national politics, especially in the long term. Many of these consequences were difficult to predict in May 1940, and were certainly more complex than popular mythology would suggest. It will be shown, for example, that in the early weeks of his premiership, Churchill was by no means a universally acclaimed war leader, and that his position of unassailable authority was only gradually built up through a mixture of skill and good fortune. The legacy of Chamberlain's downfall, it must be remembered, was such that pre-existing political tensions could not be easily forgotten even at a moment of supreme crisis. In particular, the Conservative majority in parliament only reluctantly came to terms with the new Prime Minister and the suddenly enhanced status of the Labour party. Although the political nation was now united in its determination to defeat Nazism, as we shall see, it soon became evident that the coalition was essentially a marriage of convenience; an alliance incapable of producing much in the way of domestic bliss. In other words, 1940 established a pattern of coalition politics in which each side constantly sought to maximise party advantage. This was evident from the outset: not least in the formation of the government itself.

Churchill's first action when he returned from Buckingham Palace as Prime Minister was to write to Neville Chamberlain. 'With your help and counsel and with the support of the great party of which you are the leader', he wrote, 'I trust that I shall succeed. . . . To a very large extent I am in your hands — and I feel no fear of that.'[2] This was a striking illustration of Churchill's sense of weakness when he came to power. In forming his government over the next few hectic days, he clearly found his room for manœuvre limited by the dictates of parliamentary politics. The new War Cabinet, for example, now composed of only five members, was established on strictly party lines, rather than attempting to promote those deemed most capable of meeting the national emergency. In addition to Chamberlain and Lord Halifax, who remained as Foreign Secretary, Churchill was joined by Attlee, the Labour leader, and his deputy, Arthur Greenwood. At this level, Labour had some cause for satisfaction with its representation in the new government. Indeed, Attlee and Greenwood scored an early success. The Prime Minister initially hoped that Chamberlain would be able to serve as Leader of the House of Commons, but this idea aroused great resentment on the Labour side; rumours began to circulate on 11 May that Churchill would have to choose between Chamberlain and the Labour party. In the event, Chamberlain agreed to avoid further antagonism by accepting office as Lord President of the Council — a post that allowed him, for the time being, to retain considerable power on the home front.[3]

The appointment of three service ministers outside the War Cabinet further emphasised the all-party nature of the coalition. Anthony Eden was promoted to the War Office alongside the Labour veteran A. V. Alexander, who went to the Admiralty, and Archibald Sinclair, newly installed at the Air Ministry; the latter was one of only two Liberals to receive high office. By offering these posts to amenable colleagues, the Prime Minister also secured for himself what had been his abiding concern since the outbreak of war — control of all aspects of military strategy. Beyond this, Churchill took very little interest in the personnel of his new administration.[4] Instead, the initiative was taken by David Margesson, Chamberlain's loyal henchman as Chief Whip, now dubbed 'the parachutist' by one of his opponents. Margesson's survival helped to ensure in turn the retention of many prominent Chamberlainites. Of those most readily associated with the former regime, it was true that Lord Simon found himself removed to the Woolsack, and that Sam Hoare became a major casualty; he now had to content himself with an ambassadorial mission to Madrid, ostensibly aimed at preventing Franco from entering the war. These changes were balanced, however, by the inclusion of Kingsley Wood as Chancellor of the Exchequer — an appointment which surprised even Tory back-benchers, most of whom remained ignorant of his key role in securing his former chief's fate.

As a further consequence of Churchill's need to base his power on the Conservative majority in parliament, there were only limited rewards for the so-called 'glamour boys'. Aside from Eden, Leo Amery was rewarded for his part in the Norway debate with the India Office, and Duff Cooper went to the Ministry of Information. But Harold Macmillan, Bob Boothby and Harold Nicolson were given only junior ministerial appointments, and it soon became obvious that where possible the new Premier preferred to promote his own favoured associates. Most notable of these was Lord Beaverbrook, whose qualifications for the critical post of Minister of Aircraft Production were — according to one observer — that he was 'twenty-five per cent thug, fifteen per cent crook and the re-mainder a combination of genius and real goodness of heart'.[5] Nor was there any place for others who had helped to secure Chamber-lain's downfall, such as the Liberal MP Clement Davies, who had no strong party machine to back his claims. Attlee's determination to avoid protracted bargaining over government places — something that had blighted the formation of the 1915 coalition — also worked to Margesson's advantage. Places were, of course, found for experienced Labour figures such as Herbert Morrison, who became Minister of Supply, and Hugh Dalton, the new Minister of Economic Warfare. And, as a symbolic gesture, Churchill also appointed the powerful trade union leader Ernest Bevin, whose acceptance of the vital wartime post of Minister of Labour was conditional upon the early introduction of industrial reform.[6] But, overall, Labour received less than one-third of all government posts: there were only sixteen Labour ministers, compared with fifty-two Conservatives, and the Labour party was left particularly poorly represented among junior ministers.

It would, therefore, be a mistake to exaggerate the extent to which the coalition marked a break with the past, or represented a sudden shift in political power. The new government was clearly a sign that national unity had at last been achieved in the face of a deepening military crisis, and Churchill was given to boasting that his was the most broadly based administration Britain had ever known. 'It extends', he proclaimed, 'from Lord Lloyd of Dolobran to Miss Ellen Wilkinson.'[7] But the hard political reality was that the nation's new leader had no option other than to conciliate his former enemies. In spite of Chamberlain's fall, orthodox Conservatives still constituted the most dominant political force in parliament, and so could ensure a strong element of continuity. Altogether, two-thirds of Chamberlain's government were re-appointed and only twelve senior ministerial posts were allocated to new members coming into office.[8] The formation of the coalition, in other words, was not in itself a critical moment on the road to 1945. In practical terms, Labour had not entered as equal partners; its influence was only to grow as party leaders gradually measured up to the demands of high office. In the short term, Labour ministers were clearly in no real position to begin influencing important areas of government policy-making. Attlee and Greenwood had no direct departmental responsiblities, and, like both Morrison and Bevin, they struggled to impress for many months. For the time being, Labour had to settle for an immense psychological boost: the result, simply, of having taken a share in power at the expense of their hated opponent, Neville Chamberlain. What many Labour partisans could not understand — and this was something that threatemed an early revival of party hostilities — was why Chamberlain, having been dealt a knock-out blow, should not be removed from the ring altogether.

Churchill's first few weeks in his new post were, needless to say, fraught with difficulties. As German troops rapidly overran Allied defensive positions, the Prime Minister's energies were almost entirely absorbed by military strategy; it was during this period that he made repeated visits to the continent in an attempt to rally French resistance. At the same time, he sought to instil in the British people a firm resolve to fight on whatever the consequences. In the short term, inevitably, this meant brave words rather than action: efforts to galvanise the fighting forces abroad and overhaul the war economy at home would necessarily take time to have effect, as would the Emergency Powers Act rushed through parliament on 22 May. Churchill's task was made more difficult by the insecurity he felt in these early weeks. Hostility towards the new Prime Minister and uncertainty about the future were widespread throughout Whitehall and Westminster, in private if not in public. Many civil servants feared that Churchill's tendency to make rash decisions could lead Britain to fresh, untold disaster, and in the House of Commons Chamberlain's humiliation was not something that could be easily forgotten by Conservative MPs.

Tory distrust of the Prime Minister was partly personal. For many who had loyally followed Chamberlain over the years, the ingrained image of Churchill as a dangerous renegade could not be eradicated overnight. On the evening of 10 May Rab Butler, no doubt expecting as a staunch Chamberlainite to be removed from his junior post at the Foreign Office, lamented that 'the good clean tradition of English politics' had been sold to a 'half-breed American', the 'greatest adventurer of modern political history'.[9] On top of this, many back-benchers began to have second thoughts about the Norway debate. Neville Chamberlain was soon receiving assurances from Tory MPs that their hostile action had not been directed against him personally, but against the composition of his administration.[10] The Secretary of the 1922 Committee reported on 13 May that among the parliamentary rebels, there were 'three quarters who are ready to put Chamberlain back'.[11] This sense of guilt about Chamberlain's removal turned into anger when it sunk in that government places now had to be found for both anti-Chamberlainite Tories and Labour representatives. The bitterest criticism, however, was reserved for the promotion of Churchill's personal associates. News of the appointment of Bracken and Beaverbrook led Lord Halifax to complain in private that 'the gangsters will shortly be in complete control'.[12] Taken together, these feelings helped to explain the Prime Minister's reception when parliament met to ratify the change of government on 13 May. Churchill was listened to in stony silence by Conservative MPs, but when Chamberlain appeared 'they shouted; they waved their Order Papers, and his reception was a regular ovation'.[13] Here, then, was a division of loyalty which might not be easily resolved. Churchill, for the time being at least, was a Prime Minister without a party: it came as no surprise that he decided to turn down Chamberlain's offer of resignation from the party leadership also.

Churchill's most vocal support in these early weeks undoubtedly came from the Labour party. The Bournemouth conference had almost unanimously agreed that Labour should commit itself fully to the fight against Hitler once Chamberlain had been removed. The party's participation in government, it was added, was also designed to secure greater equality and social justice — a stipulation that was to cause increasing difficulties as the war progressed. Once the House of Commons had re-assembled after the Norway vote, the Parliamentary Labour Party (PLP), quickly adjusted itself to the problem of trying to maintain party identity while entering government. The House accepted, after some acrimonious exchanges, that Labour MPs not serving in office should continue to sit on the opposition benches; the party also established an elected 'Administrative Committee', whose members sat on the front opposition bench and from whose ranks an unofficial leader of the opposition was chosen to maintain parliamentary procedure.[14] Enthusiasm among Labour back-benchers for the new coalition was further bolstered, moreover, by the attitude of Tory MPs towards their deposed leader. Throughout May, as the majority of Conservatives persisted with their stony reception for Churchill, Labour responded with loud cheering for the Premier. This behaviour was, as Paul Addison has noted, 'less a guide to their particular feelings about Churchill than to their deep animosity against each other'.[15] Party political feeling, in other words, had not simply been cast aside because of the national emergency. With British troops being relentlessly pushed to-wards the Channel ports, one back-bencher noted that unless partisan feelings were soon smothered, all prospects for the success of the new administration would soon recede.[16]

The Prime Minister's sense of insecurity was further increased by criticism of his war policy. On the one hand, some of those excluded from the coalition — notably Clement Davies, Shinwell and Hore-Belisha — did not take long to return to the charge that Britain's war effort lacked sufficient urgency. At the other extreme, a small but vocal section of opinion questioned the wisdom of continuing the war. The pacifist case continued to be espoused at Westminster by Maxton's tiny ILP group, by several Liberal peers and by twenty or so Labour MPs who formed the so-called 'Peace Aims Group'. Notwithstanding the decision of the Bournemouth conference, the likes of Sidney Silverman and Rhys Davies stuck fervently to their long-standing policy of opposing 'imperialist war'.[17] The Peace Aims Group was led by the maverick MP for Ipswich, Richard Stokes, who had argued throughout the phoney war for a peace settlement based on clearly stated anti-communist principles. Stokes denied frequent charges of being a pacifist and, indeed, accepted that efforts to secure peace had to be shelved in the face of Hitler's attack on France, though he remained convinced that the war in the West could only benefit the Soviet Union.[18] In themselves, the various critics posed a negligible threat to the Prime Minister, especially as their views were scorned by much of the national and regional press. But Churchill still had the anxiety in the back of his mind that events on the continent might increase anti-war feeling. The potency of the sceptics was enhanced, moreover, by their tendency to gravitate towards the one major critic left outside the ranks of the government — Lloyd George.

In spite of his advanced years and isolation from the political mainstream, Lloyd George could still speak with great authority in 1940 as the man who had 'won' the Great War. Unless he was 'downed', said one of his opponents, 'you will have all the disgruntled & disappointed running after him & intriguing with him in the many opportunities which the next few months will provide'.[19] Stokes and the Peace Aims Group had certainly kept in touch with Lloyd George, encourged by his public claims during the phoney war that a negotiated peace was inevitable. Chamberlain's refusal to co-operate with the Soviet Union, he had argued pessimistically, made an outright British victory impossible.[20] Churchill feared that, if anyone, it was his former Liberal colleague who might rally support for the idea of a negotiated settlement. The Prime Minister therefore made concerted efforts to tempt Lloyd George into joining the government. Initial offers of control over food production came to nothing. Then, on 28 May, with British troops now beginning their evacuation from the Dunkirk beaches, Churchill went to the trouble of summoning Lloyd Geroge in order to offer him a place in the War Cabinet, subject to the approval of Neville Chamberlain. Aside from calculations about the future, Lloyd George found grounds for refusing in the veto provided to Chamberlain — his long-standing personal enemy.[21] In spite of this rejection, the invitation to join the coalition was left open, and in a clear illustration of his state of mind the Prime Minister confessed to Lloyd George that 'like you I have no party of my own. I have received a great deal fo help from Chamberlain . . . . I have joined hands with him, and must act with perfect loyalty'.[22]

Churchill's sense of insecurity in May 1940 should not, of course, be exaggerated. The very urgency of the military situation, with daily reports of German advances on the continent, clearly concentrated minds on the dangers ahead. The House of Commons had given an overwhelming vote of confidence in the new government, and Churchill was soon rallying support with his stirring rhetoric. Nevertheless, the Prime Minister clearly believed himself to be vulnerable. He had as yet no firm parliamentary base, and was conscious that the backing of many Tory MPs was conditional upon there being no direct clash of loyalty involving the party leader. Lloyd George could still be regarded as a potential leader for those who favoured a negotiated peace, and Churchill's hold over his colleagues on war policy was still far from unchallenged. In cabinet discussions about the Dunkirk evacuation, the Prime Minister had to take seriously Lord Halifax's claim that peace terms should be considered so long as Britain's independence remained intact.[23] The Foreign Secretary, who still commanded much loyalty and respect in Conservative ranks, was severely criticial of Churchill's 'frightful rot' about achieving total victory, and he certainly alarmed the Prime Minister by threatening to resign on this point.[24] It was only after the full extent of the evacuation from France became known in early June that the cabinet finally threw its weight behind the Churchillian line. Dunkirk, we might conclude, was a deliverance for Churchill as it was for the British nation. With over 300,000 Allied troops returning safely — far more that

originally anticipated — the evacuation not only rallied public
opinion to the view that Britain now had the means to continue the
war, it also further isolated those who favoured a negotiated peace.
But it had been a close run thing. 'I cannot say', Churchill told
Stanley Baldwin on 4 June, 'that I have enjoyed being Prime Minister
vy much so far.'[25]

It was in June 1940 that Winston Churchill became Britain's
unchallenged war leader. The aftermath of Dunkirk and the fall of
France served to sweep away any lingering doubts about his
abilities. But national relief about the 'triumph' of the evacuation
from the continent was rapidly overtaken by a more ominous
reaction — the desire to find scapegoats. Many of the troops
returning from France complained bitterly that the Allied campaign
had been hopelessly beset by shortcomings in equipment and
personnel. In taking this up and seeking to explain why evacuation
had become — in the words of one observer — Britain's 'greatest
national industry',[26] sections of the press had soon embarked upon
what became known as 'the attack on the appeasers'. The *Daily
Herald* led the way: in a series of stinging editorials, responsibility
for the retreat of British forces was placed squarely on the shoulders
of 'the men of Munich', such as Chamberlain and Kingsley Wood,
who were urged to resign immediately.[27] Other newspapers, some
of them conveniently overlooking their own record on appeasement, joined in the clamour for the elimination of the 'old gang',
and it was not long before press agitation stirred up fresh controversy at Westminster.

Some Labour MPs now began to press for the removal of senior
Tories from the government. This reflected in part a simple desire to
rub salt in the wound by completing Chamberlain's humiliation,
though there was also a genuine concern that the 'old gang' were
still hampering rather than helping the war effort. The latter theme
was also pursued by Clement Davies, who in early June started to
reconvene meetings at the Reform Club similar to those he presided
over in the run-up to the Norway debate. These gatherings brought
together not only critics such as Lloyd George but also some of
the junior Tory ministers recently brought into office, such as
Macmillan and Boothby, who were themselves anxious to improve
the speed and effectiveness of government decision-making.[28] As
discontent mounted, Chamberlain decided to take matters into

hand. Convinced that Lloyd George was behind much of the agitation and was 'waiting to inflict a mortal blow on me', the Lord President received confirmation from Margesson as Chief Whip that a major intrigue was building up. As the central target of the various attacks, he determined to seek satisfactory assurances from the Prime Minister or else resign.[29]

Churchill's attitude was to oppose all demands for recrimination. In the first place, he clearly valued Chamberlain's administrative contribution on the home front; during his frequent visits to France in May and June, he would politely ask Neville to 'mind the shop'. The Prime Minister was, therefore, prepared to give sympathetic reassurances, though he did at the same time play upon Chamberlain's vulnerability by taking the opportunity to reopen the question of Lloyd George joining the government. The Lord President now agreed to drop his opposition to this idea, subject to the press campaign for his removal being called off.[30] Within days, Churchill had taken steps to ensure that attacks on the 'old gang' were silenced. His interview with Cecil King, director of one of the most critical newspapers, the *Daily Mirror*, highlighted his thinking:

Churchill said not to forget that a year ago last Christmas they were trying to hound him out of his constituency . . . . But the men who supported Chamberlain and hounded Churchill were still MPs. A Gereral Election was not possible during a war so the present House of Commons, however unrepresentative of feeling in the country, had to be reckoned with as the ultimate source of power for the duration. If Churchill trampled on these men, as he could trample on them, they would set themselves against him, and in such internecine strife lay the Germans 'best chance of victory . . . . No, he was not going to run a Government of revenge.[31]

Churchill, in other words, believed that ultimately he had no choice but to defend his predecessor. Chamberlain's resignation, which was turned down on 8 June, was certain to divide Tory loyalties and provide a fresh focus for discontent; there were grounds for thinking that if Chamberlain went, he would soon be followed by Kingsley Wood and several junior ministers.[32]

Labour leaders were also conscious of what might follow from the elimination of the 'old gang'. Attlee and Greenwood both urged their followers not to use a forthcoming secret session debate in parliament to seek recriminations, arguing that there was no justification for altering a govenment that had so recently received a massive vote of confidence.[33] Some back-benchers, out for blood,

were not easily persuaded. Chamberlain was convinced by 'the
demeanour' of Labour MPs that a direct personal assault was
intended, and his 'friends' now showed belated signs of coming to
his aid. William Spens, chairman of the 1922 Committee, declared
in a strong public statement that attacks on certain ministers were
indefensible:

The Conservative Party — by far the strongest in the country — desires
nothing less at this grave crisis in our history than to continue to support
the present Government and to refrain from all party warfare, and certainly will not throw the first stone. But if others should be so reckless of
the national interest as to launch the suggested attack, we should have no
alternative but to defend ourselves and our leaders.[34]

In the event, the open re-emergence of party hostilities was averted
by news of Italy's entry into the war. This had the effect of distract-
ing opinion at Westminster, and provided a pretext for cancelling
the secret session debate. The 'attack on the appeasers' in early
June, therefore, failed to shake Chamberlain. Lord Beaverbrook
noted that for the time being, 'Winston can hold the bloodhounds
off', but if events continued to deteriorate, he doubted whether 'the
storm against Neville will subside for long.'[35]

   Attacks on Chamberlain did, in fact, continue for some time.
With the French army by now on the verge of collapse, the search
for scapegoats intensified. On 18 June the Prime Minister prepared
the nation for bad tidings with his 'finest hour' speech, which, with
one eye on American opinion, made clear Britain's determination to
fight on alone if necessary. At the time, however, this famous
oration stirred the public more than it did the House of Commons,
where tensions remained high. Some back-benchers were not
persuaded by Churchill's warning against the 'pernicious process'
of attributing blame for the present situation; one shouted to
Chamberlain across the floor of the House that 'you ought to be
ashamed to come here'.[36] The Prime Minister, moreover, was still
receiving a cool response from the majority of Conservative MPs,
unwilling to face up to the implications of coalition. As Hugh
Dalton observed:

They think that the Labour Party has much too large a share, both in
offices and the determination of Government policy.... The Tories,
therefore, wonder where they come in. Most of the Tories in the Government are either rebels or near-rebels. So what was the use of having been
loyal to the Old Man and Margesson in the now closed chapter of our

history? There is some danger in this situation, and it must be watched. One very obvious conclusion is that we must not push the Old Man out of the Goverment, for he would then become a centre of disaffection and a rallying point for real opposition. Leave him where he is, as a decaying hostage.[37]

This view was not shared by the Tory 'rebels'. For junior ministers such as Boothby and Macmillan, it was not Labour ministers but the large number of Chamberlainites still in office who exercised undue influence. As the military situation in France became increasingly desperate, efforts to force Chamberlain's resignation were renewed in the short-lived 'Under-Secretaries' plot'. On 17 June a small group met at Amery's house and decided to press for the replacement of the War Cabinet with a three-man Committee of Public Safety, modelled on experience of the First World War. The Prime Minister's reaction, after learning of this new move, was that 'if there is any more of this nonsense they will go'. Anyone wishing to criticise, Churchill told Amery, should resign and do so from outside; junior ministers, he added, should stick to the tasks allocated to them rather than proposing wholesale goverment reorganisation.[38] This swift action forestalled the under-secretaries, but it did not deter Clement Davies, who persisted for some time with what one minister called 'sordid gatherings at the Reform Club'.[39] In early July Davies, hoping to revive parliamentary agitation, invited all back-benchers to a meeting which proposed a 'further strengthening' of the government. The meeting was packed, however, by Chamberlain's supporters, who insisted that with the fall of France the time was inopportune for changes in personnel. 'My friends', Chamberlain told his sister with some satisfaction, 'turned up in force and bullied Clem & his friends till they dropped their resolution and adjourned.'[40]

'The attack on Neville and the "men of Munich" comes to nothing', Beaverbrook wrote on 6 July.[41] But if a month of intense agitation at Westminster had failed to dislodge the Conservative leader, the 'attack on the appeasers' was in the long term to have profound political consequences. In some ways the continuing influence of the Tory majority had been underlined. This reality of parliamentary politics, after all, was at the base of Churchill's insistence that he would stand or fall by the new government. As Rab Butler put it, if the various intrigues were taken any further, 'all we have to do is to pull the string of the toy dog of the 1922

Committee and make it bark. After a few staccato utterances it
becomes clear that the Government depends upon the Tory squires
for its majority.'[42] On the other hand, Conservative MPs themselves, still reeling from the shock of Chamberlain's downfall, were
slow to grasp the possibilities of coalition. Instead, they remained
on the defensive and in a state of some disarray: the majority were
uncertain in their dealings with the new Prime Minister, and
resentful about the need to co-operate with Labour and the Tory
'rebels'. As a result, Tory MPs proved incapable of responding
effectively to the campaign of denigration against their leader. The
events of June 1940 had therefore, above all, blackened the
reputation of the 'men of Munich'. This whole process was taken
much further by the publication of the best-selling satirical
pamphlet *Guilty Men*, which clearly struck a chord with the public;
in subsequent opinion polls a high percentage of those questioned
now favoured Chamberlain's removal from the government.[43]
Here, then, as we shall see, was a major political theme — the
alleged responsibility of Chamberlain for Britain's plight in 1940 —
that was to reverberate throughout the war years and beyond.

More immediately, Churchill's authority had been greatly
strengthened. His hold over the government had increased at
Chamberlain's expense, both because of the unpopularity of the
'old gang' and because the Lord President was now showing signs
of a serious illness that was to result in his death within a matter
of months.[44] Nor was there much to fear from critics of the
government. By giving such a positive lead to the nation, the Prime
Minister succeeded in marginalising those who still favoured a
negotiated peace. After the fall of France, there were noticeably
fewer efforts to entice Lloyd George into the fold. He had turned
down the latest offer, Churchill concluded, and would now be left
alone. In practice Lloyd George, as his own private secretary noted,
had become increasingly 'sour' in old age and obsessed by 'tactics';
his chance to influence events from inside had effectively passed.[45]
What was more, the Prime Minister's parliamentary base had
suddenly become more stable, following some remarkable scenes in
the House of Commons on 4 July.

Chamberlain had recently been warned by a journalist, Paul
Einzig, that the lukewarm attitude of Tories in the House towards
Churchill was conveying a poor impression abroad. Above all,
American journalists were interpreting it as a sign that Britain was

not united in its determination to continue the fight single-handed against Germany. Fearing that vital American support might be jeopardised, the Lord President made sure that steps were taken to orchestrate a more enthusiastic response from Conservative MPs.[46] After Churchill informed the Commons about the destruction of the French fleet at Oran, Tory back-benchers — at the instigation of the Chief Whip — rose in unison to give prolonged and enthusiastic cheering. Margesson later denied organising such a response, though, as one observer present recalled, the speech was no better than several others, and 'the occasion — the outbreak of hostilities with our old ally — hardly one for rejoicing'.[47] The hatchet had by no means been entirely buried, and, as will become clear, the mutual distrust between Churchill and the party was in many ways to persist throughout the war. But Conservatives had at last reconciled themselves to the coalition, recognising that the national interest had become paramount. The 'great invasion scare', the Prime Minister noted on 12 July, was concentrating minds enormously.

For several weeks after the fall of France, a German invasion was in the forefront of people's minds. During August the Luftwaffe began its attempt to establish aerial supremacy over Britain as an essential prerequisite of invasion; it was only later, in the autumn, after the Battle of Britain had been narrowly won, that Hitler turned to massive bombing raids on the major cities in an attempt to undermine civilian morale. With the might of Nazi Germany now directed exclusively against the British for the first time, the sense of national unity and determination to survive was greatly heightened. In these circumstances, the Prime Minister was suddenly assuming the mantle of national saviour, especially after it became clear that Chamberlain's health was deteriorating rapidly. The Lord President left the cabinet for an operation at the end of July, and though he was able briefly to return to office in September, he confided in his diary that any likelihood of 'further political activity, and even a possibility of another Premiership after the war, have gone'.[48] Churchill did have genuine fears about Chamberlain's imminent departure, which he felt might upset the balance and effectiveness of the government. But he could not be oblivious to the implications for his own personal authority. 'There are', he wrote to a colleague on 30 July, 'no competitors for my job now.'[49] On the same day, following another stirring speech which won praise from

all quarters, Hugh Dalton confirmed that the Prime Minister 'now
leads the whole House, unquestioned and ascendant. . . .'[50]
    Although the coalition was absorbed by the task at hand, all was
not well behind the scenes. The government's handling of domestic
affairs, for example, had been streamlined by the creation of five
ministerial committees, to deal with production, economic policy,
food, home policy and civil defence.[51] But in some respects the new
structure was obsolete almost before it had begun to operate. In
particular, Lord Beaverbrook — publicly, of course, one of the
heroes of the hour for his role in boosting aircraft production —
effectively boycotted and undermined the committee system,
preferring to work through more direct and personal methods.
Beaverbrook's ruthlessness in obtaining men and materials led, in
fact, to the first of a series of recurrent departmental clashes,
notably with the Labour ministers Bevin and Morrison, and it was
not long before Churchill was having to use a mixture of flattery
and cajolery in order to prevent Beaverbrook's threatened resignation.[52] Other ministers were also encountering difficulties in
attempting to meet the crisis. Duff Cooper, for example, the
Minister of Information, was coming under fierce attack from the
press over his plans to introduce greater censorship of war news.
'What worries me', wrote Harold Nicolson, junior minister at the
Ministry, 'is that the whole Press, plus certain pro-Munich
Conservatives, have banded together to bring Duff Cooper
down.'[53] Cooper was to survive, but not indefinitely.
    There were other signs at Westminster that traditional party
concerns had not been entirely cast aside. In late July the 1922
Committee met to urge the government that those evacuated from
coastal areas be given compensation 'bearing some relation
to . . . previous standard of living'. The main anxiety of Tory back-
benchers, however, was that meetings throughout the country to
prepare the public for possible invasion were dominated by
speakers with 'strong left-wing, if not actually communist, sym-
pathies' — a cause of further dissatisfaction with the Minister of
Information.[54] On the Labour side, there was some back-bench
agitation when it was announced that Britain would go ahead with
the closure of the Burma Road, by which supplies reached China
for its war against Japan. This decision was widely interpreted —
wrongly in this instance — as a reflection of the Foreign Secretary's
'appeasing' instincts, and Churchill had to move quickly to forestall
a revived attack on the 'old gang'. But, for the most part, politicians

devoted their energies to encouraging defence preparations. In an intensely charged atmosphere, critics of the government now had to tread cautiously. The former Secretary of State for War, Hore-Belisha, could not — according to Lord Beaverbrook — 'make up his mind whether to attempt to smash his way into the Government by attacking it, or whether to wheedle his way in by praising it. He has just made a speech in his constituency in which he does both of these things.' And as for Lloyd George, Beaverbrook added, the public were now divided between 'the people who think that Winston should bring him in and the other people who think that Hitler will put him in'.[55]

The coalition was thus more deeply entrenched by the time the Battle of Britain had been won. 'Politics and people can in general be said to be calm', Rab Butler told Sam Hoare, serving in Madrid, 'with the government staggering along quite normally.' Lord Beaverbrook, he noted, was 'as mercurial as ever. At present he thinks that God is guarding his factories.'[56] Beaverbrook was also intimately involved in Churchill's first major cabinet changes. With Chamberlain's sudden departure, the Prime Minister decided to make a new appointment to the War Cabinet pending the Lord President's expected return. His initial plan was to promote Herbert Morrison. Although Morrison had not been an unqualified success at the Ministry of Supply, it was felt that his populist style would pay dividends in the drive to stimulate greater war production. But this idea soon foundered. Senior Tories were adamant that the principle of party balance in cabinet representation, established when setting up the coalition, should be rigidly maintained. Beaverbrook told W. P. Crozier of the *Manchester Guardian* that 'the Tory managers, Kingsley Wood, Captain Margesson and others, held a meeting and decided that to have Morrison brought in would disturb the balance of the parties in the War Cabinet and they would not have it.' Instead, Beaverbrook's entry as a Tory representative was suggested, a proposal that caused him great merriment: 'I'll tell you one thing, Mr Crozier, I'm not nearly such a Conservative as Herbert Morrison!' Soon afterwards, the Prime Minister wrote to Chamberlain, wishing him a speedy recovery and informing him that Lord Beaverbrook had been added to the War Cabinet 'in order to get more help in the supply side of the Defence Ministry'.[57]

Within weeks, though, it became obvious that Neville Chamber-

lain — far from recovering — would have to leave politics altogether. This provided an opportunity, amongst other things, for
a more far-reaching government reshufffle. In spite of his enhanced
authority, however, the Prime Minister still found difficulty in
shaping the cabinet entirely as he wished. His desire to replace
Chamberlain with Anthony Eden was again frustrated by senior
Conservatives, who insisted that Eden did not have the necessary
background for overseeing domestic policy. Churchill eventually
agreed to appoint as Lord President the dour Sir John Anderson,
whose handling of preparations for invasion as Minister of Home
Security had recently come under attack. Anderson was subsequently to become a prominent figure on the home front, bringing
to bear his long experience as a civil servant and his vast statistical
knowledge.[58] The Prime Minister had also hoped that Beaverbrook
would assume overall responsibility for supply problems. But the
Minister of Aircraft Production resisted this idea on medical
grounds, and for once absented himself from Churchill's company
with a 'last minute political temperature'. The major change in
October 1940, therefore, was the promotion to the War Cabinet of
Ernest Bevin, in recognition of his vital role as Minister of Labour;
this was balanced by the inclusion also of the Chancellor, Kingsley
Wood. Outside the War Cabinet, further consequential changes
followed. Morrison was moved to become Home Secretary, a post
he was reluctant to accept in view of the difficulties faced by
Anderson; and the Ministry of Supply now went to Sir Andrew
Duncan, a businessman who proved far more amenable to
Beaverbrook than his predecessor.[59]

Reactions to the government changes were mixed. Some press
commentators criticised the enlargement of the War Cabinet to eight
members, depicting it as an unwelcome move away from the 1916
model. Few ministers, it was noted, were now free from departmental
duties to concentrate on the war, and the *Manchester Guardian* concluded that it was hard 'to resist the suspicion that party balancing has
had too much to do with the enlargement of numbers'. In effect, the
Prime Minister had sought not to offend any major element of the
coalition, and had done just enough to keep all parties satisfied. Eden
was comforted with the assurance that now Chamberlain was gone,
'the succession was his'. Churchill had also ensured that promotion to
the middle ranks of the government had been secured for some of his
own Tory associates, such as Oliver Lyttelton, who became President

of the Board of Trade. Orthodox Conservatives, meanwhile, were reassured by Kingsley Wood's inclusion in the War Cabinet, which was taken as a sign that Chamberlain's legacy would live on. Once again, there was some concern on the Labour benches that an opportunity had been missed to eliminate the 'old gang'. But this feeling had to be set against satisfaction with the promotion of Morrison and, above all, Ernest Bevin, now establishing himself as a powerful presence on the home front.[60]

Chamberlain's retirement opened up one further possibility for the Prime Minister — leadership of the Conservative party. Churchill naturally had doubts about assuming this new responsibility. He confided to one Tory MP that he was still intensely suspicious of the party, and his wife openly argued that to take on Chamberlain's post would undermine his identity as a national leader, capable of attracting support from all sections of the community.[61] On the other hand, the arguments for stepping into Chamberlain's shoes were compelling. The Conservatives, as we have seen, could alone provide a stable parliamentary base, and to hand the party leadership over to anyone else would needlessly establish an obvious focal point for anti-government feeling in the future. To refuse the leadership, in other words, was likely to perpetuate a situation in which Chuchill felt unable to exercise complete political control.[62] The Prime Minister therefore accepted the invitation to replace Chamberlain as Tory leader, though some commentators noted an element of uncertainty when a special party meeting was convened in October to ratify the new arrangement. Rumours that a deputy leader would be proposed by party stalwarts came to nothing, and Churchill made an unusually introspective speech in which he emphasised the importance of acting with the party's authority.[63] This new development completed a transformation scarcely conceivable six months earlier. 'You will', Sam Hoare wrote in congratulation, 'be much stronger with the Party machine behind you. . . . Besides this, it seems to me vital to the Party itself that if should have at once a popular leader at its head.'[64] The Prime Minister was now the unquestioned national and party leader, though few believed that a genuine meeting of minds had taken place. Commenting on the special party meeting that endorsed Churchill's leadership, one commentator concluded: 'No one was quite sure whether the Party had captured him, or he the Party, but all were content.'[65]

What conclusions might be drawn, then, about the early months of
coalition politics? In a private interview during July 1940, the
Prime Minister commented on how his friend Lord Beaverbrook
had become totally absorbed by his duties as Minister of Aircraft
Production. 'He won't talk of politics', Churchill explained, 'he's
wholly taken up with aeroplanes.'[66] Any assessment of Churchill's
government in 1940 must, of course, underline the extraordinary
stresses of the moment: the sense of desperation as the Germans
overran the Low Countries and France; the hasty preparations for
an invasion daily anticipated; and the unprecedented hardships
caused by aerial bombardment in the Blitz. With the benefit of
hindsight, however, 1940 nevertheless stands out as a decisive year
in British politics. In the first place, the national emergency served
to transform the public mood, a development widely commented
upon at the time. As George Orwell wrote, it was one of those
moments 'when the whole nation suddenly swings together and
does the same thing, like a herd of cattle facing a wolf. . . . After
eight months of vaguely wondering what the war was about, the
people suddenly knew what they had got to do: first, to get the
army away from Dunkirk, and secondly to prevent invasion. It was
like the awakening of a giant.'[67]

In these circumstances, the atmosphere on the home front
underwent a profound change. Pressure towards the idea of
'equality of sacrifice' suddenly became intense and, as we have seen,
there was a widespread reaction against the 'old gang', those
alleged to be responsible for Britain's desperate plight. This was the
beginning of the period, in Paul Addison's vivid description, of
'Colonel Blimp being pursued through a land of Penguin Specials
by an abrasive meritocrat, a progressive churchman, and J. B.
Priestley'.[68] Certainly Mass-Observation was already finding evidence, before the end of 1940, of a radical new spirit and a
'questioning of the status quo', with the notion of a 'people's war'
rapidly gaining currency.[69] It would, though, be misleading to
overstate the longer term significance of this shift in public
attitudes. The emotions stirred during Britain's finest hour would
inevitably, in time, be overlaid by new influences and experiences,
according to how the war unfolded; this, of course, was still
impossible to foresee at the end of 1940. Indeed, it will be argued
below that the moment of no return in the wartime swing to the left
did not occur until after 1942. And, similarly, if the Conservative
cause had suffered in public from the reaction against Chamberlain

and appeasement, then there was no reason for thinking that it might not gain from what was the one incontrovertible domestic development of recent months: the consolidaton of Churchill's authority as Prime Minister.

Churchill's ascendancy, as we have seen, was not the result of his straightforward emergence as the 'man of destiny'. Nor, indeed, was it inevitable that he 'was bound to be master in his own house once he was Prime Minister'.[70] His qualities of determination and courageous leadership were, needless to say, vital once he had come to power; above all, Churchill's reputation was based on his ability to speak to the British people in the summer of 1940 'as no one ever has before of since'.[71] But, in some ways, he was fortunate in being able to extend his authority so rapidly. In particular, it was only the unexpected departure of Neville Chamberlain that removed the conflict of loyalty facing Conservative supporters throughout the country. Even after his assumption of the party leadership in October 1940, the Prime Minister still faced sullen acquiescence from many of the Chamberlainites who held sway in the House of Commons. If Churchill was now accepted as the party's major public asset, then suspicions were sustained by growing evidence that he would not brook any form of criticism. Winston, noted one of his friends at the end of 1940, was 'getting very arrogant and hates criticism of any kind'.[72] This failing — which had underpinned much of the dissatisfaction with Chamberlain — was to lead to fresh parliamentary difficulties during 1941–42. For the time being, though, Churchill could enjoy his finest hour. At the end of the year an American journalist asked several leading politicians, including ministers, who it was felt would become Prime Minister in the event of anything happening to Churchill. 'Nobody', he recorded, 'had any idea.'[73]

A measure of the Prime Minister's position at the end of 1940 came with the sudden death in December of the British ambassador in the United States, Lord Lothian. Several possible replacements were considered. Mention was made of Stafford Cripps, at the time serving as ambassador in Moscow, but Churchill dismissed him as 'a lunatic in a country of lunatics'.[74] Lloyd George was also considered sufficiently influential to be offered the post, though his potency as a critic was not such that the Prime Minister was worried by his refusal on grounds of ill health. Lloyd George, it was now more widely believed, was suffering from 'senility, pessimism

and ambition, a fatal combination'.[75] In the end Churchill forced
the job — regarded as vital if America was to be persuaded to enter
the war — upon Lord Halifax. Armed with the knowledge from
censorship reports that the Foreign Secretary had inherited some
of Chamberlain's unpopularity, the Prime Minister brushed aside
the objections made both by Halifax and, more vociferously, by his
wife. This development further consolidated Churchill's hold over
the War Cabinet by allowing the promotion of Anthony Eden, an
aim that had been frustrated in the October reshuffle. At the same
time, the Prime Minister was careful not to give the impression of a
more concerted assault on the 'old gang'. Halifax's departure was
balanced by promoting David Margesson to the War Office; he,
in turn, was replaced as Chief Whip by another Chamberlainite
loyalist, James Stuart. In effect, Churchill recognised that any move
against his erstwhile enemies had to be gradual and piecemeal, both
because the range of talent available for promotion elsewhere in
party ranks remained limited and because only the Tory majority
could provide the Prime Minister with a secure base.

Here we come back to one of the ironies of British politics in
1940. In spite of the shock caused by Chamberlain's downfall and
death, the Conservative party remained in a strong position to
dominate coalition politics. But instead of recognising this, Tory
MPs preferred to dwell on the past, and were thrown off guard by
the new mood of hostility towards the 'old gang' and 'vested
interests'. While many Conservatives remained deeply suspicious of
the coalition, the Labour party's morale and prestige had been
much improved through entry into government. But, by the end of
1940, there were still few signs that Labour had broken out from
its bridgehead. It remained to be seen whether the party would
benefit from the new public concern about social progress; this
again would depend upon a whole host of future military and
political developments. In the meantime, the government changes
of October and December had not noticeably increased Labour
representation in the government; improvement on this score was
not to come until 1942. As a result, the party remained in practical
terms the junior partner in the coalition. Labour's difficulty in
forcing the pace over policy was made clear when Churchill resisted
proposals for a public definition of Britain's war aims.[76] Nor had
Labour ministers made the individual impact originally anticipated.
Attlee inspired no fear in his opponents; Greenwood was widely

perceived as ineffectual; and Bevin — though recognised as a powerful presence — was facing mounting criticism by the end of the year. As we shall see in the next chapter, the Labour ministers collectively faced great difficulties in coming to terms with the major domestic problem facing the coalition during 1940–41 — organisation of the war economy.

Notes

1 A. Bullock, *The Life and Times of Ernest Bevin*, Vol. II *Minister of Labour 1940–1945*, London, 1967, p. 1. On the theme of this chapter, see also L. Thompson, *1940: Year of Legend, Year of History*, London, 1966.

2 Churchill to Chamberlain, 10 May 1940, cited in Gilbert, *Finest Hour*, pp. 314–15.

3 *Channon Diary*, 11 May 1940, p. 251; Feiling, *Life of Neville Chamberlain*, p. 443.

4 *Nicolson Diary*, 13 May 1940, pp. 85–6: according to Brendan Bracken, he and Margesson sat late going through the lists — 'Winston was not in the least interested once the major posts had been filled, and kept on trying to interrupt them by discussing the nature of war and the changing rules of strategy.'

5 George Steward, Press Officer for the Prime Minister, cited in J. Colville, *The Fringes of Power: Downing Street Diaries 1939–1955*, London, 1985, p. 196.

6 Bevin to Churchill, 10 May 1940, cited in Gilbert, op. cit., p. 331: the Prime Minister readily accepted Bevin's terms, including greater power for the Minstry of Labour over war production, though he showed little inclination subsequently to act upon them.

7 *Dalton Diary*, 18 May 1940, p. 13.

8 Addison, 'Political change in Britain', pp. 471–2.

9 *Colville Diary*, 10 May 1940, p. 122. Colville, one of Chamberlain's private secretaries who stayed on to serve Churchill, himself expressed a view common among civil servants: 'He may, of course, be the man of drive and energy the country believes him to be and he may be able to speed up our creaking military and industrial machinery; but it is a terrible risk.'

10 Chamberlain diary, 11 May 1940, Neville Chamberlain papers, NC2/24A.

11 Diary notes by R. A. Butler, 13 May 1940: Butler papers, Trinity College, Cambridge, G14.

12 Diary notes by Butler, cited in A. Howard, *R.A.B.: the Life of R. A. Butler*, London, 1987, p. 94. Many Tories were particularly upset at the treatment of Oliver Stanley, one of Chamberlain's allies, who was

offered a post at the Dominions Office in such 'contemptuous' terms by Churchill that he felt it necessary to decline.

13 *Channon Diary*, 13 May 1940, p. 252. Similarly, in the House of Lords, 'Neville's name was received with a full-throated cheer, whereas Winston's name was received in silence' — Lord Davidson to Baldwin, 14 May 1940: Stanley Baldwin papers, cited in Gilbert, op. cit, p. 332.

14 F. W. Pethick-Lawrence, *Fate Has Been Kind*, London, 1943, pp. 201–2; J. Griffiths, *Pages from Memory*, London, 1969, pp. 69–70. The new arrangements were to have some unusual consequences. The Labour back-bencher Arthur Creech Jones, for example, would often sit as Bevin's PPS on one side of the House to help answer questions before crossing the floor to fire questions at the government on colonial issues — J. Parker, *Father of the House: Fifty Years in Politics*, London, 1982, p. 80.

15 Addison, 'Political change in Britain', pp. 489–90.

16 Euan Wallace diary, 13 May 1940, Bodleian Laibraty Oxford, c. 497.

17 Parliamentary Peace Aims Group, *Memorandum on Peace Aims*, 10 November 1939: Richard Stokes papers, Bodleian library, Oxford, Box 18.

18 *Forward*, 25 May 1940: 'I hate Hitlerism as much as anyone, but having spent three years of the last war as a fighting soldier I remember how after a time we all longed for a negotiated peace. Such a peace obviously is not possible now but when the first great clash of arms is over an opportunity may arise and we should be ready to seize it . . .'

19 J. A. Spender to Lord Simon, 16 May 1940: Simon papers, Bodleian Library, Ms. Simon 86, f. 86.

20 On this theme, see P. Addison, 'Lloyd George and compromise peace in the Second World War', in A. J. P. Taylor (ed.), *Lloyd George: Twelve Essays*, London, 1971, pp. 361–84.

21 *Sylvester Diary*, 29 May 1940, pp. 264–5. On 15 May Lloyd Geroge's secretary reported that he had been talking 'about giving in without fighting because he thinks we are beaten. The whole point is that he hates Neville and the Government so much he would like to see them beaten.'

22 Churchill to Lloyd George, 6 June 1940, cited in Gilbert, op. cit., p. 474; *Sylyester Diary*, 30 May 1940, p. 226.

23 See D. Reynolds, 'Churchill and the British "decision" to fight on in 1940: right policy, wrong reasons', in R. Langhorne (ed.), *Diplomacy and Intelligence During the Second World War: Essays in Honour of F. H. Hinsley*, Cambridge, 1985, pp. 147–66: 'There was no formal "decision" to fight on in June 1940, but it was far from being a foregone conclusion, as Churchill suggested. In Cabinet at the time of Dunkirk, and among a small group of M.P.s and peers, there was a considerable debate about Britain's future chances and about the possibility of a satisfactory negotiated peace, immediately or when the threat of invasion had passed'.

24 Birkenhead, *Halifax*, p. 458; Gilbert, op. cit., pp. 402–13.

25 Churchill to Baldwin, 4 June 1940, Baldwin papers, ibid., p. 469.
26 A comment made by the leading civil servant Edward Bridges: *Colville Diary*, 31 May 1940, p. 144.
27 *Daily Herald*, 5–6 June 1940. See also, for example, the *News Chronicle*, 5 June 1940: 'the failures should be dropped once and for all'.
28 Minute by A. J. Sylvester, n.d. [June 1940]: Lloyd George papers House of Lords Record office, (HLRO) G/24/1/154.
29 Neville to Hilda Chamberlain, 2 June 1940, Chamberlain papers, NC18/1/1159. Chamberlain remained unmoved by charges against the policy of appeasement; he claimed in private tht he could only respond to criticism by himself attacking those Labour ministers with whom he was now serving.
30 Chamberlain diary, 6 June 1940, Chamberlain papers, NC2/24A.
31 Hugh Cudlipp, *Publish and Be Damned!: the Astonishing Story of the Daily Mirror*, London, 1953, pp. 144–5.
32 Chamberlain diary, 10 June 1940, Chamberlain papers, NC2/24A.
33 Minute by Sylvester, 9 June 1940, Lloyd Geroge papers, G/24/1/156. Sylvester also noted the complaint of Clement Davies that 'they are still playing party politics instead of putting the country first'.
34 *The Times*, 10 June 1940.
35 Beaverbrook to Hoare, 11 June 1940: Lord Beaverbrook papers, HLRO, C/308.
36 V. 362 H. C. Deb., 5 s., cc. 51–61, 18 June 1940; minute by Sylvester, 19 June 1940, Lloyd George papers, G/24/1/165.
37 *Dalton Diary*, 18 June 1940, p. 42.
38 *Amery Diary*, 18 June 1940, pp. 625–6: '... my instinctive doubts against the urgency of the juniors proved right. However desperate the national crisis may be men cannot help thinking of themselves and Clem, Boothby, etc. had successfully frightened Attlee, Greenwood and above all Neville and roused Winston's authoritarian instincts. They had better all resign themselves for the time being to doing their work...' See also Addison, *Road to 1945*, pp. 109–10.
39 Butler to Stafford Cripps, 18 June 1940, Butler papers, E3/3, f. 146.
40 Neville to Ida Chamberlain, 7 July 1940, Chamberlain papers, NC18/1/1158.
41 Beaverbrook to Hoare, 6 July 1940, Beaverbrook papers, C/308.
42 Butler to Hoare, 20 July 1940, Butler papers, E3/8, f. 114.
43 'Cato' (M. Foot, F. Owen and P. Howard), *Guilty Men*, London, 1940, p. 125: 'Let the guilty men retire... of their own volition, and so make an essential contribution to the victory upon which we are implacably resolved'.
44 Hugh Dalton's cruel description of Chamberlain during this period was the 'Old Corpse Upstairs' — *Dalton Diary*, 4 July 1940, p. 53.
45 A. J. Sylvester, *The Real Lloyd George*, London, 1947, pp. 271–2. Churchill, Lloyd George now recognised, 'will not smash the Tory Party to save the country, as I smashed the Liberal Party' — Thomas Jones, *A Diary with Letters 1931-1950*, London, 1954, p. 465.

46 P. Einzig, *In the Center of Things*, London, 1960, pp. 209–20. Einzig,
     a journalist on the *Financial News* who brought this matter to Cham-
     berlain's attention, received an assurance from the Lord President that
     he would undertake 'to see that your impression is not confirmed by
     anything more serious'.
47 Gibert, op. cit., pp. 924–3, quoting the words of a Downing Street
     official, John Martin.
48 Chamberalin diary, 9 September 1940, cited in Feiling, op. cit., p. 451.
49 Churchill to Sir Roger Keyes, 30 July 1940, cited in Gilbert, op. cit.,
     p. 697.
50 *Dalton Diary*, 30 July 1940, p. 67.
51 See below, Chapter 3.
52 A. J. P. Taylor, *Beaverbrook*, London, 1972, pp. 414–49, gives a
     detailed account of Beaverbrook's various resignation threats.
53 *Nicolson Diary*, 3 August 1940, p. 104. For a full account of Cooper's
     difficulties as Minister of Information, see I. MacLaine, *Ministry of
     Morle: Home Front Morle and the Ministry of Inforamtion in World
     War II*, London, 1979.
54 Wallace diary, 31 July and 7 August 1940, c. 497–8.
55 Beaverbrook to Hoare, 14 August 1940, Beaverbrook papers, C/308.
56 Butler to Hoare, 6 September 1940, Butler papers, E3/8, ff. 120–1.
57 Interview with Beaverbrook on 24 August 1940: Taylor (ed.), *Off the
     Record*, pp. 198–9; Gilbert, op. cit., p. 711.
58 Calder, *People's War*, p. 119: 'before the computer was perfected,
     Anderson was a tolerable substitute.'
59 *Colville Diary*, 30 September–2 October 1940, pp. 252–5.
60 *Manchester Guardian*, 4 October 1940; *Daily Herald*, 4 October 1940.
61 G. S. Harvie-Watt, *Most of My Life*, London, 1980. pp. 37–9; Mary
     Soames, *Clementine Churchill*, London, 1979, pp. 299–300.
62 W. S. Churchill, *The Second World War*, Vol. II, *Their Finest Hour*,
     London, 1949, pp. 438–9.
63 H. F. Crookshank diary, 9 October 1940: Bodleian Library, Ms. Eng.
     Hist. d. 360.
64 Hoare to Churchill, 10 October 1940, cited in Gilbert, op. cit., p. 837.
65 *The Sunday Times*, 13 October 1940.
66 Crozier interview with Churchill, 26 July 1940: Taylor (ed.), op. cit.,
     p. 177.
67 Geroge Orwell, *The Lion and the Unicorn: Socialism and the English
     Genius*, London, 1941.
68 Addison, op. cit., p. 188; see also K. Jefferys, 'The life and death of
     Colonel Blimp'. *The Historian*, XXI, 1989.
69 Mass-Observation Typescript Report No. 496, 'Popular attitudes to
     wartime politics', 20 November 1940: Mass-Observation Archive,
     University of Sussex.
70 Addison, op. cit., p. 111.
71 I. Berlin, *Mr Churchill in 1940*, London, 1964, p. 27.
72 R. Rhodes James (ed.), *Victor Cazalet: a Portrait*, London, 1976,
     p. 231. See also *Channon Diary*, 6 November 1940, p. 273: 'Winston

trades on his position', wrote Channon, adding that 'the country does not want a dictator'.
73 R. Ingersoll, *Report on England*, London, 1941, p. 165.
74 *Colville Diary*, 12 December 1940, p. 309.
75 *Dalton Diary*, 14 December 1940, p. 121, quoting words originally used by de Gaulle about Pétain.
76 This episode is detailed in the Prime Minister's papers at the Public Record Office (PRO), PREM 4 100/4; see also below, Chapter 5.

3

Organising the war economy

The war economy loomed large in domestic political discussion during 1940–41. Military strategy and war production were, of course, inextricably linked: with Britain standing alone against Nazi-dominated Europe, domestic politics inevitably focused on how the nation's resources might be most effectively harnessed to achieve victory. Just as the government devoted much of its energy to the problems of production and mobilisation, so handling of the war economy proved to be a persistent theme of political debate at Westminster. The formation of the coalition in May 1940 brought greater determination and clarification to Britain's economic war effort. But tangible results on the battlefield were slow to materialise. Britain's military fortunes showed few immediate signs of improvement, even after the entry of the Soviet Union into the war in the summer of 1941; as a result, friends and critics of the government alike became increasingly frustrated. Controversy over the war economy, hitherto muted for fear of damaging national unity, thus became more and more difficult to contain, and, indeed, by 1942 there was talk of a developing 'production crisis'. It was only after the 'turn of the tide' that war production ceased to be contentious. The coalition's whole approach to the war economy at last appeared to be vindicated, and, as we shall see, within a matter of months political attention was shifting rapidly to questions associated with post-war reconstruction.

Much later, after the cessation of hostilities in 1945, the success of Britain's economic war effort was widely attributed to central planning. Certainly, the Second World War followed the pattern of the 1914–18 conflict, with state intervention becoming progressively more intense. By 1942 the major features of the wartime economy were in place: government controls over capital and industry; the direction of labour and the conscription for war work of both men and women; the regulation of civilian consumption through a comprehensive rationing system; and elaborate planning mechanisms which included not only new central government ministries but also the growth of regional co-ordination. For the most part, there was little direct intervention in industry. Rather, the state exercised control by drawing up production programmes, by allocating raw materials and labour, and by using its position as the dominant purchaser to fix contract prices. Managements were left free to concentrate on improving production, with their profits assured through the 'cost-plus' system. In the meantime, alternative sources of demand were suppressed through high taxation, and after 1941 'concentration' schemes were introduced to help convert 'non-essential' industries to war work, while at the same time reducing the output of consumer goods to a level consistent with the maintenance of civilian morale. In this, as in other respects, there were major departures from the economic orthodoxy of the 1930s: the previous pecking order of finance, production and manpower was now completely reversed, though it remained unclear how far the new dispensation would outlast the end of the war.[1]

The war also had profound implications for workers and working conditions. As manpower became the most scarce resource, so the high unemployment of the 1930s gradually disappeared, and the trade union movement rapidly developed in both size and industrial strength. It was true that strikes and lockouts were declared illegal for the duration, and among the sweeping new powers assumed by the state was the authority to direct anyone over age sixteen to any form of war work. But the influence of trade union leader, Ernest Bevin — invited to serve as Minister of Labour as a symbol of government co-operation with the workforce — helped to ensure that such powers were used only sparingly. At the same time the government stuck to existing collective bargaining procedures, facing down demands for statutory wage controls, and the trade unions also gained in prestige from a new pattern of industrial consultation. A Joint Consultative Committee was formed representing the Trades Union Congress (TUC) and the British Employers' Confederation, and in the regions over 6,000 Joint Production Committees were established, enabling ideas on how production could be improved to be channelled from the shop-floor. Nevertheless, industrial relations remained plagued by pre-war animosites and, above all, by the necessity for 'dilution'; in craft trades especially, the introduction of unskilled labour was often fiercely resisted. The result was that in spite of the regulations, strike activity intensified as the war progressed, though, with many disputes being settled quickly through arbitration, the average annual loss of working days was only about half that experienced in the First World War.[2]

The performance of the British war economy has recently become the subject of considerable historical controversy. In particular, Corelli Barnett has argued that the war years highlighted many of the essential features of Britain's post-1945 'industrial disease': poor management, obstructive trade unions and inadequate government initiatives.[3] Barnett's 'audit of war', however, has itself been criticised for distorting the overall performance of the economic war effort; and certainly statistical evidence does suggest that in some respects the British war economy bears comparison with other leading combatants.[4] It will be argued here, moreover, that wartime circumstances ruled out the possibility of any fundamental restructuring of Britain's industry. In the first place, the main priority of the coalition when it came to power was simply to devise measures that would ensure survival: in the desperate atmosphere of 1940–41 ministers were too preoccupied with the immediate emergency to focus on long-term planning. During this period unease about the slow move towards full mobilisation gradually intensified, but much of this criticism — though understandable — tended to overlook the realities of the industrial situation. For, in practice, while squaring up to the external threat, neither side of industry could easily forget the bitter legacy of the inter-war years, and the government's policy was thus inevitably based on a series of compromises between the supporters of capital and labour. Beneath the surface of national unity the production issue also pinpointed the deep-seated differences that continued to exist between Conservative and Labour forces over the aims and objectives of economic policy. Britain's war economy was not in any sense the product of a new consensus; there was no blueprint or model that would survive effortlessly into the post-war world. Rather, war production was characterised by a series of hastily conceived expedients, measures that might be considered remarkably successful in view of one particular factor: in May 1940 there was very little to build upon.

Throughout the phoney war, Britain's economy remained only partially mobilised. The Chamberlain government did introduce a large body of legislation when war broke out in September 1939. An Emergency Powers Act, for example, had already been agreed, giving the government extensive new authority over the economic and social life of the nation. And, as Hitler's attack on Poland proceeded, Whitehall was also able to draw on the precedent of the First World War by setting up several new departments, such as the ministries of Supply, Economic Warfare, and Food and Shipping. But Chamberlain's administration was soon being attacked for lacking both urgency and coherent leadership. The vital task of translating service needs into specific orders, and converting industry to a war footing to supply them, was originally intended for the Ministry of Supply. The Admiralty, however, insisted on retaining independent control over the shipbuilding programme. This meant — after the creation of a separate department of aircraft production in 1940 — that the Ministry of Supply was left with responsibility for the army alone; a task which in itself raised a host of difficulties. Nor did the government's central committee machinery for handling the war economy inspire much confidence. In response to parliamentary and press criticism, the Prime Minister had established a special Economic Policy Committee, but he refused to consider demands for a single minister to oversee the whole field of war production. In the meantime, the Treasury remained entrenched as the most powerful department in Whitehall, and sought to manage the war economy through the traditional peacetime methods of inter-departmental conciliation.[5]

The Prime Minister had already appointed, before the outbreak of war, a special economic adviser, Lord Stamp, who, with the assistance of professional economists recruited from outside the civil service, began to prepare a 'survey of war plans in the economic and financial sphere'. Stamp clearly enjoyed the confidence of Chamberlain and his senior officials, and, indeed, early in 1940 the Prime Minister seriously considered promoting his new adviser to the top spot at the Treasury. This plan would have meant both sacking the Chancellor, Sir John Simon, and removing Stamp's peerage by special Act of Parliament, and had to be abandoned after the controversy surrounding the dismissal of the War Minister, Hore-Belisha. In consequence, Stamp's influence on the war economy remained limited: he insisted on continuing with his duties as a railway director at the same time, and the committee he chaired was balanced by a separate ministerial committee under the Chancellor. The professional economists charged with working on the Stamp survey were stunned to find that, when making suggestions for boosting manpower levels, the most frequent official response was that such things could not possibly be contemplated as there was a war on.[6]

Chamberlain's government, therefore, gave the appearance of administrative activity, but without major departures from pre-war orthodoxy. Sir John Simon's cautious war budget proposed only modest increases in direct taxation; government expenditure amounted to £20 million a week at the beginning of the war, and had risen to only £33 million six months later, much of the increase resulting from price rises.[7] Moreover, with the government assuming that the war would last for at least three years, the production of munitions and the mobilisation of manpower proceeded at a leisurely pace. Individual departments continued with their own self-contained initiatives, and on occasions even competed for scarce resources. At the same time, little was done to interrupt the production of many non-essential items.[8] After six months of phoney war, the numbers in the armed forces had risen fourfold, to close on 2 million, but there were still over 1 million men registered as unemployed. Chamberlain, in short, saw no need for wholesale economic planning. His administration was primarily concerned with supplying the specific items required by the services, such as aircraft and guns, rather than with the overall planning of resources. The Prime Minister's only reason for doubting such a strategy was the rise in the cost of living, soon proceeding more rapidly than in the early months of the Great War and conjuring up the spectre of similiar industrial unrest.

There were, in fact, few signs of any real inprovement in the tense pre-war relationship between Chamberlain and the trade unions. The Prime Minister, concerned that inflation would increase strike activity, initially urged government departments to increase co-operation with the TUC. But, in practical terms, closer collaboration remained elusive, and many union leaders continued to be profoundly suspicious of Chamberlain. During the spring of 1940 Ernest Bevin, as head of the Transport Workers, led a deputation to the Home Office on the topic of civil defence, only to be told by officials that allowing trade unionists to involve themselves in this sort of work raised the problem of fifth column activity. Bevin thundered: 'Go and tell the Home Secretary that it was not the working class in Norway that sold out to Hitler. . . . And, while you're about it, tell the Home Secretary to advise Mr Chamberlain that he'll never win this war without the trade union movement.'[9] Hence, it came as no surprise that the TUC refused to support legislation designed to increase government powers over the direction of labour; only in May 1940, with disaster in Norway looming, did the Ministry of Labour go beyond its voluntary methods to the introduction of measures for the conscription of workers.[10] With manpower shortages now beoming impossible to ignore, and with other pressures building up — notably a drain of foreign reserves and a growing shipping shortage — the strain on the wartime economy was suddenly becoming intense. The need for more far-reaching measures was at last being recognised, if not directly acted upon, just at the time when Chamberlain was unexpectedly forced to resign.

The coalition brought new resolve to the handling of Britain's war economy. Within two weeks a new version of the Emergency Powers Act had extended the goverment's powers over persons and property, and Ernest Bevin, now joining the government as Minister of Labour, was soon winning praise for his speed in producing plans for the mobilisation of manpower and labour.[11] The importance of central planning in terms of physical rather than fiscal resources was at last recognised. Indeed, when the government announced its modified central committee structure in June 1940, the role of the Treasury was clearly downgraded, and the Chancellor of the Exchequer was for the time being excluded from the War Cabinet. With manpower becoming the key economic priority, it was the Minister of Labour who now had to come to the forefront. Bevin's bold assumption of the role of government spokesman for the working class was in time to win him many admirers; indeed, he gradually emerged as the dominant political personality on the home front. But this reputation was not easily won. In the summer of 1940 Bevin was faced with acute shortages of labour in vital munitions factories, and his abrasive style of leadership and intolerance of criticism served only to exacerbate existing difficulties. Labour ministers, having accepted a share of responsibility for domestic policy, soon found themselves being blamed for failing to overcome the problems bedevilling war production. By the autumn of 1940 the coalition honeymoon — the sense of relief that came with the new government — was over, and criticism was beginning to resurface.

Three particular types of problem came to be identified. In the first place, concern was expressed that the level of war production was not being raised quickly enough. Lord Beaverbrook's triumph in boosting aircraft production, though vital to the outcome of the Battle of Britain, was achieved at the cost of holding back re-equipment of the army, and led to complaints that the overall production effort was being hampered by fatigue and absenteeism — the natural result of excessive working hours.[12] Alleged production deficiencies led, secondly, to renewed party tensions at Westminster. Tory and Labour supporters, anxious not to yield any advantage, were soon lining up behind the respective interests of captial and labour. It was not long, for example, before Bevin was coming under attack for relying on 'voluntaryism' rather than taking up the government's extensive powers of industrial conscription.[13] Finally, there were problems of leadership and co-ordination. The Prime Minister could not easily reproduce his own control over strategy in the field of war production. He was constrained both by the need to compromise between his coalition supporters, and by the knowledge that to introduce a clear-cut chain of command might involve bringing forward a leader of almost comparable status on the domestic front. The result was that the government's machinery for handling the war economy became a prime target for critics. Within months, the committee structure announced in June was considered to be seriously deficient. The Lord President's Committee, for instance, instead of co-ordinating the whole system, found itself dealing with only minor policy issues, and was further hamstrung by the illness of its chairman, Neville Chamberlain. In the meantime, the remainder of the committee structure became deadlocked: above all the Production Council was unable to impose necessary priorities in war production in the absence of Beaverbrook, whose dislike of working through committees was such that he refused to attend after the first meeting.[14]

Once the immediate threat of invasion had passed, press commentators and critics at Westminster felt less inhibited about voicing their concerns publicly. Labour ministers, in particular, suddenly found themsevles on the defensive. Arthur Greenwood, for example, was attacked for failing to give any strong lead as chairman of the cabinet's Economic Policy Committee. But the strongest criticism, without doubt, was directed towards Bevin, who was accused of insufficient urgency in transferring workers to essential war industries.[15] The minister preferred to use voluntary co-operation in mobilising manpower; an approach seen by some as part of a concerted effort to exploit wartime conditions by securing advances for the trade union movement. Sir John Wardlaw-Milne, an influential Conservative MP and chairman of the Commons Select Committee on National Expenditure, received wide publicity for his accusation that the failure to utilise compulsory powers was a root cause of continued hold-ups in production.[16] The plain speaking of the Select Committee, a group of thirty mostly Tory back-benchers, came close to rekindling party warfare, though in general production deficiencies were a convenient focus for disgruntled critics in all parts of the House. It was this belief, that Churchill's handling of the war economy left much to be desired, which led to the unlikely alliance of 'Arsenic and Old Lace' — the Labour critic Manny Shinwell and the senior Tory Lord Winterton.[17] By the end of 1940 the government recognised, with dissatisfaction becoming more widespread, that it would have to find new ways of improving war production.

The cabinet's initial response, agreed in December, was to reorganise the central committee machinery. In brief, the Production Council was to be abolished, and replaced by a remodelled Production Executive. This would have similar functions — of allocating materials, plant and labour in order of priority — but would be balanced by the introduction of a new Import Executive.[18] The linchpin of the new system, however, was to be the Lord President's Committee, which in its new capacity would settle any internal disputes and take charge of general economic policy. Indeed, under Sir John Anderson, the Committee was to become, after 1941, the driving force in the coalition's domestic policy. In accepting these new procedures, the Prime Minister entertained hopes that Lord Beaverbrook might play a more prominent role. If Churchill was opposed to the idea of a single overriding ministry, for much the same reasons as Neville Chamberlain, then he was prepared to see his friend become *de facto* overlord of war production. But Beaverbrook resisted. He remained scathing about any centralised committee structure, which, as a businessman, he believed slowed down effective action.[19] He was also reluctant about working more closely with Bevin. The two men had already developed a strong personal antipathy, and this soon acquired a political edge as Beaverbrook tried to persuade the Minister of Labour about the need for industrial conscription.[20] Bevin stuck to his guns on this point, though he was persuaded by a report from the Manpower Requirements Committee — pointing to shortages in industry and the services over the next six months — that an amendment to his voluntary approach had become unavoidable. Hence, in January 1941, the government announced two new aspects of policy. Responsibility for the economic war effort would in future rest with the new Executives, of which Bevin became chairman, while the Lord President's Committee would play a wide-ranging co-ordinating role.[21] And, henceforth, more emphasis would be placed on bringing workers from non-essential trades into war employment, with new powers being vested in the Ministry of Labour.[22]

Reactions to the new proposals were only cautiously favourable. *The Economist*, while recognising that a move had been made towards full mobilisation of manpower, argued that the government still had only 'half a plan'.[23] This theme was taken up in a wide-ranging Commons debate on economic policy. Bevin, having been returned unopposed as MP for Wandsworth back in June 1940, had not found it easy adapting to the rituals of parliamentary life, and he hardly helped his cause with a poor speech, delivered slowly from an official brief. 'Everybody yawned', noted John Colville, 'and the incorrigible Mr Austin Hopkinson even suggested rudely that to save Mr Bevin trouble the Clerk of the Table should read the speech for him.'[24] This left the way open for critics, led by Shinwell, to claim that the coalition had mobilised no more than 60–70 per cent of the nation's available labour and resources.[25] The number of open critics remained negligible; the urgency of the war in early 1941 still provided a powerful incentive for unity. But, as the war progressed, the handling of the production issue was becoming the source of growing irritation at Westminster, and this was increasingly coming to have a party dimension. James Griffiths, speaking from the Labour benches, warned that further moves towards industrial conscription would not be well received unless accompanied by countervailing measures. 'If there is to be, as there must be, the fullest use of the industrial and economic resources of the country', he argued, 'these resources must be owned and effectively controlled by the nation and organised for the benefit of the nation.'[26] Here, then, was a clear illustration of the constraints within which coalition policy operated: ministers knew that to force the pace too quickly in their efforts to boost war production would raise a host of divisive, unwanted controversies, especially at a time when censorship reports made it clear that both sides of industry believed the other to be profiting from the war.[27]

Strike activity, though in theory illegal, was, in fact, becoming more widespread by 1941. Many local disputes were settled quickly by arbitration, but unrest was gradually mounting among transport workers, dockers and coalminers; the latter, in particular, having fallen behind in the wages' league between the wars, were set on catching up some of the lost ground. During the emergency of 1940 the level of industrial unrest had diminished, but in 1941 some 110,000 working days were lost and, indeed, by 1942 the number of man-days lost had risen in excess of corresponding pre-war figures.[28] Whereas employers complained about absenteeism and lack of commitment, many workers felt that the 'cost-plus' system — by assuring profits without the danger of being undercut by competitors — was responsible for management inefficiency and poor planning. But wage disputes and dilution caused the major problems. The most serious dispute in 1941 took place in the shipyards on Clydeside, where Mass-Observation found great tension simmering below the surface: 'The peacetime discipline of the sack for slacking is no longer operating. Some men exploit this, remembering with natural bitterness the long periods of unemployment and ill-use that they received from the shipyard employers before the war. Underlying all is the men's feeling that after the war they'll be back on the scrap-heap, where they were before.'[29] In spite of co-operation to defeat the external enemy, therefore, the war had clearly not eradicated many of the traditional animosities that beset industrial relations. Whenever deficiencies in war production were raised, the two sides of industry quickly fell back on recriminations. Mass-Observation found that a sizeable minority thought worker's wages were too high, though far more people interviewed believed employers were still taking excessive profits by circumventing wartime regulations. In the egalitarian atmosphere of 1940–42, many were in favour of a 'standard wage policy', and opinion was equally strongly in favour of the nationalisation of war industry.[30]

Concern about industrial relations and the spiralling pattern of wages also provided the context for changes in the government's fiscal policy during the spring of 1941. Although physical controls and 'manpower budgeting' were becoming the central instruments of policy, finance still, of course, had its part to play. With Chamberlain in power, the major objectives of the Treasury had been to prevent inflationary price rises and to meet the cost of the war as far as possible from increased taxation. After May 1940, however, — as we have seen — the Treasury became less influential; indeed, the Chancellor, Kingsley Wood, entered the War Cabinet in October 1940 only as a counterweight to Bevin's inclusion. Wood's cautious instincts helped to ensure an element of continuity in Treasury thinking. Initially, he was not prepared to raise income tax by more than another 1s in the £; he did increase Excess Profits Tax to 100 per cent, though the impact of this was later to be softened by various concessions. These changes allowed prospective war expenditure for the year to increase from £2,000 million to £2,800 million, but parts of the Chancellor's budget were nevertheless criticised by Labour back-benchers as regressive, amounting to an assault on working-class wage-earners.[31] By mid-1940, moreover, it was becoming clear that such an orthodox approach was no longer sufficient. Above all, new departures in policy were needed to combat rising inflation. Hitherto, price fixing, food subsidies, rationing, and the urging of wage restraint had all been used to hold down prices, but, with growing demands on labour and wage increases above the level of the retail price index, a fresh approach had become imperative.[32]

The government's budgetary policy had, in fact, been the subject of sustained criticism since the outbreak of war. The lead in this context, as is well known, had been taken by Keynes, who followed up his press campaign in *The Times* by publishing an influential pamphlet in 1940, *How to Pay for the War*. In this, he criticised the traditional Treasury method of assessing government revenue according to what the taxpayer would bear, as this would only ever provide about half the required expenditure. Instead, the problem should be tackled from the opposite end. By estimating national income first, it would then be possible to calculate the level of taxation required to raise government revenue without creating

inflation. Increased taxes, he argued, could be made more acceptable by promises to repay part of them after the war.[33] Keynes was
brought into the Treasury as a special adviser in July 1940, and
found that officials were more sympathetic to his ideas for closing
the gap between taxation and expenditure than they had earlier
been to his plans for reducing unemployment. Hence, the budget of
April 1941, was to mark a turning point in public finance. In order
to close the'inflationary gap' — roughly estimated by Keynes at
£500 million — the Chancellor still placed some reliance on
voluntary savings. But the standard rate of income tax went up to
10s in the £, creating 4 million new taxpayers, and a limited scheme
for compulsory savings was introduced. This was offset to an
extent by making a portion of increased tax repayable after the
war, in the form of 'post-war credits', and by mitigating the effects of the Excess Profits Tax. For the first time the budget was
worked out within a national income accounting framework rather
than being simply a balance sheet of government income
and expenditure.[34]

This new effort to stimulate the war economy was generally well
received. 'The House and country', said Brendan Bracken, 'take a
masochistic pleasure in it, like flagellating friars.'[35] In the longer
term, though, the 1941 budget was arguably only a small step on
the way to a 'Keynesian revolution' in economic policy-making;
indeed — as will be shown below — in many ways such a process
was still incomplete by the end of the war.[36] Kingsley Wood and his
leading Treasury officials remained committed to many orthodox
tenets of pre-war economic policy, as was made particularly clear
during ministerial disputes over wages policy throughout 1941.
The government came under increasing attack as prices rose for its
alleged lack of a wages policy. In response, it was agreed to issue a
white paper confirming the coalition view that the responsibility for
checking high wages increases rested jointly with employers and
trade unions, through the collective bargaining process. By the end
of 1941, however, the Chancellor was alarmed by high wage settle-
ments in engineering, agriculture and shipbuilding; these, he believed, posed the threat of a new inflationary sprial. With the
support of the President of the Board of Trade, Sir Andrew Duncan,
Wood now proposed the introduction of some form of statutory
wage restraint, only to come up against fierce opposition from
Labour ministers. Bevin, in particular, stressed that voluntary co-

operation was the only viable policy. To introduce state regulation, he claimed, would inevitably arouse political controversy between the parties, and would lead to demands from the left for further restrictions on profits. The chancellor's idea was shelved, but not entirely ruled out if future circumstances demanded reconsideration.[37]

In the seconed half of 1941 war production returned to the centre of the domestic political agenda. At the Ministry of Labour, Bevin could take satisfaction from the fact that his first year in office had seen a rise of over 1 million men in the armed forces, and nearly 750,000 men and women in the munitions industry.[38] But unease at Westminster continued unabated. Concern among back-benchers was, if anything, intensified; after Hitler's attack on the Soviet Union, demands for assistance by the Russians served to exacerbate Britain's production difficulties. There was also a tendency in the Commons to concentrate not on past successes but on what remained to be done. In June 1941 the chairman of the Select Committee on National Expenditure, Wardlaw-Milne, wrote to the Prime Minister expressing anxiety based on inside knowledge, and in a subsequent debate he followed this up with a hard-hitting speech claiming that the nation had still reached only 75 per cent of its maximum productive capacity.[39] Wardlaw-Milne's concerns were echoed by several hitherto loyal supporters of the coalition. The most common complaint, now voiced from all sides of the House, was the absence of a single minister to oversee the whole field of war production. In again setting his face against this proposal, the Prime Minister displayed a degree of intolerance reminiscent of his predecessor. Resentment among MPs was increased when it was learnt that Churchill had summoned Wardlaw-Milne, lost his temper and had threatened to abolish the Select Committee unless it stopped asking 'damned silly questions'. In response, Wardlaw-Milne said he would publish details to support his contentions about production levels, adding that many of those in the know were agreed that his was a generous assessment.[40]

It was no surprise, therefore, that in mid-1941 ministers were themselves admitting, at least in private, that 'output is not what it should be, and nothing to boast about'.[41] Mass-Observation found that poor industrial relations were becoming endemic, and the respective causes of management and workers continued to find expression at Westminster. John Colville noted in June 1941 the first signs of a new 'class feeling between the two sides of the House. The Tories, conscious of the great sacrifices they are making financially and of exceedingly high wages being paid to war workers, are cantankerous about the many reports of slackness, absenteeism, etc, in the factories. The Labour Party resent this criticism and blame the managers and employers for any shortcomings.'[42] Behind the scenes, Tory back-benchers made no secret of their belief that failures in war production owed much to Bevin's refusal to take up compulsory powers. During July there was much speculation that the 1922 Committee were intriguing to remove Bevin from the Ministry of Labour. 'Tory back-benchers', reported Hugh Dalton, 'are making a great set against Bevin, who has been offered Halifax's job but said, "If I go out at all, I'll go out through the front door, not the back, and tell the public why." '[43]

The government's central machinery also remained the subject of disquiet. By the spring of 1941 Lord Beaverbrook had determined to leave the Ministry of Aircraft Production, believing that his task there was complete. After much persuasion from Churchill, he agreed to accept the anomalous position of Minister of State, vested with vaguely defined powers over the three supply ministries. Within weeks, however, Beaverbrook was again restless, and sought more orthodox departmental responsibilities. Brendan Bracken jibed that at present 'he takes up more of the P.M.'s time than Hitler'.[44] Only when he became Minister of Supply at the end of June was Beaverbrook able to channel his energies into a new enthusiasm — that of maximising material aid to Britain's new ally, the Soviet Union. In the meantime, confidence in the committee structure adopted at the beginning of the year was on the wane, and the Prime Minister came under attack in July for failing to use the opportunity of a cabinet reshuffle to appoint a Minister of Production. Churchill knew that the major contenders for such a post, Bevin and Beaverbrook, would stir up the wrath of their political opponents, but he was coolly received when he tried convincing the House that the machinery introduced in January was working effectively. Among a series of critical speeches, the chairman of the 1922 Committee, Erskine Hill, made the point that it was now the government alone which refused to acknowledge failings in war production.[45]

By the autumn production difficulties were coming to a head.

Churchill was conscious of the rising tide of parliamentary discontent, and his task was made no easier by internal wrangling as
Beaverbrook accused Bevin of refusing demands for labour made
by the Ministry of Supply; this running dispute was to be settled,
temporarily, only when Beaverbrook went to Washington in
December to iron out supply difficulties with the Americans.[46] In
the meantime, the imminence of a fresh manpower shortage — with
another 2 million men needed in the forces and the war industries
by mid-1942 — convinced Bevin of the need for fresh measures of
compulsion. Having rejected Wardlaw-Milne's earlier claims about
the war economy, the minister himself advanced the view that
production levels had to be raised by 30 per cent over the winter,
and the Lord President's Committee devised a package of measures
that were incorporated in a new National Service Bill.[47] This
foreshadowed a tightening up of the system of reservation by
occupation; the introduction of conscription for women to serve in
the auxiliary forces; and the placing of all men between the ages of
eighteen and sixty under statutory obligation to undertake some
form of national service. When the new measures were announced
in early December 1941, there was a broad measure of agreement
about the need for some such action, though complaints continued
about men and machinery standing idle and about the inadequacy
of regional organisation. The nature of Bevin's proposals, moreover, also led to a novel development — open defiance of coalition
policy along straight party lines.

The compulsion of workers was still viewed, at the end of 1941,
with suspicion by Labour supporters. The party's Administrative
Committee, which included ministers as well as back-benchers,
came to the view that the government should provide a quid pro
quo for introducing 'stern measures of compulsion'. The Emergency Powers Act, it was argued, had not been used as expected to
introduce controls over management; the country would welcome
the new measure, but Labour should make clear its disappointment
'about the failure to control management & to secure equality of
sacrifice'.[48] After a heated debate, the parliamentary party agreed,
by a majority of two to one, to accept the new National Service Bill,
but also to make known deeply felt reservations. Hence, on 2
December the Labour spokesman, Jim Griffiths, called for national
control of the armaments industry, transport and coal.[49] The
following day, however, attitudes hardened. Following an inept

performance by Anderson in presenting the government's case, over thirty left-wing Labour MPs, led by Sidney Silverman and George Daggar, decided to press an amendment calling for immediate 'public ownership and control of all industries vital to our war effort'. This led to bitter arguments within the party, and naturally proved particularly embarrassing for Labour ministers, pledged as they were to defend coalition policy.[50] On the final morning of the Commons debate, Attlee threatened resignation unless he had the party's backing for the new legislation. Despite this, and an undertaking from Bevin to consider any proposals for nationalisation that would increase war production, the feeling persisted in Labour ranks that more should be done to impose equivalent sacrifices on all sections of the community, and forty MPs went ahead to vote in favour of the unofficial amendment . This, by a long way, was the most serious anti-government vote since May 1940.[51]

In private, some MPs believed that the Labour revolt marked 'the equivalent of the figures which brought down Neville', taking into account Churchill's enormous prestige.[52] Though an exaggerated view in retrospect, at the time the minortiy vote had some serious implications. In the first place, Labour's action provided the clearest illustration yet of the extent to which war production remained a matter for partisan disagreement. Many Conservatives clearly saw the issue as another attempt to exploit the war for socialist purposes. 'What', questioned one, 'would have been said if the Conservatives had made it a condition of their joining Asquith in the last war that he should accept Protection?' In the House, Erskine Hill firmly stated that the 1922 Committee would oppose any such 'controversial' proposals, and he subsequently led a back-bench deputation which received an assurance from Sir John Anderson that there would be no nationalisation by stealth.[53] The mask of party unity, therefore, was clearly slipping in the case of war production. Equally disturbing for the coalition was the growing belief on the Labour side that it was being forced to accept unpalatable demands as the price for national unity. This inevitably placed great strain on the party's leaders. As one junior minister put it: 'Those of us in the Govt. could not be expected to go on indefinitely voting against the Party without serious consequences. . . . If the Party broke the Government the country would never forgive it.'[54] This pinpointed a potential danger that was to persist, as we shall see, until beyond the Beveridge debates in 1943, though in the short term the argument was quickly defused: the Labour dissidents agreed to accept the National Service Bill, while reserving the right to campaign for public ownership. This outcome did not represent any change of heart. Rather, the focus of political debate was suddenly, and very dramatically, shifted by the announcement of Japan's attack on Pearl Harbour and America's entry into the war. 'All this row', Hugh Dalton noted,' . . . is now blown away by the war news.'[55]

Britain's economic war effort had, by any standard, improved considerably in the period between Dunkirk and Pearl Harbour. Manpower budgeting had become the driving force in determining every facet of the war effort, and in the process the basis had been laid for a higher degree of mobilisation — either in uniform or war work — than achieved by any of the other major combatants.[56] After the defeat of Hitler was eventually completed in 1944–45, the government was able to proclaim that its handling of the war economy had been a triumph for national sacrifice and careful planning, and in the euphoria of victory there was little reason to question this impression of sustained achievement. Looking back as the war in Europe drew to a close, *The Economist* noted in a leading article that some of the government's achievements — such as the compulsory mobilisation of women — were regarded as unthinkable before the war. But, it went on, these achievements should not be allowed to obscure the very protracted development of British mobilisation, which did not, in fact, reach its peak until 1943. After two years of war, it had to be remembered, the country's manpower was only two-thirds mobilised; the Minister of Labour was still refusing to take up his powers of industrial conscription; and the government had only recently modified its timid fiscal policy by introducing the technique of budgeting on the national income. The article went on:

Mr Lloyd George once said that it was the critics who won the last war, and the record of battles fought and battles won against the passivity of Ministers is the critics' claim to have played their part in this war too. There is, indeed, a regular sequence of events in these matters. In the first stage, the outside critic points out a difficulty that will inevitably arise and suggests a remedy. The Government replies that the need may never arise and that, in any case, any fool can see that the suggested remedy is politically impossible and administratively impossible. In stage two, the emergency arrives and the remedy is pressed with more insistence. The

Government now says that . . . there is no time to deal with the matter thoroughly, and an appeal for the voluntary and unorganised co-operation of the public will have to be made. Some matters never get beyond this second stage, but for those that do, the third stage is the belated acceptance by the Government, under further pressure, of the remedy suggested in the first place. Some time later there follows stage four, in which a White Paper is issued to illustrate the magnificent results achieved by the energy and forethought of His Majesty's Government. There is an element of caricature in this description, but not a very large one. It has been the path pursued in finance, in manpower, in production, in rationing and the organisation of civilian consumption, in war damage legislation and — more recently — in the preparation for post-war reconstruction.[57]

The factors that delayed full mobilisation of Britain's war economy have already been noted. Aside from the failings of the Chamberlain regime, the coalition faced an uphill struggle from the outset. In the midst of a grave emergency during 1940–41, politicians and civil servants had to react under great pressure to constantly changing circumstances, devising new methods and procedures as events demanded.[58] But behind this, as we have seen, came the dictates of coalition. Ministers recognised that war production could be maximised only with the consent of public and political opinion. It was for this reason that Bevin sought to extend industrial conscription only when he was convinced that working-class opinion would deem it inevitable. To develop controversial initiatives might also, as the debates of December 1941 demonstrated, place an acute strain on coalition unity. Both Conservative and Labour ministers, therefore, had to settle — however reluctantly at times — for compromise measures. Conservatives such as the Chancellor were frustrated in their desire for statutory wage restraints, and consequently had to accept a mild degree of inflation; Labour ministers, in turn, made no headway in attempting to revise the restrictions imposed by the notorious 1927 Trades Disputes Act.[59] These political differences could not go on being concealed indefinitely, and indeed, as we shall see in the next chapter, during 1942 the coal industry was to become the source of a fierce row about the future direction of Britain's economy.

To speak of the Second World War as a lost opportunity for major industrial reorganisation, along the lines advanced by Corelli Barnett, thus distorts the reality of coalition politics. Britain's economic war effort, if it was to achieve victory over Hitler, had to be based on an acceptance of fundamental industrial and political differences. Coalition policy, in other words, reflecting as it did deep-seated differences in industry and society, simply had no option other than to seek temporary and artificial solutions. This helps to explain why wholesale industrial reorganisation — whether in terms of equipping management to face new technological challenges or removing trade union restrictive practices — never reached the government's agenda, even in the second half of the war after military victory had become more certain. In 1941, when the Axis powers were still formidable opponents, there were several signs that the industrial balance in Britain had shifted, and had tilted towards the workforce in a manner inconceivable in the era of Neville Chamberlain. Full employment, high wages and much greater consultation between unions and government were all the products of total war, but there were no guarantees that such advances would be secure after hostilities had ceased. Both sides, in industry as well as politics, remained suspicious and vigilant, determined not to make concessions which might leave themselves and their supportes at a disadvantage in the post-war world.

In the struggle for party advantage, it was Labour who had gained the psychological upper hand. By the end of 1941 Bevin still had many detractors, and — as we have seen — Labour supporters were deeply unhappy about the introduction of industrial conscription without any restrictions on capital in return. But if the left made the most vocal protests, in many ways the right had more to complain about in the organisation of the war economy. Indeed, as the doctrine of central economic planning had inexorably taken hold, so the Conservative party had been pushed more and more on the defensive. Certainly, in the interests of national unity, Tory supporters had acquiesced in a whole range of measures that had hitherto been anathema. Higher rates of income tax; excess profits duty at 100 per cent; increased wage rates in industry and a rationing system based on 'fair shares for all' — all these could be taken as signs of 'creeping socialism'. The all-embracing nature of the war economy — affecting as it did the lives of every individual citizen — therefore played a central role in the wartime swing to the left, giving respectability to state planning and reinforcing the radical trends set in motion by the fall of Chamberlain and the emergency of 1940.

What was more certain, however, was that by the end of 1941 Britain's sense of heightened national unity, the Dunkirk spirit, was beginning to dissipate. With the entry into the war of the Soviet Union, and latterly the United States, relief about no longer 'standing alone' gave greater scope for the public expression of dissent and political disputation. During the following year, unease continued to intensify around what some came to call 'the production crisis', but this in itself now became only one aspect of a much wider concern at Westminster — anxiety about the Prime Minister's leadership, such as had not been seen since Churchill came to power. If improved war production was an essential prerequisite of success on the battlefied, then something was clearly amiss, for early in 1942 British forces sustained a period of unrelenting military set-backs. At home, the result was to be a year of prolonged political disturbance, bringing together all the discontents manifested since the formation of the coalition. Over Christmas 1941 the Prime Minister decided to put his production difficulties behind him, and went on a lengthy trip to Washington to discuss future strategy with President Roosevelt. But in his absence a storm of criticism developed. 'His Majesty's Government has had a shock', wrote one observer after a secret session debate in late December, adding that if the Prime Minister was not careful, 'he won't have a Government to come back to'.[60]

Notes

1   The standard text remains the volume in the official history of the war by W. K. Hancock and M. Gowing, *British War Economy*, London, 1949.

2   On Bevin and the trade unions, see Bullock, *Bevin*, which firmly locates the wartime economy in its political context.

3   Barnett, *Audit of War*, e.g. p. 304: '... by the time they took the bunting down from the streets after VE-Day and turned from the war to the future, the British in their dreams and illusions and in their flinching from reality had already written the broad scenario for Britain's descent to the place of fifth in the free world as an industrial power ...'.

4   See the critical commentaries by Paul Addion, T. C. Barker and Margaret Gowing in *Contemporary Record*, I, 2, 1987. Professor Gowing argues (p. 18): 'An audit, being a systematic examination of accounts, should not fill up the debit side and leave the credit columns

empty. Barnett does so as he tell one gloomy story after another and implies that Britain's dependence on United States aid was total. . . . The general impression he conveys of Britain's war effort greatly under-rates its achievement. . . . There are alternative hypotheses, besides the misdeeds of the New Jerusalemites, for Britain's relatively low postwar economic performance.'

5 D. N. Chester, 'The central machinery for economic policy', in D. N. Chester (ed.), *Lessons of the British War Economy*, Cambridge, 1951, pp. 5–6.

6 A. Booth, 'Economic advice at the centre of British government, 1939–1941', *The Historical Journal*, xxix, 3, 1986, pp. 656–63; see also A. Cairncross and N. Watts, *The Economic Section 1939–1961*, London, 1989, pp. 10–23.

7 R. S. Sayers, *Financial Policy, 1938–1945*, London, 1956, pp. 23–44.

8 See two further volumes in the official history series — H. M. D. Parker, *Manpower: a Study of War-Time Policy and Administration*, London, 1957, pp. 61–86; and E. L. Hargreaves and M. Gowing, *Civil Industry and Trade*, London, 1952, pp. 14–19.

9 Cited in P. Lewis, *A People's War*, London, 1986, p.111.

10 Addison, *Road to 1945*, pp. 59–60.

11 E.g. *News Chronicle*, 20–23 May 1940; *The Economist*, 25 May 1940, ran the headline 'Mobilisation at last!'.

12 A. J. Robertson, 'Lord Beaverbrook and the supply of aircraft, 1940–1941', in A. Slaven and D. H. Aldcroft (eds), *Business, Banking and Urban History: Essays in Honour of S. G. Checkland*, Edinburgh, 1982, pp. 80–100.

13 Bullock, op. cit., pp. 42–4.

14 Booth, op. cit., p. 664: of the other main committees, the Economic Policy Committee met only four times before September 1940, and conducted only low-level business, and the Food Policy Committee under Attlee's chairmanship was deadlocked over food imports.

15 See, for example, the comments of the *Manchester Guardian*, 10 October 1940, and *The Observer*, 1 December 1940.

16 V. 367 H. C. Deb., 5 s., c. 610, 4 December 1940; House of Commons, *Third Report from the Select Committee on National Expenditure*, Session 1940–41, 19 December 1940, p. 14.

17 E. Shinwell, *Conflict Without Malice*, London, 1955, p. 151; Earl Winterton, *Orders of the Day*, London, 1953, pp. 260–2.

18 Chester, op. cit., p. 8.

19 Taylor, *Beaverbrook*, pp. 462–5: 'I am not a committee man', he told Churchill, 'I am the cat that walks alone.'

20 War Cabinet minutes, 19 November 1940, PRO CAB 65/9; *Dalton Diary*, 11 December 1940, pp. 117–18.

21 Sir J. W. Wheeler-Bennett, *John Anderson, Viscount Waverley*, London, 1962, pp. 258–9.

22 Bullock, op. cit., pp. 46–9.

23 *The Economist*, 25 January 1941.

24 *Colville Diary*, 21 January 1941, p. 339.

25 V. 368 H. C. Deb., 5 s., cc. 125–32, 21 January 1941: 'Instead of active and unified policy, we have seen the Government resorting to a series of makeshifts, futile expedients and trifling devices, improvising without the vestige of plan . . . and, what is worse, constantly waiting to be stimulated by this House and by pressure of public opinion.'

26 Ibid., c. 148.

27 *Colville Diary*, 5 February 1941, p. 353.

28 'Trade stoppages — Weekly Return to the Minister of Labour', 1940–42, PRO LAB 10/132.

29 Cited in Lewis, op. cit., p. 128.

30 Mass-Observation, *People in Production*, London, 1942, cited in Calder, *People's War*, pp. 299–300.

31 Sayers, op. cit., p. 45.

32 On the greatly increased cost of food subsidies — one of the main devices used by the government to disguise the level of inflation — see the official history by R. J. Hammond, –Food, Vol. I. *The Growth of Policy*, London, 1951, pp. 182–206.

33 J. M. Keynes, *How to Pay for the War*, London, 1940.

34 R. S. Sayers, '1941 — the first Keynesian budget', in C. Feinstein (ed.), *The Managed Economy: Essays in British Economic Policy and Performance since 1929*, Oxford, 1983, pp. 107–17.

35 *Colville Diary*, 7 April 1941, p. 372.

36 A. Booth, 'The "Keynesian Revolution" in economic policy-making', *Economic History Review*, XXXVI, 1, 1983, pp. 103–23. See also below, Chapter 7.

37 Minutes of the Lord President's Committee, 8 and 24 December 1941, PRO CAB 71/2.

38 Bullock, op. cit., p. 64.

39 Wardlaw-Milne to Churchill, 21 June 1941, PRO PREM 4 86/2; V. 373 H. C. Deb., 5 s., c. 336, 10 July 1941.

40 Notes by A. J. Sylvester, 16–18 July 1941, Lloyd George papers, HLRO, G/24/2/133–5.

41 Hankey to Hoare, 18 May 1941: Lord Hankey papers, Churchill College, Cambridge, 4/33.

42 *Colville Diary*, 19 June 1941, p. 401.

43 Dalton Diary, 14 July 1941, p. 251. See also Harvie-Watt, *Most of My Life*, p. 58.

44 *Colville Diary*, 5 June 1941, p. 395; Taylor, op. cit., pp. 467–73.

45 V. 373 H. C. Deb., 5s., cc. 1274–1371, 29 July 1941. On this occasion, the Prime Minister's reputation was tarnished by his refusal to recognise production difficulties, though Bevin managed to make his best impression yet in the House — Sylvester notes, 31 July 1941, Lloyd George papers, G/24/2/142.

46 Taylor, op. cit., pp. 498–502. The Prime Minister had tried to prevent any further discussion on production matters — Churchill to James Stuart (Chief Whip), 6 October 1941, PRO PREM 4 86/4.

47 *The Times*, 14 November 1941; minutes of the Lord President's Committee, October–November 1941, PRO CAB 71/2.

48 K. Jefferys (ed.), *Labour and the Wartime Coalition: from the Diary of James Chuter Ede, 1941–1945*, London, 1988, 27 November and 1 December 1941, pp. 24–5.
49 V. 376 H. C. Deb., 5 s., cc. 1039–47, 2 December 1941: 'If we say to the people of this country that besides conscripting man-power we are developing the Government's powers to take over wealth, privilege and economic power, we shall give them an incentive which I do not feel is contained in this Measure.'
50 Notes by Sylvester, 4 December 1941, Lloyd George papers, G/24/ 2/198.
51 *Chuter Ede Diary*, 3 and 4 Decemebr 1941, pp. 26–30.
52 Notes by Sylvester, 5 December 1941, G/24/2/199. Chuter Ede recalled that many years ago Churchill said that fifty Tories voting against the government would produce a Minister of Supply, adding that thirty Labour dissidents at present would 'Kill this Govt.' — *Diary*, 3 December 1941, p. 27.
53 Headlam diary, 4 and 16 December 1941: Durham Record Office, D/He 37.
54 *Chuter Ede Diary*, 3 December 1941, p. 27.
55 *Dalton Diary*, 8 December 1941, p. 331.
56 By various other standards, however, the British war economy did not match that of its rivals. In 1943, for example, Germany was the most highly mobilised of the powers in terms of national income share; the American economy compares favourably to the British when considering domestically financed supply of the war effort; and from 1941 to 1944 Soviet resources were employed in the defeat of Hitler with much greater intensity than those of either Britain or the USA. Britain was also most heavily dependent on external resources: mainly owing to the Lend–Lease programme, by 1944 some 40 per cent of Britain's armaments were coming from overseas — M. Harrison, 'Resource mobilisation for world war II: the U.S.A., U.K., U.S.S.R., and Germany, 1938–1945', *Economic History Review*, XLI, 2, 1988, pp. 182–91.
57 *The Economist*, 9 December 1944.
58 E. A. G. Robinson, 'The overall allocation of resources', in Chester, op. cit., pp. 34–5.
59 P. Goodhart, *The 1922: the Story of the Conservative Backbenchers' Parliamentary Committee*, London, 1973, pp. 109–10: in the autumn of 1941 the 1922 Committee refused even to discuss the Trade Disputes Act with union representatives, and Churchill urged the TUC to refrain from pressing the matter 'in the national interest'. Trade unions in the public sector had, in fact, been prominent in exposing inefficiencies in industry. The civil service unions in 1941 wanted the suspension of those sections of the Trade Disputes Act which prevented their affiliation to the TUC; they felt they were being unfairly treated if they could not negotiate directly with management at the local level, as their private sector counterparts could do — J. M. Lee, *The Churchill Coalition 1940–1945*, London, 1980, p. 94.

60 Notes by Sylvester, 18 December 1941, G/24/2/205. The same point was made in the *Channon Diary*, 18 December 1941, p. 315: 'Of course, the Members behaved rather like schoolboys with the Head-master away', but there was no doubting the seriousness of the situation: 'The Government, as it is, is doomed: I give it a few months. No Government could survive such unpopularity for long.'

4

'Parliament is given over to intrigue'

In January 1941 Harry Hopkins, President Roosevelt's aide, reported back from a visit to Britain that Winston Churchill '*is* the government in every sense of the word....' After his role in the crisis of 1940, the idea of the Prime Minister ever being challenged as war leader seemed inconceivable. Criticism of the government, however, did resurface and increase steadily during 1941: production difficulties, as we have seen, were a principal cause of dissatisfaction. Equally important, military success remained elusive, even after Britain, having stood alone against Hitler for a year, was joined in the struggle by the Soviet Union and the United States. In retrospect, this widening of the conflict to a global scale marked a crucial turning point in the history of the war. With the vast economic and military resources of the Americans in particular behind the Allied cause, Churchill and his government could at last have some confidence in the prospect of ultimate victory. But in the short term things went from bad to worse for the British. Indeed, only days after the Japanese attack on Pearl Harbour, two of the Royal Navy's premier battleships were sunk as the Japanese began an advance that threatened the entire British position in the Far East. At a time when expectations had been raised, this news was doubly difficult to bear. The effect at Westminster was to produce a period of sustained and unprecedented unrest; for the first time since coming to power in May 1940, the Prime Minister found his whole war strategy coming under intense scrutiny.

Nineteen forty-two was thus to become, contrary to popular mythology about Churchill's unchallenged ascendancy, a year of political crisis. Pressure on the Prime Minister mounted as British forces suffered a series of humiliating reversals. The Allied garrison at Singapore fell to the Japanese in February, and during the summer the fortress of Tobruk was captured as part of a relentless German advance in North Africa. With the overnight emergence onto the political scene of Sir Stafford Cripps, Churchill was faced with a novel situation — how to deal with a potentially serious contender for his job. And the ebbing of confidence in the government was compounded by a perceptible sharpening of conflict on the home front between the major coalition partners; indeed, the trend towards discussion of future domestic policy was becoming irresistible by the end of the year. In the event, much of the direct criticism of the government was to be swept away and quickly forgotten with the 'turn of the tide' at the end of 1942. The Prime Minister's leadership was finally vindicated by General Montgomery's victory in North Africa, which was soon to be followed by news of successful Soviet resistance around Stalingrad. But, as this chapter will demonstrate, such an outcome had been uncertain for much of the year, and it did not mean that the coalition would henceforth be free from serious controversy. Rather, just as the economic war effort gave way in late 1941 to military strategy as the major cause of contention in British politics, so this in turn was replaced at the end of 1942 by the issue that was to reverberate for the remainder of the war years — reconstruction.

The crisis of 1942 developed from failings on the battlefield. At the beginning of 1941 the Prime Minister's critics remained weak and ineffective. In the House of Commons, Richard Stokes made little headway in trying to rally those members, mostly in Labour and ILP ranks, who were not 'bitter-enders' on the war issue. Few backbenchers were prepared to voice any doubts about military strategy openly, and those that were — such as Shinwell, Hore-Belisha and Clement Davies — clearly had 'no cement to bind them together'.[1] But the patience of loyal coalition supporters was increasingly tested as the year progressed. On top of the horrors of the Blitz and the unremitting shipping losses in the Atlantic, British forces were pushed on the defensive in North Africa and the Balkans. As news filtered through that troops were to be evacuated from Greece at the end of April, John Colville reported a strong tendency 'to discontent visible in the House and in the country'. Any worsening of the military position was always likely to unsettle public and parliamentary opinion, and some members of the government itself were now reported to believe that 'this cannot go on. They are likening it to Asquith's Coalition. They say [the present government] cannot win the war and there must be a change.'[2]

In reality, back-bench anxiety during the spring of 1941 was directed not towards the Prime Minister, but — as it had been in Chamberlain's early days — to allegedly negligent ministers. The chief target was the Foreign Secretary, Anthony Eden. He had spent several weeks in the Balkans attempting to rally Allied forces, and now found himself under fire in attacks that were clearly motivated in part by the desire of Chamberlainite Tories to settle old political scores.[3] Churchill's rhetoric, however, served to calm fears. His insistence that criticism be made an issue of confidence in the government, moreover, made it unlikely that murmurings of discontent would be pushed any further, for fear of damaging national unity. In a two-day Commons debate on the war situation, the only major attack was made by Lloyd George, who, in what was to be his last significant parliamentary speech, reasserted his belief that Britain needed new allies, and had to reconstruct its government machinery to fight the war more effectively. It was a measure of how far Lloyd George's potency as a critic had declined that the Prime Minister was able to compare this speech with those of Marshal Pétain in the final days before the collapse of France. As press commentators noted, there was no real comparison between the situation in May 1941 and the debate which almost exactly a year previously brought down Chamberlain. The government now received an overwhelming vote of confidence, with only a handful of MPs voting against Churchill or abstaining.[4]

But criticism inevitably resurfaced when the defeat in Greece was followed by a fresh set-back — evacuation from Crete. In some of the fiercest fighting of the war, some 13,000 Allied troops were killed as the Germans launched their assault on the island; another 16,000 were evacuated, with the British Expeditionary Force (BEF) now acquiring the new nickname of 'Back Every Friday'. At Westminster, it was becoming increasingly difficult to give the Prime Minister the benefit of the doubt. 'On all sides', wrote Chips Channon in early June, 'one hears increasing criticism of Churchill. He is undergoing a noticeable slump in popularity and many of his enemies, long silenced by his personal popularity, are once more vocal. Crete has been a great blow to him.'[5] Much of the press now became more openly critical of the government, and it was no coincidence that the ministerial reshuffle carried out shortly afterwards centred on the removal of the hapless Minister of Information, Duff Cooper.[6] Although the majority of back-benchers remained earnest supporters of the coalition, there were now more and more clouds on the horizon. As we have seen, dissatisfaction with the government's handling of war production was becoming widespread, and matters were not helped by the Prime Minister's evident disdain for any form of criticism, however well-intentioned. Churchill's attitude — encapsulated by the remark to his secretary after one episode that he 'didn't give a damn what the House thought as there was a bloody war on' — was resented in parliament as a repetition of one of Chamberlain's worst failings.[7]

The slow sea-change in political opinion continued after Hitler's attack on the Soviet Union. At one level, the Prime Minister's immediate declaration of full support for the Russians helped to bolster his public popularity. But at the same time, with the burden of resistance to Hitler now shifting away from Britain, critics of the government naturally felt less inhibited in voicing their concerns. Harold Macmillan, serving as Beaverbrook's deputy, wrote in October 1941 that parliament had become restive and the press hostile, largely because of the government's production failings and its slowness in sending supplies to assist the Soviet Union. All the symptoms were now developing, he claimed, which marked out the Asquith coalition (between parties) and the formation in 1916 of the Lloyd George coalition (of personalities).[8] Within six months, therefore, during the course of 1941, there had been a perceptible change in the political atmosphere. *The Economist* in summing this up and trying to pinpoint what had happened, made the case that some of the instinctive unity of 1940 had now been lost; criticism had become more widespread than at any time since the fall of Chamberlain, and in spite of Churchill's immense popularity, the government had been pushed onto the defensive.[9] Nor, as we shall see, was the Prime Minister's cause immediately helped by America's entry into the war in December 1941; instead of bringing sudden benefits, it was followed by a series of disastrous military set-backs in the Far East. Pressure for change now became so irresistible that within weeks Churchill was forced to carry out, against his wishes, the most far-reaching government reshuffle since the formation of the coalition. The scene was set for the crisis year of 1942.

During Churchill's absence in the United States over Christmas, a small group of Conservative MPs was called together by the chairman of the 1922 Committee, Erskine Hill. It was unanimously agreed that unless changes were made urgently, such as the separation of the powers of Prime Minister and Minister of Defence, then the government was doomed. The general feeling of the meeting, according to the diarist Chips Channon, was that there was no point 'the P.M. coming back and making one of his magical speeches. This time it would serve no purpose. The Government must be reformed, and that soon.'[10] This revival of anti-Churchill feeling — never far from the surface among the Chamberlainite loyalists who dominated the 1922 Committee — was clearly sparked off by concern about the position in the Far East. But it also reflected what R. A. Butler called the party's 'curious inverted conscience'. Tory back-benchers, noted Butler, 'saw things going very badly for the country and their own interest. . . . They began to search their conscience as to whether they had told the truth to Chamberlain. They came to the conclusion that they hadn't and that they must therefore tell the truth to Churchill.'[11] In this frame of mind, the 1922 Committee took the lead in attacking the Prime Minister when he returned from Washington. Behind the scenes, Tory MPs requested that a forthcoming debate on the military situation should not be turned into a vote of confidence by the government, as many members would feel obliged to take up the challenge or least abstain. Hence, an unexpected challenge to Churchill's authority had suddenly arisen, unimaginable only months earlier. In late January Channon reported that 'the ineffectual Whips are in a frenzy and a first class crisis, no doubt chuckled on by the Germans, is upon us'.[12]

The Prime Minister was, at least initially, downcast by this turn of events. On 21 January he told Anthony Eden that the majority of the Conservative Party hated him; he would, he claimed, gladly relinquish his burdens to make way for a younger man.[13] But this mood was quickly overtaken by a determination to hit back at the critics. Shortly afterwards, Erskine Hill was summoned. Churchill, according to his PPS, was 'foaming with rage', and complained that it was disgraceful to come back to the scurvy treatment of a snarling House of Commons', adding that he alone stood between the Tory party and political extinction, and that in view of their record on appeasement they had no right to complain.[14] Thus chastened, and divided about the exact changes they hoped to bring about, the Tory critics hastily retreated. After the Prime Minister gave an effective defence in the House, Erskine Hill recanted and — in the words of Channon — 'tried to insinuate himself with the government'. Labour MPs also rallied to the defence of the coalition. Many were convinced by the new assertiveness of the Tories that there was, as one said, 'a ramp aimed at discrediting our Party & our men in the Government'.[15] As a result, open criticism was confined to a familiar band of critics. But the resounding vote of confidence received by the government served only to conceal a new element of uncertainty. Not only had old appeasement wounds been reopened but dissatisfaction was continuing to take hold, fuelled further by another telling attack on production failings by the chairman of the Select Committee on National Expenditure, Wardlaw-Milne. One of those who supported Churchill in the lobby reflected that 'a few more votes such as today's — unless he can show some successes and a greater efficiency — will be the end of Winston.'[16]

In early February the Prime Minister hoped that limited changes in personnel would forestall any further agitation. To this end, he had already offered the post of Minister of Supply to Sir Stafford Cripps, the recently returned British Ambassador in the Soviet Union. Cripps had been serving in Moscow since 1940, and so had hitherto escaped all responsibility for the shortcomings of the coalition. In spite of his association with socialist extremism in the 1930s, and his expulsion from the Labour party for advocating a 'popular front' against fascism, Cripps was widely acclaimed by much of the press as the new man of 1942. He arrived back in Britain at a crucial moment in the war effort, his reputation enhanced by his part — largely exaggerated at the time — in cementing the Anglo-Soviet military alliance. Cripps, of course, had a reputation for austerity: he was, writes Angus Calder, 'a teetotaller and vegetarian, and somehow it showed'. But in the circumstances of the hour this served only to increase his public appeal, especially for those willing to contemplate further sacrifices if only it would bring an improvement in Britain's fortunes. Cripps could not help but be influenced by his astonishing reception; alongside his clear sense of public duty, he also harboured the highest personal ambitions. After some thought, he declined to serve at the Ministry of Supply on the ground that this did not involve a seat in the War Cabinet. The Prime Minister, according to Hugh Dalton, did not take kindly to this rebuff, and could subsequently be found 'ramping round denouncing Cripps with every kind of imprecation'.[17] Churchill's anger reflected in part a recognition that he was now confronted with a potential rival. After a powerful speech calling for closer Anglo-Soviet co-operation, opinion polls showed that Cripps was making a serious inpression on public opinion. By sections of the press, he was now being hailed as the only man who could bring greater efficiency and urgency to the war effort on the home front. The Prime Minister, conscious of the danger of leaving Cripps outside the government where he might rally dissident opinion, was soon looking for ways to 'enlarge the bait' in order to bring him into office.[18]

In the meantime, the government was running into further trouble over its handling of the war economy. On 4 February it was confirmed that a new Ministry of Production would finally be established, to be presided over by Lord Beaverbrook. Such a ministry had, of course, been long advocated by back-bench opinion, but the government's announcement was nevertheless coolly received in the Commons. The reasons for this were both personal and political. Labour members, in particular, were suspicious of Beaverbrook and his methods, and waited upon a more precise definition of the new minister's powers before judging the likely impact on war production. At the time of the announcement, Beaverbrook's executive role was, in fact, still being worked out behind the scenes amidst fierce political and departmental wrangling. Beaverbrook had insisted that the production brief, in order to operate effectively, must include controlling powers over each of the supply ministries; in practice, frustrated by the limitations of his previous posts, he was now pushing to become overlord of war production.[19] Resistance to his plan, however, was intense, and was led by Ernest Bevin, who, having enhanced the role of the Ministry of Labour, had no intention of relinquishing control over questions affecting manpower. Since May 1940 Labour control over manpower had been an unwritten assumption of coalition co-operation, and when Bevin made it clear he regarded this as a resignation issue, the Prime Minister had little choice but to give way. Beaverbrook was, thus, presented with an ultimatum: to accept limited powers or else resign. He reluctantly agreed to proceed, but when the powers of the new ministry were outlined as a 'foreign office of supply', primarily to deal with the United States, back-bench critics were quick to seize on inconsistencies.[20] In spite of sustained pressure on this point stretching back to 1940, there was still to be no unified control over the whole war economy.

By mid-February the 'production crisis' was itself becoming entangled in renewed unease about the military position. Public opinion was outraged when it was learnt that two German battleships had sailed, apparently unscathed by Allied attacks, from Brest through the Channel to home ports. And tensions were heightened when it was confirmed that Japanese advances in the Far East had resulted in the capture of Singapore, forcing the surrender of thousands of troops in what Churchill was later to describe as the greatest military disaster in British history. Pressure on the Prime Minister either to reduce his own burden of work, by appointing a new Minister of Defence, or else to carry out a major government reshuffle, now became irresistable. 'Parliament', noted the Labour minister Chuter Ede, 'is given over to intrigue'. Various factions, he noted, favoured particular changes, though most members were united in their anger when Churchill implied that the House was in a mood of panic.[21] The Prime Minister was, in fact, already well advanced in a plan to reshape his adminstration as the best means of defusing tension. His main objective was to find a place in the War Cabinet for the man of the moment, Stafford Cripps. Beaverbrook, however, complicated matters by standing out against the inclusion of Cripps, who, he claimed, 'was not like Bonar Law who held the stirrup for Ll[oyd] G[eorge]'.[22] After resuming his complaints about the limited powers of the production ministry, Beaverbrook stormed out from a heated encounter with Churchill and finally acted upon one of his regular threats to resign. Whatever the cause of this action — and failure to secure control over war production was arguably uppermost — the effect was to clear the way for the completion of cabinet changes. The Labour leader, Attlee, also had suspicions about Cripps, whom he regarded as a maverick Independent. As Beaverbrook put it, 'having excommunicated Cripps in the peace, he is not going to make him assistant pope in the war.'[23] But, with his own status enhanced by the title of Deputy Prime Minister, Attlee dropped his objections: the way was clear for Cripps to join the government.

Hence, on 19 February, a new War Cabinet was announced.

Labour's deputy leader Arthur Greenwood was sacked; he had long been considered ineffectual as minister in charge of reconstruction. This move was balanced by the removal from the cabinet of the Tory Chancellor, Kingsley Wood, who did, however, remain at the Treasury. Under Churchill's leadership, the War Cabinet now consisted, on the one hand, of Eden, Sir John Anderson and Oliver Lyttelton, Beaverbrook's replacement as Mininster of Production; and, on the other, Attlee, Bevin and Cripps. The latter's inclusion as Lord Privy Seal and Leader of the House of Commons was widely welcomed as the centrepiece of the reshuffle. In private, however, the major coalition partners were less enthusiastic. Labour members, said one, felt 'they had been "had" over the dropping of Greenwood'.[24] Tory MPs, in turn, were alarmed by the exclusion of Kingsley Wood and, above all, by the treatment of the former Chief Whip David Margesson, who in further consequential changes outside the War Cabinet was sacked from the War Office.[25] It was no coincidence that when the Commons next met to ratify the changes, Chuter Ede found the House 'in a sullen mood in which Party feeling showed itself more than I have known since May, 1940'. For the most part, however, parliamentary opinion agreed that the new War Cabinet should be given its chance to improve Britain's military fortunes. The full-scale debate on the fall of Singapore, therefore, took place in an atmosphere of anti-climax, and the Conservative MP Beverley Baxter was over- heard commenting on the ease with which the Prime Minister had satisfied his critics. 'Never', he said, 'had so many bears been satisfied by the throwing of so few buns.'[26]

In the long term the restructuring of the government was to have major implications for coalition politics. On the surface the new War Cabinet looked, according to one of those present at its first meeting, 'very much like the old one'.[27] But, on closer inspection, there were clear signs of a shift in the balance of forces — a direct result of the reopening of old wounds in the Conservative party. As we have seen, since coming to power Churchill had moved only slowly and reluctantly against his former enemies in the party, conscious of the need to base himself upon the Tory majority in parliament. But in the highly charged atmosphere surrounding the fall of Singapore, he was without doubt influenced by the recent behaviour of the 1922 Committee. As one Tory MP noted, 'the Municheers had raised the trouble in the House; the result of the changes was that the Municheers had gone, Kingsley Wood from the War Cabinet and Margesson from the Government. The new men were all anti-Municheers.'[28] The inevitable, if inadvertent, consequence of Churchill's determination to strike back at the Chamberlainites was thus a strengthening of Labour's influence in the coalition. 'The staggering fact', concluded Rab Butler, 'was that a revolt of the Right had brought about a War Cabinet more to the Left.'[29]

Beaverbrook's unexpected departure clearly contributed to this outcome. Moreover, with so few anti-appeasement Conservatives available for promotion, Attlee was able to press hard for getting rid of 'some more of these bloody Tories', and so improve Labour's share of posts in the government as a whole. Hugh Dalton, for example, now went to the Board of Trade, a vital home front post, thereby helping to place Labour ministers in a stronger position to influence domestic policy.[30] There remained, in addition, the enigmatic Cripps, who, if nothing else, seemed certain to encourage demands for social reform. In retrospect, therefore, February 1942 stands out as an important staging post on the road to 1945. More immediately, opinion was divided as to whether the government changes would forestall further criticism or undermine the idea of Churchill's indispensability. But, as one commentator observed, rarely in British political history had the fortunes of an individual been so dramatically transformed: after being for so long an outcast, Cripps now suddenly 'finds himself with the ball at his feet'.[31]

Sir Stafford's first inclination, surprisingly enough, was to run off with the ball. Within weeks of entering the War Cabinet, he had volunteered to go on a personal mission aimed at breaking the constitutional deadlook in India, which had been made urgent by Japanese advances in the Far East.[32] This decision was greeted with some bewilderment in political circles since his recent promotion had been intended to stimulate the war effort on the home front. In the absence of the Lord Privy Seal critics and friends of the government alike pensively awaited further war news. For the time being, the Prime Minister remained on the defensive. Lord Hankey, one of those removed from office in the February reshuffle, claimed during March:

One hears nothing but abuse of Winston wherever one goes — in Clubs, Government offices, Parliamentary lobbies, Fleet Street, private houses, and I am told even in the Services. Absolutely the only thing that keeps the Government in office is the difficulty of finding a successor to the Prime Minister.... Cripps is the favourite, but he is a dark horse.... I imagine nothing decisive can happen politically until [he] gets back, but ... I should not be surprised if the situation blew up at any time.[33]

In the event, the reputation of Cripps received a set-back when he proved unable to persuade Congress leaders in India to accept British terms for independence. Nevertheless, after returning to England, he continued to receive a reception in the Commons which equalled that accorded to the Prime Minister, and opinion polls now showed him alongside Eden as the most credible likely successor to Churchill in the public mind.[34]

Cripps, therefore, continued to wait in the wings, encouraged by growing evidence of an ebbing of confidence in the Prime Minister. The clearest sign of this in the spring of 1942 was the so-called 'Palace Revolt' — a movement led by Lord Hankey, who carried weight as a former Secretary of the Cabinet with experience stretching back to the First World War. Hankey had become increasingly disillusioned with the higher strategical direction of the war effort and, after his removal from office, he began proposing a series of changes in machinery which, in effect, would have curtailed Churchill's powers. He wanted, for example, to abolish the Defence Committee and replace it with a Supreme General Staff, over which the Prime Minister would have no executive authority.[35] Churchill was clearly alarmed by criticism from 'the professionals', and it was only after much thought that he excluded from a radio broadcast the claim that he would not consent to bearing 'the burden of responsibility in times like these without ... the means of taking decisions'.[36] What caused particular concern was the knowledge that, in pressing for a reduction of the Prime Minister's powers, Hankey had the support of influential Tory peers such as Viscount Swinton and Lord Salisbury. The latter, of course, had been instrumental in leading opposition to the Chamberlain government, and was considered by Beaverbrook to be a 'dangerous foe', capable of moving opinion within the party.[37]

There was, in fact, by this stage, one Tory MP confirmed, a good deal of 'anti-P.M.' feeling in the party but as yet no unanimity as to who should replace him.[38] On the Labour side also it was becoming ever more difficult to maintain party discipline in the face of agitation against the government by separate groups of malcontents: peace-by-negotaition supporters, pacifists and advocates of a more vigorous war policy, notably Shinwell and Aneurin Bevan.[39] In effect, with the war going so badly, the reservoir of loyalty built up by Churchill in 1940 was slowly trickling away. There was, it was true, still no agreement among the disaffected as to whether curbing the Prime Minister's powers, stimulating war production or changing the composition and leadership of the government itself constituted the most urgent requirement. It was noticeable, however, that the parties at Westminster — unable to see any immediate improvement — more and more vented their frustrations on each other. In the spring of 1942 the government suffered its first by-election defeats at the hands of Independent candidates, who, unlike the major parties, were not bound by the terms of the electoral truce. In consequence, a strong feeling developed that Labour was being denied the benefits of disaffection on the part of voters. At the party's annual conference, an executive resolution to extend the truce — to include endorsement of any official candidate nominated by the incumbent party when a seat fell vacant — was passed by the barest of majorities.[40] The Conservative party, in turn, dug its heels in during May 1942 in what became the fiercest domestic dispute since the formation of the coalition — the controversy over fuel rationing.

The coal industry had caused considerable headaches for the government since the outbreak of war. Miners' representatives were determined to improve wages and conditions, which had not recovered relative to other workers since the General Strike. But, with an ageing and declining workforce, the demands of war had resulted in a decline of productivity, exacerbated by sharp rises in consumption.[41] Hugh Dalton, as the new President of the Board of Trade, was soon convinced that fuel rationing provided the only equitable solution, and made a provisional announcement to this effect in March 1942. But before the government could finalise its plans a strong body of resistance build up among coal-owners and Tory MPs. This was partly due to a suspicion — not without foundation — that rationing was the thin end of a wedge aimed at nationalisation, though Dalton was careful to present his plan in terms of administrative rationality. On a more self-interested level, Rab Butler also observed that 'the Tories are against fuel rationing because they are afraid that it will mean that they won't get enough for their country houses.'[42] Opposition to Dalton's plan was chan-

nelled through the 1922 Committee, whose new vice-chairman, Sir
Arnold Gridley, proposed an alternative policy designed to increase
coal production; he also warned the minister that at least fifty MPs
would enter the opposition lobby if the government pushed ahead
with its plan unamended.[43]

By mid-May, after some acrimonious exchanges in the Commons, Dalton was reconsidering his options. In spite of support in
cabinet from Bevin and Cripps, the prospects for a full rationing
scheme became more remote after the Prime Minister declared his
opposition. 'People like Shinwell . . . can criticise and oppose all
they want', he complained in private, 'but the poor, down-trodden
Tory is not allowed to open his mouth to the Government without
loud cries of protest being raised.'[44] In these circumstances, Dalton
was forced to shelve rationing and decided to focus instead on the
idea of limited state intervention aimed at increasing production.
The government's white paper of early June thus espoused the
principle of 'dual contol': the state would assume responsibility for
mining operations, while owners retained control of all financial
matters. This compromise, while acceptable to Conservatives, was
poorly received by miners' officials and Labour opinion. In the
House, Labour back-benchers claimed that the government had run
away from its own arguments in favour of rationing; although only
eight MPs went into the opposition lobby when the crunch came,
it was widely believed that Dalton had given way to the 1922
Committee.[45]

The fuel rationing controversy had, within a matter of weeks,
clearly developed into a test of party strength. Hugh Dalton was
openly told by one Tory MP that 'they acted as they did because
they felt that the Labour Party in the Government was getting too
much of its own way.'[46] There was little doubt that Conservatives
had greater cause for satisfaction with the outcome; 'the ghost of
Neville Chamberlain', as Angus Calder puts it, 'was still master of
the Commons.'[47] Tory opinion had conceded the creation of a new
department to oversee the mines, the Ministry of Fuel and Power,
but to set against this rationing had been relegated to an annexe of
the white paper as a remote future contingency. 'Dual control',
moreover, avoided altogether contentious questions of ownership,
wages and conditions, and was therefore difficult to interpret as a
first step towards nationalisation. In fact, Labour members, feeling
humiliated and convinced by this episode that economic and social

reform was being shelved, from this time on began to put greater pressure on their ministerial leaders to produce tangible results as the price for continued participation in the coalition.[48] More immediately, the rationing controversy, helped to rekindle Conservative fears about Stafford Cripps. If his failure in India had undermined his credibility on the left, then his strong support for rationing clearly aroused the suspicions of the 1922 Committee.[49] This was to have important knock-on effects in the summer of 1942, when the Prime Minister suddenly faced the most open challenge yet to his leadership.

On 21 June the North African fortress of Tobruk, with its 30,000 Allied defenders, was captured by the Germans. This unexpected loss, coming as it did out of the blue after a period of sustained setbacks, inevitably provoked renewed doubts about the government's handling of the war effort. The Prime Minister, visiting the United States when the news came through, cannot have been encouraged by reports in the American press predicting the downfall of his government. Certainly, Tobruk caused a profound shock. Amongst ministers, even Ernest Bevin — not usually given to pessimistic predictions — was sufficiently alarmed to question whether the coalition could survive this fresh blow.[50] According to Bevin's version of events, he was now approached about participation in an alternative government by Lord Beaverbrook, who, since his resignation in February, had embarrassed Churchill with his support for the immediate opening of a Second Front in Europe.[51] In the House of Commons wild rumours circulated, and the tension was heightened when the prominent Tory MP Sir John Wardlaw-Milne declared his intention to move a vote of no confidence in the government. As we have seen, Wardlaw-Milne, in his capacity as chairman of the Select Committee on National Expenditure, had become increasingly disillusioned and outspoken about the government's shortcomings in mobilising the war economy. His decision to confront the Prime Minister openly was prompted in part by the Select Committee's recent uncovering of appalling deficiencies in tank manufacture. This, Wardlaw-Milne believed, was decisively affecting the North African campaign. He thus launched his attack on the government confident of receiving support both from established back-bench critics and from members of the Select Committee.[52]

The level of unease in the Commons did not, of course, escape
the attention of the Leader of the House. Cripps sensed that Tobruk
offered new possibilities. He now urged one associate to sound out
members of the cabinet about his possible succession to the leadership and, after the government suffered a resounding defeat in the
by-election at Maldon on 26 June, he felt emboldened to report to
Churchill that 'something is wrong and should be put right without
delay'. The Prime Minister reacted furiously to these strictures, and
there ensued what he later described — with masterful understate-
ment — as a 'stern discussion' between the two men.[53] As anger
about Tobruk began to subside, it became evident that Cripps had
made his move prematurely. The 1922 Committee, having burnt its
fingers earlier in the year, decided to oppose the Wardlaw-Milne
motion. Many Tories still hoped to see a reduction in the Prime
Minister's powers, but few wanted the responsibility for a rerun
of May 1940, especially as the most likely Tory alternative was
Anthony Eden, an equally distrusted figure.[54] The Labour party
also agreed not to press for a fresh investigation into armaments
production, and the minority who urged support for the vote of
censure were taken to task by Labour ministers at a heated party
meeting. Ernest Bevin, it was reported, 'weighed in with a tremen-
dous speech which shattered his opponents. He warned the Party
that the Wardlaw-Milne group wanted to get Labour out of the
Govt. We had to watch those members of our Party who ran with
this gang.'[55] The Prime Minister thus had less to fear than
originally seemed likely, though it was with the unexpected outcome of the famous Norway debate in mind that MPs packed into
the House to hear Wardlaw-Milne propose his motion on 1 July.

The censure debate of July 1942 was in many ways over almost
before it had begun. After some fifteen minutes of careful and well-
received criticism, which pushed ministers onto the defensive,
Wardlaw-Milne made his celebrated *faux pas*. The suggestion
that the King's brother, the Duke of Gloucester, be appointed
Commander-in-Chief of Britain's armed forces provoked a remarkable outburst of sustained ironical cheering. 'I at once saw
Winston's face light up', reported Chips Channon; 'he knew that
he was saved.'[56] Although Wardlaw-Milne recovered to hit hard
at production policy, the damage was irreparable. His mistake was
compounded by the seconder, Sir Roger Keyes, who actually con-
tradicted the motion by calling upon the Prime Minister to exercise

greater, not less, responsibility. In these circumstances, it hardly mattered that Oliver Lyttelton, replying for the government, made what he later described as 'a proper balls of it'.[57] The House was counted out in confusion in the early hours of the morning with two MPs coming to blows, and the debate nearly collapsed before Wardlaw-Milne formally moved his motion for a second time. On the following day stinging attacks were made on the government by Aneurin Bevan, now emerging as 'snarler in chief' in the Commons, and by another disaffected back-bencher, Hore-Belisha.[58] But the outcome was no longer in doubt. The Prime Minister was sufficiently confident in winding up the debate that he managed to avoid any real explanation for the disaster in Libya. The government defeated the motion of censure by 475 votes to twenty-five, with an estimated thirty to forty abstentions.[59]

The Tobruk debate was obviously a resounding triumph for Churchill. He was fascinated to be told of a historical parallel — the minority vote of twenty-five exactly equalled that registered against Pitt in 1799, after a similarly protracted series of military defeats. On closer inspection, however, there were still causes for concern in the political situation. The Prime Minister was well aware that the mishandling of the censure motion had persuaded many waverers, notably members of the Select Committee, to rally behind the government. In view of the disastrous mistakes made by Wardlaw-Milne and Keyes, the real surprise was that as many as twenty-five back-benchers were prepared to go into the opposition lobby — a considerable increase in open dissent when compared with the vote in February. Churchill was also fortunate in that the supporters of the censure motion, spread as they were across the parties, lacked any strong sense of unity.[60] Nor, in spite of the vote of confidence, had the doubts of large numbers of MPs been overcome. Among Conservatives, there was a widespread feeling that had a motion been proposed demanding the overhaul of production techniques, many more would have entered the opposition lobby. And Labour members were now equally impatient for some sign that matters would improve. One of those who supported the Prime Minister concluded that never before 'have so many Members entered a division lobby with so many reservations in their minds'.[61] In this light, the Tobruk debate had, in effect, only provided the government with a further breathing space. Churchill's PPS was convinced by recent proceedings that unless

Britain's military fortunes improved dramatically over the next few months, the writing was on the wall.[62]

The problems besetting the government were brought to a head and resolved in the autumn of 1942. During August the Prime Minister was out of the country, reorganising the Allied High Command in the Middle East and informing Stalin that there would be no Second Front in Europe for the foreseeable future. Britain's military strategy — and Churchill's political future — was instead tied up with the fate of a joint Anglo-American operation designed to push back the Germans in North Africa, Operation Torch. In the meantime critics of the government sought more effective means of co-ordinating opposition. Lord Hankey, for example, led moves to bring together newspaper editors, servicemen and MPs in an attempt to show that 'something must be done to improve the organisation of the war effort and the planning of strategy'.[63] Walter Elliot, a prominent Tory back-bencher, noted in a radio broadcast that parliament was loath to rise for its annual hoilday in August. 'For nobody', he declared, 'likes the way that things are shaping. Rommel dug in at El Alamein — the Japs reaching up the mountains in New Guinea — and in Russia, the Germans developing a thrust which . . . bids fair to carry them to the Caspian.'[64] But familiar obstacles continued to lie in the path of critics. In particular, how could disparate opposition groups be brought together and who — in the event of change becoming inevitable — could replace the Prime Minister?

With these problems in mind, a small group of senior Tories spent much of the summer recess trying to build up the prospects of Anthony Eden. The Foreign Secretary, as we have seen, still had few friends on the 1922 Committee, and his political standing tended to fluctuate. But his public popularity remained consistently high, and before one of his foreign trips earlier in the year, Chuchill had, in fact, advised the King to send for Eden in the event of his own death. The Foreign Secretary appeared to offer something new to the likes of Sir Edward Grigg, one of those removed from office in February, and Lord Astor, whose *Observer* newspaper had in recent months become more openly critical of Churchill. 'What is needed', Astor urged in private, 'is a younger man who will be backed by a small War Cabinet and who will create a single General Staff. . . . We do not need a superman.'[65] It rapidly became clear, however, that

Eden could not be relied upon to spearhead an alternative administration. From private soundings, Eden's real concern appeared to
be that Beaverbrook, still at loose outside the government, might
try to rally support behind the cause of a negotiated peace. In view
of this fear, Lord Astor was informed that the Foreign Secretary
was still prepared to 'prop up Winston on the latter's terms'.[66]

The loyalty of Stafford Cripps was much less certain. Over the
summer a series of dinners was arranged with the aim, according to
Rab Butler, of enabling Cripps to improve his standing among
Conservative MPs. At these, Cripps aired his view that the Prime
Minister would be pushed aside in due course, lacking as he did any
real understanding of the home front. Thereafter, he envisaged a
joint government headed by Eden, Lyttelton and himself.[67] The
Lord Privy Seal was equally open about his ambitions among
Labour supporters. During August he was reported to be discussing
with family and friends whether he should resign from office,
thereby leaving himself free to rally oppostion and voice openly his
concerns about coalition policy, both in terms of strategy and what
he saw as a lack of genuine commitment to post-war planning.[68]
Although public support for Cripps had declined from the dizzy
heights of the spring, it remained unclear how much support he
could rely upon in political circles; his own uncertainty on this
point was reflected in the emphasis given in his speeches to the idea
of a new centre party, based on progressive elements in both
Labour and Conservative ranks.[69] Cripps continued, nevertheless,
to figure prominently in the intense speculation about the future.
One Labour MP. voiced the opinion that the Prime Minister was
being left 'high & dry' by successive military defeats, and would
not be saved by the loyalty of cabinet colleagues unless matters
improved. Of the alternatives, he added, Tory distrust of Eden was
still likely to 'bring Cripps to the top'.[70]

When asked years later to reflect on his most anxious period of
the war, Churchill did not refer, as might be expected, to the danger
of invasion in 1940 but pointed without hesitation to the months of
September and October 1942. Certainly, when parliament reassembled briefly in early September, the Prime Minister received a rough
ride. He was not well received when outlining his recent negotiations in the Middle East and Moscow, and he was caught off guard
by an open call for his resignation from Aneurin Bevan.[71] At this
stage, however, the pressure on Churchill was temporarily relieved

by a remarkable example of naivety and misjudgement on the part of the Leader of the House. When the Prime Minister had finished speaking the following day, MPs left the chamber in large numbers for lunch. Hugh Dalton, taking up the story, noted that 'Cripps — silly ass — instead of saying that this shows the House is completely satisfied . . . preaches a priggish sermon on the duty of MPs to stay and talk. He is rapidly losing all that is left of his "mystique".'[72] Certainly, feelings ran high in all parts of the House. The 1922 Committee responded by making a formal complaint to the Chief Whip, asserting that the prestige of parliament had been seriously impaired. Labour memebers were equally angered. One bluntly voiced a common view: that a man who lunched 'on two nuts & half a carrot' had no right to upbraid others for their eating habits. The prospects for Cripps now looked less rosy than earlier in the year, though public reaction to his plain speaking was generally favourable.[73]

In spite of this episode, the Lord Privy Seal decided to act upon his misgivings. He now wrote to the Prime Minister, detailing a list of concerns which, he said — if not remedied — would lead to his resignation; chief among these were the demand to remodel the machinery for handling the war effort to include a War Planning Directorate, and the need for a bold programme of social re-construction.[74] Cripps did agree, after persuasion from colleagues, to delay his resignation at least until the outcome of the impending battle in North Africa became known. In early October Churchill told Eden that if Operation Torch turned out to be a failure, he would be 'done for'. This pessimism was shared by his close associate Brendan Bracken, who believed the Prime Minister 'must win his battle in the desert or get out'. When asked whether this exaggerated the position, he retorted that if Cripps 'pulls out, there'll be a hell of a row'. The prospect of a leading minister — and potential rival — resigning in the wake of another military defeat thus made Churchill more than usually anxious as he awaited news from the battle-front. At first, this was far from encouraging.[75] But finally, in early November, it became clear that Montgomery's troops were in the process of overwhelming the Germans at El Alamein. In the long run, this victory was to help transform the course of the war. Its immediate impact or British politics was decisive. For the first time in over a year, the Prime Minister could face the Commons confident that there was — as he put it — 'some sugar on the cake'.

Critics of the 'higher direction of the war', Hugh Dalton noted, were suddenly sunk out of sight and mind. 'Crazy Cripps', he went on, 'will have to think again about the prospect of the P.M. falling from power and find some new excuse for his own resignation from the Government.'[76] In the event, resignation was not necessary. Two weeks later Churchill carried out a small ministerial reshuffle: Cripps was removed from the War Cabinet and sent reluctantly to the Ministry of Aircraft Production. The political crisis of 1942 was over.

One obvious question arises from this reassessment of the events of 1942: could the Prime Minister have fallen from power? The critics of the government have generally been dismissed by historians of the war years. Alan Bullock, for example, has argued that, having failed to shake Churchill in the Tobruk debate, 'there was nothing the critics could do except wait until the Government either began to win the war or plunged the country into some final disaster.'[77] As we have seen, the Prime Minister had, by his courageous example in 1940, built up an unrivalled authority; the government's commanding majority gave him almost unprecedented executive power, and the number of open critics at Westminster always remained small. At the same time, however, it was clear that under the impact of a series of military defeats — in Greece, Crete, Singapore and Libya — the patience of the most loyal coalition supporters was being stretched to the limit. For as long as military victory evaded British forces, Churchill, like his predecessor, would be vulnerable to even small shifts in parliamentary opinion.

The fall of Neville Chamberlain — after only one major reversal in the Norway campaign — had followed on from a minority of Conservative MPs deciding to switch their allegiance. As the political atmosphere became more and more highly charged with news of defeat in 1942, so disaffection spread again through Tory ranks: orthodox Chamberlainites, leading peers and Wardlaw-Milne's Select Committee followers all came to have grave doubts, further exacerbated by Churchill's dictatorial style of leadership. The coalition did, it was true, have an extra cushion provided by Labour backing, but this had to be balanced against the possibility of the government coming to grief over a domestic controversy. It was in recognition of these underlying political realities that the Prime Minister pointed with hindsight to the autumn of 1942 as his

most anxious months of the war. He sensed that the Tobruk debate
had offered only a breathing space, and that news of another British
military defeat might act as the final straw. The Labour minister
Chuter Ede, looking back at the end of the year, commented that
after Tobruk 'misgivings were profoud', and were not eased by the
months of stagnation which followed. 'This apparent inaction', he
added, 'further tried our faith. Had anyone seen an alternative to
Churchill the Government would have fallen.'[78]

Here we run up against one of the dominating features of British
politics in 1942 — the assumption that Churchill was indispensable. Shortly before the Tobruk debate, Chips Channon wrote that
'there *is* nobody else — if only Mr Chamberlain was alive. Many a
member who voted against him would now willingly withdraw his
vote.'[79] Chamberlain's death, as we saw earlier, had eased Churchill's rise to untrammelled power, though on closer inspection the
idea of indispensability might be regarded as something of a
double-edged sword. Neville Chamberlain, after all, had been
regarded as an irreplaceable leader by his own supporters for much
of his premiership, whereas Churchill, of course, was widely
distrusted by the political nation before he assumed the reins of
power. In this sense, the shortcomings of Cripps were unimportant,
or at least must be balanced against his potential, untested in the
event, to take over as an alternative leader, committed to new
departures both abroad and at home. Cripps had no firm party
base, but then neither had Churchill before May 1940; and
although public enthusiasm for Cripps had waned as he became
more identified with the policies of the government, he was still
receiving — again like Churchill in 1939 — strong backing from
sections of the national press. The Prime Minister himself certainly
did not believe that Cripps posed a negligible threat, and was
conscious that as Britain came to rely more and more on her major
allies, the notion of his indispensability was losing ground. As one
writer put it in mid-1942: 'When the public begins to say of a
leader, "But who could possibly replace him?", it means that the
possibility is occupying the public mind and the change is
coming.'[80] The major coalition partners may, of course, have stuck
to Churchill even in the event of defeat in North Africa. But it was
not simply a question of staying loyal to the Prime Minister or
awaiting 'some final disaster'. With the backing of the Russians and
Americans, it was widely assumed in 1942 that Hitler would untli-

mately be defeated. The issue at stake, therefore, was how long political opinion in Britain would tolerate defeat on the battlefield before forcing some further change, whatever the consequences.

The likely outcome of an extended political crisis, exacerbated by the resignation of the Leader of the House of Commons, can only remain a matter of speculation. What the events of 1942 had made clear, though, was that the Prime Minister faced an increasingly uphill struggle in reconciling the competing claims of party spokesmen on the home front. Early in the year Hugh Dalton, commenting on the tense atmosphere at Westminster and in Whitehall, wrote that 'we just don't deserve to win the war. We are all fighting each other instead of the enemy, and with such zest.'[81] The reality was that the major coalition partners had found the experience of co-operation uncomfortable from the very beginning. Conservatives had reluctantly acquiesced in new measures of state intervention and economic planning, but drew the line at Dalton's fuel rationing scheme. In many ways the party had been in a state of disarray since the fall of Chamberlain, uncertain how to respond to the profound social changes taking places and wavering in its uncertain loyalty to the Prime Minister. During the autumn of 1942 one leading Tory wrote to the Chief Whip 'that as an effective body of opinion in the House or the Country, the Conservative Party have ceased to exist'.[82] In spite of the manifestly radical mood of the public, which we shall examine in a later chapter, Labour supporters felt equally frustrated. The fuel rationing controversy was regarded as a sign of Conservative determination to resist fundamental reform, and Labour ministers were coming under increasing pressure to demonstrate that the coalition would seriously consider the whole question of post-war reconstruction.

The Prime Minister had survived the traumas of 1942; after El Alamein, his leadership was never again to be questioned. But one thing he was powerless to prevent was a burgeoning debate, at many different levels of British society, about the shape of the post-war world. Churchill, preoccupied as he was with matters military, believed that discussion about reconstruction was irrelevant until the Nazi menace had been defeated; it was also, he felt, undesirable, since it was likely to stimulate further the revival of party hostilities. By the end of the year, however, he could no longer stem the tide. As soon as military victory looked more certain, whatever the time scale involved, it was inevitable that a new phase in the history of the coalition would begin to open up. Instead of military strategy and war production — the themes that had held sway since May 1940 — national attention, sensing some light at the end of the tunnel, would naturally now switch to consideration of the domestic future. But that this happened so rapidly after the victory at El Alamein, and with such intensity as to set a clear pattern for the remainder of the war years, was due in no small measure to one man — Sir William Beveridge.

Notes

1 Notes by A. J. Sylvester, 14 March 1941, Lloyd George papers, G/24/2/45; Stokes to Lloyd George, 3 April 1941, Lloyd George papers, G/19/3/25.
2 *Colville Diary*, 23 April 1941, p. 377; notes by Sylvester, 23–25 April 1941, Lloyd Geoge papers, G/24/2/68–70.
3 *Dalton Diary*, 28 April 1941, p. 190. See also *Channon Diary*, 6 May 1941, pp. 302–3, which reports the irreverent claim of one of Eden's opponents that in the present situation, the nation wanted 'a Panzer Government, not a Pansy Government'.
4 *The Times*, 8–9 May 1941, reported that only three MPs, D. N. Pritt, William Gallacher and Alfred Salter, voted against the government, with two ILP members as tellers. Lloyd George and Manny Shinwell abstained.
5 *Channon Diary*, 1 and 6 June 1941, p. 307.
6 Cooper was replaced by Churchill's protégé, Brendan Bracken. Overall the reshuffle had little effect on the party balance of the coalition. On the hardening of newspaper attitudes in 1941, see Cockett, 'Government, press and politics', pp. 175–202.
7 *Colville Diary*, 18 August 1941, p. 428. Lord Hankey, an increasingly disenchanted member of the government, had earlier observed that there was a 'good deal of murmuring among the Service Staffs both military and civilian at Winston's dictatorial methods, and one hears repeated a saying attributed to A. J. B[alfour] that he is a "genius without judgement"' — Hankey to Hoare, 18 May 1941, Hankey papers, HNKY 4/33.
8 Macmillan to Beaverbrook, 13 October 1941, cited in Taylor, *Beaverbrook*, p. 494.
9 *The Economist*, 1 November 1941.
10 *Channon Diary*, 9 January 1942, p. 316.
11 Butler to Hoare, 6 March 1942, Butler papers, G14, ff. 33–4.
12 *Channon Diary*, 20–22 January 1942, pp. 317–18.
13 Eden diary, 21 January 1942, cited in R. Rhodes James, *Anthony Eden*, London, 1986, p. 262.

14 Harvie-Watt, *Most of My Life*, p. 74: Churchill's poor reception in the House led him to decry what the called 'a hostile Parliament and a guilty Parliament', adding that 'a General Election might be necessary'.

15 *Chuter Ede Diary*, 27 January 1942, p. 42. Jack Lawson MP spoke in even stronger terms: '... the 1922 Committee were appeasers, pro-Chamberlain and anti-Churchill. They would try to step in at some appropriate moment & save Hitler's skin.'

16 Headlam diary, 29 January 1942, D/He 38.

17 Calder, *People's War*, p. 313; *Dalton Diary*, 4–5 February 1942, pp. 360–2. G. M. Thomson, *Vote of Censure*, London, 1968, p. 77, summarises the appeal of Cripps as follows: 'He had a notable power of lucid and compelling speech and a character which seemed to reproach, in its crystalline integrity, the dusty compromises of public life.'

18 James Stuart (Viscount Findhorn), *Within the Fringe*, London, 1967, p. 120; Mass-Observation Typescript Report No. 1166, 'Sir Stafford Cripps', 23 March 1942.

19 Taylor, op. cit., pp. 508–12; Bullock, *Bevin*, pp. 149–50. Churchill told Beaverbrook that he had expended much energy on this issue and could do 'no more for him': an illustration of his own vulnerability at this time – M. Gilbert, *Road to Victory: Winston S. Churchill 1941–1945*, London, 1986, p. 55.

20 *Channon Diary*, 4 February 1942, p. 320: '... the reshuffle is inadequate and reminiscent of Mr Chamberlain's last, and fatal, attempt to reorganise his government'.

21 *Chuter Ede Diary*, 15–18, February 1942, pp. 50–1; V. 377 H. C. Deb., 5 s., c. 1682, 17 February 1942.

22 Hore-Belisha diary, 22 February 1942: Churchill College, Cambridge.

23 Taylor, op. cit., pp. 513–20.

24 *Chuter Ede Diary*, 25 February 1942, p. 57: at the party meeting one Labour MP complained that 'if we accepted these changes we lost all for which we had asked: (a) Reconstruction; (b) India; (c) prestige because we had lost more than any other party'. Attlee retorted that he had done his best, and had been told when pushing for party representation that 'he could only put 100 votes in the lobby'.

25 Butler to Hoare, 6 March 1942, Butler papers, G14, f. 34: Margesson was not considered effective at the War Office, and had been harmed by scurrilous attacks on the 'Baldwin–Chamberlain Old School Tie Clique'; what particularly angered Tories was the manner in which Margesson found out that he was to be replaced by his own Permanent Secretary, P. J. Grigg.

26 *Chuter Ede Diary*, 24–25 February 1942, pp. 54 and 58.

27 D. Dilks (ed.), *The Diaries of Sir Alexander Cadogan, 1938–1945*, London, 1971, p. 437.

28 *Chuter Ede Diary*, 23 February 1942, p. 54, citing the view of Major Vyvyan Adams, Conservative MP for Leeds West and a long-standing opponent of appeasement. See also the entry for 25 February, p. 57, where Rab Butler refers to the anxiety that there were no 'orthodox'

Tories left in the War Cabinet: 'Churchill was not orthodox; Eden was not liked; Anderson had never called himself a Tory; Lyttelton nobody knew & he was regarded as a city shark!'

29 Ibid., 27 February 1942, p. 60.
30 *Dalton Diary*, 20 February 1942, p. 373; Pimlott, *Hugh Dalton*, p. 345.
31 *The Economist*, 28 February 1942. See also 'Home Intelligence Weekly Report', 25 February 1942, PRO INF 1/292, which reported the strong public backing for the inclusion of Cripps, on the grounds that at last 'a personality is looming up who should really be able to take some of the strain off the Prime Minister's shoulders and could, if necessary, succeed him'.
32 For a full discussion of the Cripps mission to India, see R. J. Moore, *Churchill, Cripps and India, 1939–1945*, Oxford, 1979.
33 Hankey to Hoare, 12 March 1942, Hankey papers, HNKY 4/34.
34 *Nicolson Diary*, 23 April 1942, p. 223; N and J. Mackenzie (eds), *The Diary of Beatrice Webb*, Vol. IV, *1924–1943*, London, 1985: diary entry for 1 May 1942, p. 481; 'Home Intelligence Weekly Report', 28 May 1942, PRO INF 1/292.
35 Roskill, *Hankey*, pp. 549–53.
36 Gilbert, op. cit., pp. 107–8.
37 Beaverbrook to President Roosevelt, cited in Thomson, op. cit., p. 146. Beaverbrook himself was thought to be behind much of the intriguing at this time — see R. Boothy, *Boothby: Recollections of a Rebel*, London, 178, p. 183. Taylor, op. cit., pp. 530–3, claims that his main purpose was to promote the Second Front, though 'he was not alone in sometimes doubting whether Churchill would survive'.
38 *Dalton Diary*, 25 March 1942, p. 403, for the view of A. C. Spearman, MP for Scarborough. See also *Chuter Ede Diary*, 11 March 1942, p. 63, which cites J. P. Thomas, MP for Hereford on the Tory party being in a bad way: the 1922 Committee spent its time bemoaning the excess profits duty and deciding to entertain Churchill 'to lunch at 11/– a head although more than half of them didn't like him or his principal supporters in the Govt . . .'.
39 Ibid., 15 February and 26 March 1942, pp. 50 and 57–8. Disquiet about the military position was such that Attlee felt compelled to urge one of Labour's senior back-benchers, Jim Griffiths, that 'it is at the present time essential that our leading men should give a strong lead to the weaker brethren' — Attlee to Griffiths, 19 March 1942: James Griffiths papers, National Library of Wales, B3/10.
40 On the electoral truce, see below, Chapter 6.
41 The background to the fuel rationing controversy is fully detailed in the relevant official history by W. H. B. Court, *Coal*, London, 1951. Chapters VI–IX.
42 *Dalton Diary*, 6 May 1942. See also Pimlott, *Dalton*, pp. 351–8.
43 Goodhart, *The 1922*, pp. 114–18; *Dalton Diary*, 9 May 1942, p. 427.
44 Crozier interview with the Prime Minister, 29 May 1942: Taylor (ed.), *Off the Record*, p. 333 .

45 *Chuter Ede Diary*, 8–11 June 1942, pp. 76–8.

46 Hugh Dalton, *Fateful Years*, p. 400.

47 Calder, op. cit., p. 328.

48 For example, Labour MPs denounced proposed pension increases as wholly inadequate, and in July fifty back-benchers were to vote against the government in an effort to secure further increases.

49 Goodhart, op. cit., p. 120: the 1922 Committee came close to requesting that the Tory MP Gerald Palmer, who acted as PPS to Cripps, should be asked to resign.

50 Diary notes, 21 June 1942: A. V. Alexander papers, Churchill College, Cambridge, AVAR 6/1.

51 Bullock, op. cit., pp. 177–8. Bevin, needless to say, would have nothing to do with any intrigue proposed by Beaverbrook.

52 M. Philips Price, *My Three Revolutions*, London, 1969, p. 279. Philips Price, Labour MP for the Forest to Dean, recalled that Churchill was at first truculent about the claims of the Select Committee, but promised to investigate the idea of creating a scientific general staff. Philips Price was originally supportive of the Wardlaw-Milne motion, but eventually decided to abstain from voting in the censure debate.

53 Addison, *Road to 1945*, p. 205; W. S. Churchill, *The Second World War*, Vol. IV, *The Hinge of Fate*, London, 1951, pp. 354–6.

54 *Channon Diary*, 25 June 1942, p. 353: he for one would never 'vote against Winston to make Anthony King'.

55 *Chuter Ede Diary*, 30 June 1942, p. 82.

56 *Channon Diary*, 1 July 1942, p. 334. The fullest description of the debate remains Thomson, op. cit., pp. 192–207.

57 *Channon Diary*, 1 July 1942, p. 334.

58 Campbell, *Bevan and the Mirage of Socialism*, pp. 114–16; M. Foot, *Aneurin Bevan*, Vol. I, *1897–1945*, London 1962, pp. 372–8.

59 *The Times*, 4 July 1942, analysed the division lists to show that the minority vote consisted of eight Conservatives, eight Labour, two Liberals, six Independents and three ILP members (twenty-seven including tellers).

60 *Chuter Ede Diary*, 4 July 1942, p. 84, cites the claim of one Labour MP: ' "When I read the motion & noted the names attached to it, I could not help asking myself if these hon. members who have no confidence in the Govt, have any confidence in one other." Certainly no sound Labour man could have felt confidence in company with Wardlaw-Mile who wanted still further to aristocracise the Army; and Roger Keyes who wanted to dismiss Morrison for releasing strikers . . . .'

61 Headlam diary, 2 July 1942, D/He 38.

62 Harvie-Watt, op. cit, p. 93.

63 'The war machine', report of meeting, 30 July 1942: Hankey papers, HNKY 13/2.

64 Walter Elliot, broadcast of 8 August 1942, cited in *Long Distance*, London, 1943, p. 74.

65 Memorandum by Lord Astor, 13 August 1942: Viscount Astor papers,

Reading University, MS 1066/1/823.
66 'Note on Nancy Tree's views about A[nthony] E[den], August 1942, Astor papers, MS 1066/1/823.
67 Typed diary notes, July 1942, Butler papers, G14, ff. 58–60.
68 *Dalton Diary*, 24 August 1942, pp. 479–80. Dalton also heard from the journalist Maurice Webb that Tory MPs led Cripps on and later laughed at his expense. Bevin said they had tried to convince him also of how they saw him as a future leader. 'But he said, "You can't catch an old dog like me as easily as that. I am not Stafford Cripps."'
69 See, for example, 'Lord Privy Seal's speech', delivered to the Fabian Society on 29 May 1942: Cripps papers, Nuffield College, Oxford, Ref. 1170.
70 Ivor Thomas to Tom Jones, 13 August 1942, copy in Astor papers, MS 1066/823.
71 Campbell, op. cit., p. 118, interprets this as Bevan being able to use romantic rhetoric because of Churchill's indispensability, though it might be argued that Bevan was simply reserving his bitterest attacks for the time when they might have most effect.
72 *Dalton Diary*, 8 September 1942, p. 490.
73 James Stuart minute to the Prime Minister, 9 September 1942, PRO PREM 4 60/4; *Chuter Ede Diary*, 20 September and 27 November 1942, pp. 97 and 110; 'Home Intelligence Weekly Report', 17 September 1942, PRO INF 1/292.
74 Cripps to Churchill, cited in C. Cooke, *The Life of Richard Stafford Cripps*, London, 1957, pp. 298–9.
75 Gilbert, op. cit., p. 237; Lord Moran, *Winston Churchill: the Struggle for Survival, 1940–1965*, London, 1966, pp. 91–6 — Bracken said that Churchill found the suspense of waiting 'almost unbearable', and when the news looked bad angrily asked, 'Haven't we got a single general who can even win one battle?'
76 *Dalton Diary*, 8 November 1942, p. 515.
77 Bullock, op. cit., p. 180.
78 *Chuter Ede Diary*, 31 December 1942, p. 115.
79 *Channon Diary*, 23 June 1942, p. 353.
80 The view of Osbert Sitwell, cited in Thomson, op. cit., p. 183.
81 *Dalton Diary*, 6 February 1942, p. 362.
82 Goodhart, op. cit., pp. 123–5: 'You yourself are well aware', added Lord William Scott, 'of what the P.M. thinks of the Tory Rump: he may not say so himself, but . . . his satellites are not so careful of their tongues.' Churchill had in fact asked the Cheif Whip himself at one point, what 'does the great Conservative Party think it is doing? It is like a whale stuck in the mud and unable even to flap its own tail' — Stuart, op. cit., pp. 88–93.

5

The New Jerusalem?

After the publication of the Beveridge Report in late 1942, reconstruction became the central theme of wartime politics. The report has long been seen as a vital turning point in economic and social policy. In the second half of the war, according to this line of thinking, Churchill's coalition took up the Beveridge plan by laying the foundations for the welfare state — accepting the idea of full employment, comprehensive social security, a national health service, and improved education and housing. The reforming instincts of the wartime government have become deeply embedded in the historiography of the period, from Paul Addison's notion of a new 'consensus' emerging between left and right through to Corelli Barnett's lament that the oppportunity for wholesale industrial regeneration was lost. 'Instead', he concludes, 'all the boldness of vision, all the radical planning, all the lavishing of resources, had gone towards working the *social* miracle of the New Jerusalem.'[1] This chapter sets out to challenge the notion of the war giving rise to a New Jerusalem, arguing instead that the coalition programme for reconstruction always promised more than it delivered. Wartime reforms were not as far-reaching as often supposed, in part because deep-seated differences continued to exist between the two major coalition partners. The idea of a wartime consensus, in other words, sits uneasily with the strong element of partisan disagreement which — as we have seen — had never entirely disapppeared and which intensified as the war progressed.

Reconstruction, it will be shown here, fell broadly into two stages. For more than two years after Churchill came to power, in May 1940, the government's energies were directed almost exclusively to matters of military strategy and production. In this early part of the war the Prime Minister — who in Hugh Dalton's words was 'alllergic to post-war policy' — succeeded in his aim of avoiding sensitive domestic issues that might threaten the unity of the coalition, and with it his leadership.[2] As the military position gradually improved, however, the government came under increasing pressure to act. The publication of Beveridge's immensely popular report brought reconstruction to the centre of the political stage, and the appointment of Lord Woolton to the newly created Ministry of Reconstruction in November 1943 represented a serious attempt to co-ordinate the various wide-ranging proposals for reform. The second half of the war thus witnessed an active phase of reconstruction, with the government outlining its commitment to reform in a series of white papers. But these departures, it will be argued, did not necessarily imply a radically new approach to social policy. The coalition was, if anything, characterised by prevarication in domestic policy; in spite of enormous pressure the Beveridge Report was not implemented before the end of the war, and the white papers tended to reflect the limits of agreement between Conservative and Labour supporters.

The Labour party, in line with its attitude during the early part of the war, on the whole accepted coalition policy as a minimum instalment of reform. The government's white papers promised more than might be secured if — as was felt likely — Churchill was returned to power at the end of the war. Hence, Labour concentrated its energies on pushing the Tories towards the implementation of agreed policies, while making clear its own preference for more fundamental social change. The Conservative party, on the other hand, believed that coalition policy had defined the maximum instalment of reform possible for a post-war administration. The white papers were acceptable only after several consessions had been made to party concerns, and the new attitude towards reform after 1943 was heavily coloured by a desire not to be seen opposing measures that had received widespread public acclaim. The element of electoral calculation was particularly strong in the approach of the Tory Reform Committee, a group of forty mostly younger MPs who emerged as strong critics of coalition policy, but who subsequently swung round to strong backing for the white paper reforms — even where these fell short of their original demands.[3] The advocates of social progress, moreover, remained very much a minority in Conservative ranks. Partly differences over reconstruction in the early years of the war, we might conclude, gave way after 1942 to what was only a temporary, artificial consensus.

Conservative and Labour members in parliament were henceforth agreed that reconstruction had to be faced, but they were not agreed on the need for a fundamentally new approach to social welfare. This line of argument can be developed first by outlining government policy in the early part of the war, and then by examining the major themes in the reconstruction process during 1943–44.[4]

Planning for reconstruction did not proceed far before the end of 1942. There was, of course, an obvious reason for this: the gravity of the military situation, especially in the year of Britain 'standing alone', left ministers with little time to plan for an uncertain future. In January 1941 the Labour veteran Arthur Greenwood was appointed Minister without Portfolio, charged with responsibility for reconstruction questions — a reflection of the low priority accorded to post-war matters at this early stage of the war. Greenwood had been regarded throughout Whitehall as unsuccessful in attempting to stimulate war production, and he found similar difficulties in providing a lead on reconstruction. The new ministerial committee over which he presided met only four times before his dismissal in February 1942.[5] One of the major stumbling-blocks facing Greenwood had been the knowledge that Churchill was opposed to the discussion of any politically contentious themes. The Prime Minister, consumed as he was by matters of military strategy, was consistently opposed to demands for an outline of 'constructive peace aims'. If Britain surrendered, Churchill declaimed angrily, then she would soon discover for what she was fighting. A cabinet committee was, in fact, established in 1940 to consider war aims, but, as Duff Cooper noted, this was 'too much an apple of discord to throw into a Coalition Cabinet'. By early 1941 the committee had been wound up, much to the annoyance of Labour back-benchers.[6]

Churchill had, if nothing else, recognised that reconstruction was a question of particular interest to Labour ministers. Greenwood's responsibilities were eventually passed on to another middle-ranking Labour figure, Sir William Jowitt, though he was not given a place in the War Cabinet, and, like his predecessor, he had few executive powers. Other Labour representatives such as Attlee and Bevin, in the meantime, often justified their participation in the coalition as a means of securing advances in economic and social welfare. But their enthusiasm should not be confused with an ability to dominate policy. Jowitt's Reconstruction Committee, on which Labour ministers were carefully balanced by Tory counterparts, could only co-ordinate work going on elsewhere; it was still widely accepted that responsibility for particular issues rested with individual government departments. By this standard, it .was Conservative rather than Labour ministers who held the upper hand: education, housing and health, as we shall see, were all policy areas entrusted to Tory representatives by 1943.

In response to the new and widespread interest in creating a better Britain, a cause vociferously taken up by the press and a multitude of pressure groups, planning for reform did begin in various parts of Whitehall. But in each case progress was slow. At the Board of Education, for example, the Conservative minister, Ramsbotham, was removed in 1941 after publicising proposals for reform that had been rejected before the war. His successor, R. A. Butler, was chosen primarily because on his past record, at the India Office and Foreign Office, he seemed less likely to depart from Churchill's injunction that the education department should stick to the task at hand — evacuation and it attendant problems for schoolchildern.[7] Similarly, in town and country planning, ministerial initiatives did not meet with Churchill's approval, and were effectively vetoed for the foreseeable future. More promising on the surface was discussion about medical reform, which had become widespread amongst specialist groups and interested observers under the impact of war. The experience of the Emergency Medical Service, in particular, had highlighted the deficiences of the pre-war hospital system, and, by 1941 the National Liberal minister in charge of health, Ernest Brown, had publicly announced a long-term commitment to reform the hospitals and maintain wartime standards. But legislation remained a long way off: progress had not been made on other crucial issues, such as health insurance, and Labour ministers were soon attacking Brown for being over-conciliatory to the voluntary hospital sector. By 1942 medical reform had been shelved again.[8] Thus, before the turn of the tide in the war, the story of reconstruction was one of a separate series of departmental accounts. There was no overall sense of direction or urgency in government planning, and the only common theme was the lack of progress towards measures that might actually reach the statute book.

Reconstruction planning was constrained not simply by Churchill's hostility but also by party differences. The absence of any major initiatives in the first two years of coalition clearly reflected the mood of the Conservative majority in parliament. As we have seen, Tory back-benchers were resentful of what they saw as the socialistic trend of wartime controls over the economy, and were determined to limit, where possible, the influence of Labour ministers. Hugh Dalton had discovered to his cost how uncompromising Conservatives could be over future policy when he produced plans to reorganise the coal industry. The only source of a more progressive party approach at this stage was the Post-War Problems Central Committee, established under the chairmanship of Rab Butler in 1941. Butler was convinced that the war made necessary the creation of a new and distinctly Conservative social policy, accepting an enhanced role for the state while defending the place of liberty and diversity. His committee operated through a network of specialist groups investigating a variety of policy issues, but, far from meeting the chairman's initial hopes, it had only mixed success in influencing the reconstruction process. The desire to represent all shades of party opinion made policy-making difficult; the committee's place in the party hierarchy was never clearly defined; and its published findings were generally undistinguished, attracting attention as examples of reactionary — as much as advanced — Conservative thinking.[9] Indeed, by the end of 1942 some elements within the divided Tory ranks were throwing their weight behind fledgling right-wing groups such as the National Society of Freedom.[10]

The Labour party had also established a variety of policy groups early on to discuss post-war policy. These also were beset by problems of personality and uncertainty about the future, though Labour did have the advantage that wartime experience was enhancing the popularity of some of its pre-war ideas, for example the need for a comprehensive national health service.[11] Policy discussion in both parties had only limited bearing on government planning, which was more directly influenced by specialist interests such as the religious denominations in education or the medical profession in health care. The importance of such discussion lay, rather, in highlighting the very different perceptions of the future that lay concealed beneath the mask of coalition unity. Labour back-benchers, reflecting the mood of the rank-and-file away from

Westminster, grew increasingly impatient with what they saw as deliberate stonewalling over reconstruction; pending the outcome of Beveridge's investigation, for instance, government spokesmen deprecated any full discussion of social insurance. From mid-1942 onwards especially, after the Tory revolt over coal rationing, the PLP was determined to exhort its representatives in government to secure more tangible results in social policy. Hence, in July more than fifty Labour MPs voted to condemn the latest changes in the pensions sytem — the largest anti-government vote recorded since the outbreak of war.[12]

In practical terms, given the composition of the government, Labour ministers were still in no position to seize the initiative. Rather, they found themselves on a tightrope: pledged, on the one hand, to defend coalition policy, but forced to recognise, on the other, that sooner or later party opinion would demand substantive changes on the home front. The day of reckoning was brought much closer once Britain's war fortunes finally showed signs of improvement. At the end of 1942 one Labour minister warned privately that the party would create further trouble unless 'something on account' was provided in social policy, adding that Labour feared, in particular, a repetition of 'the 1918 trick' — keeping them in governmnet until victory was assured and then pushing them out to restore pre-war standards.[13] Certainly, the battlelines were now being more openly drawn in public. In a debate on reconstruction shortly before, the Labour critic Aneurin Bevan caused a stir in the Commons with a stinging attack on his coalition partners: 'The British Army are not fighting for the old world. If the hon. Members opposite think we are going through this in order to keep their Malayan swamps, they are making a mistake. We can see the Conservatives crawling out of their holes now. In 1940 and 1941 they would not have dared to say these things.'[14] It was against this background, of an already burgeoning debate about the post-war world, that Sir William Beveridge forcefully added his voice to the clamour for action.

It was not intended that the Beveridge Committee should produce a major blueprint for social reform. Beveridge, whose long career as a public servant stretched back to the days of the Edwardian Liberal reforms, had been a leading critic of Chamberlain's economic war effort, and was subsequently drafted into the Ministry of Labour to provide specialist advice on manpower and labour questions. Ernest Bevin, however, soon grew tired of his restless and egotistical charge, and decided that the best way to occupy Beveridge was to offer him the chairmanship of what appeared to be a minor committee set up to investigate insurance benefits. Bevin telephoned Arthur Greenwood: 'You remember this 'ere social security business? I've got just the man for you. I'm sending Beveridge round in the morning.'[15] After recovering from this indignity, Beveridge quickly sensed the opportunity to press for far-reaching domestic reform. Within weeks he was using his personal domination of the new committee to sketch out radical proposals, much to the alarm of his Whitehall colleagues, who in the event dissociated themselves from the eventual findings. But Beveridge was scarcely concerned that the report became tied to his name alone. Having culitvated press contacts to ensure wide publicity, the Beveridge scheme was received with remarkable public acclaim, its publication at the end of 1942 coinciding with the very moment when impoved war fortunes allowed the British people to look forward with optimism for the first time since the outbreak of war.[16]

At the heart of the Beveridge Report was the call for a comprehensive system of social security, based on subsistence rate benefits 'from the cradle to the grave'. What made the plan so wide-ranging was the claim that any system could only be effective if accompanied by a new health service and by full employment, though Beveridge left others to work out the details of these additional proposals. With the benefit of hindsight, the report stands out as a central foundation of Britain's post-war welfare state. But Beveridge's biographer, Jose Harris, has cautioned against exaggerating its significance in the context of wartime social policy. The importance of the report, she has shown, lay less in the originality of its ideas than in its successful synthesis and transmission of plans to rationalise the disjointed insurance schemes that existed before the war. Above all, the press and public response to the Beveridge Report was such that the coalition came under sustained pressure to give serious — rather than token — attention to the problems of reconstruction, though, as we shall see, the introduction of concrete reform proposals was still to be a protracted and problematic process.[17]

The initial response of the government and the political parties at

Westminster perfectly exemplified their attitudes towards social reform in the first half of the war. Among Conservative ministers, the Chancellor Kingsley Wood — as the head of the department which had most distanced itself from Beveridge's ideas — spoke out strongly in the cabinet. He argued that no account had been taken of the uncertain post-war economic situation, and the popular expectations might be raised beyond levels which realistically could be satisfied. Labour ministers, by contrast, expressed support for the plan but — with the exception of Herbert Morrison — were anxious that calls for immediate action might pose a threat to the unity of the coalition.[18] The inevitable result was prevarication. The cabinet agreed to welcome the report in principle, but also to undertake its own detailed investigation. In the meantime there could be no question of legislation: given the uncertainty of the post-war situation, it was 'impossible at this stage to establish any order of priority or to enter into definite commitments'.[19] This, Churchill told his PPS was as far as he was prepared to go, adding that the trouble with Beveridge was that he was 'an awful windbag and a dreamer'.[20]

The government's compromise itself reflected party political reactions to the report. With some minor reservations, Labour members responded enthusiastically to what amounted to a more detailed exposition of aims proposed by the party in general terms for many years.[21] But on the Conservative side a committee of back-benchers had reacted by submitting a secret report to the Prime Minister, attacking the whole notion of social security. In the first place, the committee stressed that the major financial priority after the war must be the reduction of wartime levels of taxation, not the redistribution of income implied by the Beveridge scheme. Moreover, there were grave objections to the state assuming overriding responsibility in this area: the uniform provision of subsistence benefits, it was claimed, would undermine the national character by removing incentives to individual initiative.[22] The Beveridge Report thus brought to the surface and pinpointed the tensions of coalition politics. The government had been 'bounced' by Beveridge into modifying its previous policy of playing down reconstruction. But at the same time Churchill had been forcefully reminded by the committee of Tory MPs — claiming to represent 90 per cent of back-benchers — that the majority party in the Commons was not prepared to concede ground to its coalition partner. In these circumstances, it was not surprising that the government ran into trouble when the report came to be discussed in parliament during February 1943.

At the start of the debate, it was intended that MPs would simply welcome the report in general terms as a suitable basis for future action. This approach was reluctantly accepted by most Conservatives, anxious not to be seen blocking a proposal that had such widespread public approval. The only open criticism came from Sir Herbert Williams, who, in the words of one observer, could champion 'the Bolshevik Revolution and still win the loyal Tory votes of South Croydon'.[23] Several other spokesmen, however — while professing support — could barely conceal their animosity towards the report and the manner in which it had been produced. A group of Tory industrialists did, in fact, put down an amendment calling for the postponment of legislation, though this was not pressed after the government's spokesmen, Sir John Anderson and Kingsley Wood, created the definite impression that any such eventuality was unlikely before the end of the war.[24] The party's negative attitude was offset to an extent by the first parliamentary appearance of the Tory Reform Committee — the dissident 10 per cent of back-bench opinion — whose members urged a more positive approach to Beveridge reform. Tory Reformers nevertheless lined up behind the majority of the party when it became clear that Labour members, alarmed by the speeches of Anderson and Wood, would press for the immediate introduction of legislation. For Labour, the whole episode suddenly sharpened the tension between ministers, aiming to maiximise concessions from within the coalition, and back-benchers, determined to make immediate reform the price of remaining in government. The result was that Labour's amendment produced the largest anti-government vote of the war period, with ministers and almost all back-benchers marching into different lobbies.[25]

What, then, were the implications of the Beveridge episode? In the short term, the continued participation of Labour within the coalition looked in doubt. A government created ostensibly as a symbol of national unity could clearly not survive many such acts of defiance, and Labour ministers were particularly fearful of the consequences. What back-benchers failed to see, wrote Hugh Dalton, was that their refusal to support coalition policy posed the danger of Churchill calling a general election on the question of

Fig 2 Just to show they mean business

whether planning for peace was more important than winning the war, with the likely outcome that 'the Labour Party would be scrubbed out as completely as in 1931'.[26] This possibility gradually receded. The PLP, which received some stern lectures from Morrison and Bevin — the latter of whom refused to attend party meetings for several months afterwards — eventually backed down and agreed to accept the government's undertaking to examine further the Beveridge plan. Labour's enthusiasm for the report, in the heat of the moment, thus rebounded to an extent, though in the longer term, once the immediate crisis had passed, the parliamentary debate proved to be a critical turning point in underlining the wartime swing to the left. James Griffiths, the mover of Labour's amendment, commented to Beveridge at the time that the division in the Commons made the return of a Labour government after the war a certainty and, as we shall see in the next chapter, the government's handling of events in early 1943 did indeed produce a long-lasting cynicism about Tory plans for post-war recon-struction.[27] Many Conservatives subsequently tried to create a more positive public image, and at the party's first wartime conference shortly afterwards Tory Reformers were allowed to proceed with a resolution welcoming the Beveridge scheme.[28] But, in private, great scepticism remained. Several months later, Rab Butler could still be found observing that there was within the party 'a feeling that Beveridge is a sinister old man, who wishes to give away a great deal of other people's money'.[29]

The Beveridge Report did not produce any immediate shift in coalition policy. In the year following the heated parliamentary debate of February 1943, the government moved only slowly towards the introduction of a reconstruction programme. In spite of the now intense pressure for action, the Prime Minister con-tinued to set his face against reform. It was true that in March 1943 Churchill devoted a major radio broadcast to what he called a 'four year plan', outlining his own vision of future economic and social recovery. But it would be misleading to interpret this initiative as 'the first popular proclamation of the new consensus', marking a return to Churchill's Liberal reforming days. The small print of the speech committed the Prime Minister to nothing more than 'preliminary legislative preparation'; he clearly envisaged that the plan would only begin to operate when the war had ended. Only days after the broadcast, Churchill conceded in a private interview that major legislation was unlikely. He greatly resented, he said, being constantly told about the need for post-war plans when 'we had nothing like won the war. People were always getting ahead of events.'[30] The substance of domestic policy thus remained unaffected. A new Reconstruction Priorities Committee was established to consider further the government's reaction to the Beveridge plan, but the new machinery proved unwieldy in operation, and the only minister to take a lead on social issues — Herbert Morrison — was quickly rebuked by the Prime Minister for launching a 'Midlothian campagin' of progressive speeches.[31] 'The truth was', commented Rab Butler, 'that since the Beveridge Report debate Ministers had great terror of doing anything at all.'[32]

 After the impact of Churchill's broadcast wore off doubts about the government's intentions came to the fore. Press commentators urged that now was the time for action, not words. The Prime

Minister, it was noted, had not accepted the central Beveridge recommendation of a minumum subsistence income; no declarations had been made about the crucial area of economic policy; and the whole question of town and country planning was still being shelved.[33] By the summer dissatisfaction was again becoming vocal on the Labour back-benches, and in late June 1943 Attlee, Morrison and Bevin submitted a forceful paper to the cabinet entitled 'The Need for Decisions'. This argued that future planning would be fatally prejudiced unless the government made its own detailed financial forecasts, followed by firm decisions about which items of policy might be acted upon before the end of the war. Any future administration, it concluded, would be hopelessly impeded unless clear commitments were made on a variety of issues, such as land use, development rights, the reorganisation of transport, water supply and the electricity industry.[34] It was the Chancellor, Kingsley Wood, who provided ammunition for Churchill's negative response. The Labour ministers, Wood noted, were ignoring the amount of detailed work already proceeding, for example on the Beveridge scheme. The 'four year plan', moreover, would involve consideration of several major measures, and could be judged by the electorate only at the end to the war.[35] Any further discussion was postponed over the summer, and Herbert Morrison was left to complain about the lack of constructive measures and the 'slowing down influence of Kingsley Wood and such like people'.[36]

The influence of the Treasury continued to grow after Wood's sudden death in the autumn of 1943 and his replacement by the Lord President, Sir John Anderson. It did not go unnoticed that home policy was now being more firmly entrusted than ever to the minister whose inept performance had exacerbated tensions during the Beveridge debate six months earlier. *The Economist* summed up how far the mood of frustration had spread:

Like the policemen in 'The Pirates of Penzance', Ministers say in chorus 'We Go, We Go', but, like Gilbert's constables again, they do not go; no visible headway is made. Worthy White Papers on education, the health services, workmen's compensation, pensions, social insurance . . . and the rest of the Beveridge proposals are, and will be, ably produced; ground work is laid upon ground work. But the questions that matter most to the people of this country, the questions of highest policy — the prevention of want, the use and control of the land, the realities of demobilisation, industrial re-equipment — all these must apparently remain without even interim replies, and certainly without legislative answers, so long as the voice of Downing Street cannot find time from its vast strategic exercises to speak or to choose a spokesman in its stead.[37]

The Prime Minister was certainly reluctant to yield ground when cabinet discussion resumed on 'The Need for Decisions'. 'Was he not always taking decisions?', he questioned, and he taunted Labour ministers by noting that there were obvious objections to forwarding legislation if, as seemed increasingly likely, Labour co-operation would not continue after the war.[38] Nevertheless, under sustained pressure, Churchill did make two decisions which helped to determine the course of reconstruction policy for the remainder of the war.

The first was to accept that plans must now be considered for the period of transition between war and peace. Attlee, using his new found influence as Anderson's successor as Lord President, managed to convince Churchill that several issues could be tackled without serious controversy. The Prime Minister, conceding that he had been 'jostled and beaten up by the Deputy Prime Minister', now ordered schemes to be prepared for the transition period. Indeed, the Churchillian imagination, having taken on board a new idea, soon ran away with itself. The government, he claimed, should make every effort to prepare 'a great book, the Book of the Transition, like the War Book, running to perhaps a thousand closely printed pages or taking the form of a number of Reports and precise plans contained in drawers, one above another, so that, if any amateurish critic says, "You have no plan for this or that", it would be easy to pull out a drawer, bring out a paper, and say, "Here it all is."'[39] In a subsequent speech, the Prime Minister publicly announced his initiative under the slogan 'food, work and homes for all', but once again his interest in the whole area of domestic policy soon dwindled. Little more was heard of the 'Book of the Transition', and attention quickly turned to what seemed the more important of Churchill's two decisions — the formation in November 1943 of a Ministry of Reconstruction.

The appointment of Lord Woolton at the head of the new ministry was widely welcomed as a sign that Churchill was at last taking the task of reconstruction seriously. 'He has left it very late indeed', wrote one commentator, 'and the number of people who are frankly cynical about the possibility of any real reconstruction emerging from Mr Churchill's Government, or from his party, is

already very large. . . . Whether Lord Woolton will measure up to
his task will be one of the most interesting and important specula-
tions of the next few months.'[40] The Prime Minister, however, was
quite candid about why Woolton had been chosen: he was not only
an independent acceptable to both wings of the coalition but he
also had a reputation as a strong non-socialist, and would, therefore, resist attempts by Labour ministers to dominate the new
Reconstruction Committee through which the minister would
work. For his own part, Woolton was by no means keen to leave his
post at the Ministry of Food, where he had built up an enviable
reputation. In the first place, he suspected — rightly in the event, as
we shall see — that he would now be drawn into partly political
in-fighting; indeed, the activities of the new Reconstruction Committee were to be circumscribed by the need to avoid altogether
contentious issues such as the future control of industry. The
executive powers of the new ministry, moreover, were themselves
limited. Far from being given a brief to devise and implement his
own programme of reconstruction, Woolton's task was primarily
to co-ordinate and clarify proposals coming from specific departments.[41] This alone, Woolton realised, would make it difficult
for the new ministry to live up to the nation's high expectations.
In reality, at the time of his appointment, concrete proposals
for reform were still very thin on the ground. On the committee
devising the King's Speech for the new parliamentary session, Rab
Bulter noted that ministers could come up only with variations
upon ' "We have an Education Bill". When they came to including
something else they couldn't find it. . . .'[42]

The 1944 Education Act was to be the first major item of coalition
policy to reach the statute book, though educational reform only
slowly came to the forefront of the political agenda. After taking
over at the Board of Education, Rab Bulter initiated a long series of
negotiations aimed at overcoming the major obstacle to reform —
the uncertain future of religious education. Between the wars the
Anglican and Roman Catholic owners of the voluntary schools
found it increasingly difficult to keep pace with developments in
state education. At the same time, however, Nonconformist opinion continued to give a lead to those who opposed the granting of
further government aid to the voluntary bodies without a corresponding increase in state control. The Education Minister needed

all his diplomatic skills to reconcile such divergent viewpoints. He refused to be provoked by the intransigence of Catholics hostile to further control, even when they appeared to regard him — as in the case of one representative — as 'a forthcoming ox who was about to be laid upon the faggots'.[43] And Church of England opinion was similarly reticent until Bulter forced Anglican managers to recognise their failure as a building body, pointing out that less than 200 of the Church's 9,000 elementary schools had been built since 1905.[44] Nevertheless, by the end of 1942 the Board had devised a plan broadly acceptable to Anglicans and Nonconformists, if not to Roman Catholics. Under this scheme, the voluntary bodies were given the option of choosing between 'controlled status', which relieved the owners of their financial obligation but vested control over the appointment of teachers in the local authority and stressed non-denominational religious instruction; or — with the Catholics in mind — 'aided status', which allowed finanical aid for only half the cost of maintaining a church school where the power to appoint teachers and provide denominational instruction was retained. The religious dimension was regarded as an essential precondition to proceeding with the wider reforms that Butler and his officials now drafted into an Education Bill: secondary education for all children, the raising of the school-leaving age and the introduction of part-time 'continuation schools'.[45]

Once the Board had settled its ideas, there were, of course, still several hurdles to be overcome before legislation became practicable. At the same time as negotiating with the various educational interests, Butler was also looking for ways of tackling the obvious political obstacles to reform — securing approval from cabinet colleagues, and then finding sufficient basis for agreement between the Conservative and Labour wings of the coalition. The Prime Minister posed a particular problem, and had warned Butler in September 1941 that he would not tolerate the revival of denominational or political controversy. Butler, in response, was careful not to seek cabinet backing until he was confident that support from prominent Anglican Tories for 'controlled status' would sway Churchill. Thereafter, the Prime Minister's indifference was only likely to present problems in the event of a major public controversy arising.[46] Greater difficulties arose, in fact, at meetings of the Lord President's Committee, where sharp divisions emerged along party lines. These divisions were gradually narrowed, how-

ever, partly because the 'Cecil gang' — Selborne and Cranborne —
eventually reconciled themselves to the proposed religious settlement, and partly because of the feeling that education was the most
suitable topic for early action. Ernest Bevin, at a series of critical
meetings, hammered home the latter point. He was, in the words of
Chuter Ede, a tough statesman capable of giving the Tories 'a good
kick up the pants' when necessary — a tactic which succeeded when
the Lord President's Committee gave permission to proceed with
outline legislation in December 1942.[47] The Board thus issued a
white paper in the summer of 1943 and was soon ready to enter the
parliamentary arena. Butler's only real concern with his colleagues
was now that unless he kept proceeding quickly, the Prime Minister's
'sinister bodyguard' — Beaverbook and Cherwell — might take
charge of revitalising export trade, and education would be 'pushed
out of the picture'.[48]

When it came to soothing party fears, Butler's principal concern
was that Conservatives had no real enthusiasm for educational
reform. The President of the Board had long since been aware of
the 'abysmal ignorance of the Tory M.P.s on education', and held
back until prompted by Bevin for fear that the party would refuse
to give its support. During 1943 Butler had to spend much time
making sympathetic noises to the Conservative rank-and-file.
He reassured the 1922 Committee that the position of the Public
Schools would be safeguarded after the war; he deliberately stressed
the themes of diversity and variety in state provision; he gave
in to the party view on maintaining fees in a small number of
'direct-grant' secondary schools; and he emphasised the broad
acceptability of the religious provisions. Most Tories, 'like the
Prime Minister', Butler noted, 'are satisfied that the established
Church and the Cecil interest have accepted the need for a
measure of this sort'.[49] When the Education Bill came before
parliament at the end of 1943 Conservative MPs, in fact, took
very little interest in anything except the religious settlement.
Members of the Tory Reform Committee were critical on certain
points, such as the failure to include a firm date for raising the
school-leaving age but, on the whole, back-benchers were prepared
to acquiesce quietly. The main danger as the bill proceeded to
the committee stage in early 1944, noted the President, was simply
that the Tories were getting bored by the whole thing.[50]

Opinion in the Labour party was much more receptive to reform.

At the parliamentary stage, Labour members voiced the complaint that in certain respects the Board's plan did not go far enough. The most strongly felt reservations were over the retention of fees in direct-grant secondary schools and the absence of any projected date for raising the school age, and on both these points the party did not hesitate to force divisions at the committee stage.[51] In stressing the consensual nature of educational reform, much has been made of the fact that Labour accepted the so-called 'tripartite' system of secondary schooling, implicit though not spelt out in the legislation. Some sections of party opinion, notably the National Association of Labour Teachers, already believed that genuine equality of opportunity was possible only if all children attended a single, multilateral secondary school. But mainstream opinion in the war years was content to see the old division between elementary and secondary schooling finally abolished; concern about the failings of the secondary modern school within the tripartite structure was only to surface widely after the war. Nor did this necessarily mean hostility to multilateral schooling. The latter was generally regarded as a useful addition, though for the time being the main goal was that of achieving parity between the different types of proposed institution.[52] This controversy, moreover, barely surfaced in 1944, and should not obscure a more important reality. The Conservative party, as Butler himself conceded, had by a variety of means 'been brought to think the reforms less awful than they might'.[53] Labour, on the other hand, was keen not to hold up this long-awaited first item of coalition reconstruction policy, especially as the bill promised early implementation of what had been the party's minimum demands for twenty years.

The war was, thus, crucial in explaining the success of educational reform. It pressurised the Board of Education into producing plans that had been resisted before 1939, though it was doubtful whether the end result represented a radical departure in policy. Butler himself, in fact, reflected that he was largely 'codifying existing practice', and giving practical shape to reforms long canvassed in the educational world. He also remained convinced that he had safeguarded his party's essential interests — diversity within the state sector, the place of religious instruction and the autonomy of the Public Schools. As he told one colleague, public opinion was generally content with moderate reform, 'if only it is dressed up in the dress of non-privilege and social equality'.[54]

It is also worth remembering that education had come to the forefront for negative as much as positive reasons. In June 1942 Butler noted that 'my only competition appears to be Sir William Beveridge, whose shield is fortunately tarnished by grimy coal and oil stains.'[55] The President reaped the benefit after the Beveridge Report was 'bruited abroad', thereby offending Westminster and Whitehall convention, though Butler's major advantage in seeking priority was that educational reform was likely to cost much less than a comprehensive scheme of social security. This argument weighed heavily with the Treasury, as it did with the Lord President, Anderson, who told Butler he would rather provide money for education than 'throw it down the sink with Sir William Beveridge'.[56] Above all, the only really contentious theme in the education debate, as we have seen, was the denominational issue, which had always been divisive within — as much as between — the parties. Educational reform, in other words, was exceptional because it had mininally disruptive effects on the balance of the coalition. The government, Butler concluded, 'have been prompted to come the way of education because it has been very difficult to obtain agreement between the parties on any matters which involve property or the pocket...'.[57]

Nowhere was Butler's claim more clearly borne out than in the case of medical reform. The Beveridge Report was again crucial in this context: its call for a comprehensive national health service helped to revive and extend plans for hospital reform that had lost their way since 1941. The government accepted the principle of reform early in 1943, and although Ernest Brown ran into difficulties in his subsequent negotiations with the medical profession — and, indeed, was removed from office at the end of the year — the Ministry of Health was able to publish a white paper on the proposed health service in February 1944. This development has traditionally been seen as an important pointer towards the welfare state. On this view, the white paper was the obvious precursor to the legislation passed by the Labour government after 1945, having overcome the wartime obstruction caused less by political opinion than by professional interest groups.[58] More recently, though, emphasis has been placed on the important differences between the coalition plan of 1944 and Labour's subsequent legislation,[59] and an analysis of health policy in its political context brings out not only the ambiguity of official policy but also an increasing level of controversy beneath the surface of party agreement. The white paper, though symbolically important as the first detailed outline of coalition intentions, carried insufficient weight to stem a mounting tide of criticism. During the course of 1944, as we shall see, the prospects of early legislation rapidly receded, with the result that wholesale medical reform proved as elusive as other features of the reconstruction programme.[60]

The background to the white paper itself reflected the balance of coalition forces. Paul Addison has argued that Labour ministers played a major part in the formation of the government's health scheme, and could justifiably claim that the white paper brought close to realisation one of the party's most consistent aims over the past two decades.[61] In practice, though, Labour ministers felt they were accepting an interim measure but no more. Ministerial discussions on this topic had a strong ideological tone, with Kingsley Wood's call to extend the pre-war panel system being countered by Bevin's desire for a centrally controlled medical service.[62] The real stumbling-block on the Reconstruction Committee, noted Lord Woolton, was the reluctance of Labour ministers to accept modifications put forward by Conservatives such as Butler, relating, in particular, to the proposal for new health centres.[63] At the last moment Churchill, urged on by Beaverbrook, attempted to reopen the whole debate, only to be firmly told by Attlee that such a move would force Labour ministers to renew their demands for a full-time salaried service and for other policies 'far more repugnant to Conservative feeling'.[64] As a result, the white paper in its final form, while accepting the need for change, remained hesitant on a variety of contentious issues, notably the administrative structure of the proposed service and the relationship between the hitherto separate voluntary and local authority hospitals. Certainly, for the Minister of Reconstruction, who introduced the white paper in the Lords, the essence of the plan was not a break with the past but a natural evolution for the existing system.[65] This view was echoed in the Commons by Brown's successor, Henry Willink, a commercial lawyer who had been acting as special commissioner for housing in London since becoming a Tory MP in 1940. Willink was also able to point out that the white paper was intended as a consultative document rather than a final official statement — a crucial factor in view of subsequent developments.[66]

In February 1944 there was some hope that the white paper might proceed in the same way as the Education Bill, at that time rapidly passing through Parliament. The Conservative party had initially been sceptical about medical reform when Beveridge first made it a serious possibility. The secret committee of back-benchers reporting to the Prime Minister had interpreted the idea of a national health service in a singularly narrow fashion, calling for an extension of health insurance which would be compulsory only for those earning a limited income. A scheme covering the whole population, it was claimed, would 'so narrow private practice as to virtually destroy it, with an inevitable lowering of standards in the medical profession'.[67] With reconstruction now firmly on the agenda, however, the party's public transformation on the issue of national insurance was matched by a new commitment to medical reform. There were some complaints, put most forcefully by the chairman of the back-bench Social Services Committee, that the voluntary hospitals would be undermined and gradually forced into the state sector. But, on the whole, Conservatives accepted the white paper as a further instalment of the government's social programme, worthy of at least restrained approval.[68] The Labour party came to the same conclusion, but for different reasons. Although the new plan fell short of the party's declared policy in several important respects, it was decided to endorse the white paper as a step in the right direction. Labour speakers made it clear they would accept no further compromises but, on the whole, agreed with the party's Public Health Advisory Committee that the priority was to ensure the introduction of legislation without further amendment by professional or political opposition.[69]

Labour fears were borne out in the following year. For several months after the publication of the white paper, medical reform did not come before the cabinet or leading ministers. Instead, Willink decided to enter into a new round of private negotiations: with the voluntary hospitals and local authority associations; and with a special negotiating committee of the medical profession. This meant not only that legislation before the end of the war became unlikely but also that fresh ideas crept into the ministry's thinking. Under pressure from the British Medical Association, which feared the introduction of a state-salaried medical service, Willink now made several modifications to the white paper. The adminstrative role of local government, for example, was to be weakened at the expense of the professional organisations, and new financial provision was to be made for the voluntary hospitals.[70] Above all, the minister made it clear that doctors in the proposed health centres would not become local salaried employees, and would remain free to continue private practice alongside their public work.[71] These changes, which were not announced before the breakup of the coalition and only began to filter out through press leaks, were clearly made in deference to political as well as medical opinion. Willink later recorded, in his unpublished autobiography, that the Conservative party would not have accepted the emasculation of the voluntary hospitals during the war.[72] Hence, by the spring of 1945, as we shall see in a later chapter, the minister was being fiercely accused by Labour of having 'surrendered' to the doctors. As the official historian of the NHS concludes:

> Although a skilful cosmetic exercise, the 1944 White Paper signified little progress in resolving acute disagreements over the future direction of policy. The planners notably failed to bring the profession and the voluntary hospitals round to their way of thinking. . . . while the fragile agreement between the coalition partners over the White Paper broke down. Thus in the last year of the coalition the two partners kept their separate counsels. The line followed by Willink . . . represented capitulation rather than the emergence of consensus.[73]

In the eighteen months after the publication of the Beveridge Report, therefore, Churchill's government — contrary to the received impression — moved only tentatively towards the creation of a 'New Jerusalem'. Under pressure from reconstruction enthusiasts, and spurred on by the embarrassment of the Beveridge debate in parliament, the coalition had outlined some broad objectives for the future. This in itself was an advance on pre-war orthodoxy, but 'the white paper chase' did not imply binding, irreversible commitments for the post-war world. Ideological differences between the parties were still so strong that there was agreement neither upon the long-term aims of domestic policy nor about the best way to proceed before the war ended. Apart from the 1944 Education Act, which, as we have seen, was the product of exceptional circumstances, reconstruction had barely proceeded beyond the planning stage. No official policy had yet been outlined on national insurance; the likelihood of the health service becoming a reality had receded; and the nation still awaited ministeral pronouncements on the vital themes of economic policy

and physical planning. Much of the national press, having given a
lead to the movement for social change, was soon resigning itself to
the likelihood that promised legislation would not be achieved
under the present Prime Minister, whatever might be said in radio
broadcasts or public speeches. Beveridge himself wrote in despair
to the editor of *The Times*: 'It seems to me that any Government
under Winston will not do more for social progress than they are
driven to by opposition and peace-making.'[74] The reason for this
was simple: in spite of all the external pressures, Churchill and his
party were not convinced about the need for a brave new world.
Tory Reformers had tried, without success, to influence mainstream
opinion, but were forced to concede that the 'old blunderbores'
were still in control. Political consensus — a new harmony of
purpose between the parties — was not a characteristic of British
politics in 1943–44.

  After the high hopes that greeted Lord Woolton's appointment
at the end of 1943, Hugh Dalton was writing six months later
that the 'post-war Reconstruction machine seems badly blocked
again'.[75] It was no surprise that, with the benefit of hindsight,
Woolton found little cause for satisfaction in his work at the
Ministry of Reconstruction. Aside from the attitude of the Prime
Minister and the party in-fighting that characterised coalition,
Woolton recalled other factors that constrained his work: the
need to operate without knowledge of precisely when the war
would end; the difficulty of calculating costs; and the increasing
certainty that the ending of hostilities would be followed by a
general election.[76] The last point was of particular importance.
After the Allied landings on the continent in June 1944, the ending
of the war suddenly looked imminent; thereafter, the problem
of securing agreement on the home front became far more acute.
This soon became evident, both among senior ministers and in
the House of Commons, though the transition of a final stage in
wartime politics — leading to the break up of coalition — was,
in fact, already well under way at another level to which we shall
now turn our attention: that of local politics.

Notes

1 Barnett, *Audit of War*, p. 304.
2 Dalton, *Fateful Years*, p. 410.

3 For the background to the committee, see J. D. Hoffman, *The Conservative Party in Opposition, 1945–51*, London, 1964, pp. 40–2.

4 Two important themes, employment policy and town and country planning, are dealt with separately below — see Chapter 7.

5 Addison, *Road to 1945*, p. 167.

6 *Nicolson Diary*, 16 July and 3 December 1940, pp. 102–3 and p. 130; *Colville Diary*, 10 August 1940, pp. 215–16; v. 369 H. C. Deb., 5 s., cc. 1416–7, 13 March 1941.

7 See original manuscript of Chuter Ede diary, 21 July and 8 August 1941 — BL, Add. Ass. 59690, pp. 6 and 28, where Butler notes that 'whispers of displeasure at Ramsbotham's advanced ideas' had been conveyed to him. Lord Butler, *The Art of the Possible*, London, 1971, p. 90, describes Butler's encounter with Churchill: '"You will move poor children from here to here"', and he lifted up and evacuated imaginery children from one side of his blotting pad to the other; "this will be very difficult."'

8 C. Webster, *The Health Services since the War*, Vol. I, *Problems of Health Care: the National Health Service before 1957*, London, 1988, pp. 24–34.

9 J. A. Ramsden, *The Making of Conservative Party Policy: the Conservative Research Department Since 1929*, London, 1980, pp. 97–8. For fierce criticisms of a report on education as 'quasi-fascist', see D. W. Dean, 'Problems of the Conservative sub-committee on education, 1941–1945', *Journal of Educational Administration and History*, III, 1, 1970, pp. 26–35.

10 Sir J. H. Morris-Jones, *Doctor in the Whips' Room*, London, 1955, p. 120.

11 Labour's sub-committees are dealt with in I. H. Taylor, 'War and the development of Labour's domestic programme, 1939–45', unpulished Ph.D. thesis, University of London, 1978, esp. pp. 48–52.

12 *Chuter Ede Diary*, 29–30 July 1942, pp. 87–9.

13 Ibid., 7 August and 27 November 1942, cited in K. Jefferys, 'British politics and social policy during the Second World War', *The Historical Journal*, XXX, 1, 1987, p. 127.

14 V. 385 H. C. Deb., 5 s., c. 138, 12 November 1942; Bevan was replyig specifically to a speech by Lord Croft which had defended the Empire and implied that there was no need for a new order after the war.

15 Notes by R. A. Butler, 1941: Butler papers, G16, f. 100.

16 The deliberations of the Beveridge Committee are fully recorded in PRO CAB 87/76–8.

17 J. Harris, 'Social planning in war-time: some aspects of the Beveridge Report', in J. Winter (ed.), *War and Economic Development*, Cambridge, 1975; *William Beveridge*, Oxford, 1977; 'Some aspects of social policy in Britain during the Second World War', in W. J. Mommsen (ed.), *The Emergence of the Welfare State in Britain and Germany*, London, 1981.

18 Addison, op. cit., pp. 220–4.

19 War Cabinet minutes, 15 February 1943, PRO CAB 65/33.

20 Harvie-Watt, *Most of My Life*, p. 117. Churchill's attitude is also evident in his note circulated to the cabinet on 19 February 1943, reprinted in *The Hinge of Fate*, p. 862.

21 Taylor, 'War and Labour's domestic programme', pp. 70–6.

22 Secret Conservation Committee, 'Report on the Beveridge proposals', 19 January 1943: Conservative party archive, Bodleian Library, Oxford, Box 600/01. For a detailed study of this report, see H. Kopsch, 'The approach of the Conservative party to social policy during World War Two', unpublished Ph.D. thesis, University of London, 1970, pp. 109–23.

23 V. 386 H. C. Deb., 5 s., c. 2016, 18 February 1943; Cassius (Michael Foot), *Brendan and Beverley: an Extravaganza*, London, 1944, p. 51.

24 V. 386 H. C. Deb., 5 s. c. 1614, 16 February 1943.

25 The amendment calling for immediate implementation was defeated by 338 votes to 121; the minority consisted of ninety-seven Labour MPs, who were joined by Liberals, Independents and members of the ILP.

26 *Dalton Diary*, 18 February 1943, p. 555: '... many of our colleagues are complete innocents, while a small minority is fixedly set on breaking up the Government. Master Shinwell today has been rushing around with a maninacal glint in his eye. He reminds me of the chap who was determined to set fire to the house and burn it down for his own delight.'

27 Griffiths, *Pages from Memory*, p. 72.

28 *The Times*, 21 May 1943.

29 Diary notes by Butler, 9 September 1943, Butler papers, G15, f. 81.

30 Addison, op. cit., p. 227; Crozier interview with Churchill, 26 March 1943 — Taylor (ed.), *Off the Record*, p. 345.

31 'Herbert Morrison is bidding for the Treasuryship and, some say, the Leadership. His technique is to make speeches on other people's subjects, and to please the very gullible "Times" by being so intensely reasonable' — notes by Butler, 25 May 1943, Butler papers, G15. f. 37. B. Donoughue and G. W. Jones, *Herbert Morrison: Portrait of a Politician*, London, 1973, pp. 323–5, describe his campaign in more altruistic terms.

32 *Chuter Ede Diary*, 19 March 1943, p. 129.

33 *The Economist*, 1 May 1943.

34 'The Need for Decisions', memorandum by the Deputy Prime Minister, the Minister of Labour and the Home Secretary, 26 June 1943, PRO CAB 66/38.

35 'Paper on the need for decisions', Kingsley Wood minute to Churchill, 1 July 1943, PRO PREM 4 87/8.

36 Crozier interview with Morrison, 2 July 1943 — Taylor (ed.), op. cit., p. 371.

37 *The Economist*, 2 October 1943.

38 War Cabinet minutes, 14 October 1943, PRO CAB 65/36; *Chuter Ede Diary*, 15 October 1943, p. 147.

39 Harris, *Attlee*, pp. 225–7; Crozier interview with Churchill, 22

October 1943 — Taylor (ed.), op. cit., pp. 379–80. The Prime Minister had one reservation about the new plan. When the idea of Beveridge becoming involved was raised, he said 'Beveridge! He sticks his nose into too many things!'

40 *The Economist*, 20 November 1943.

41 Lord Woolton, *The Memoirs of the Rt. Hon. the Earl of Woolton*, London, 1959, pp. 259–72.

42 *Chuter Ede Diary*, 1 November 1943, p. 150.

43 Note by Butler, 18 February 1942, PRO ED 136/226, cited along with other references hereafter in K. Jefferys. 'R. A. Butler, the Board of Education and the 1944 Education Act', *History*, LXIX, 227, 1984, p. 421.

44 See original Chuter Ede diary, 14 and 29 May 1942, BL Add. Mss. 59693, pp. 27 and 49.

45 For a full description of the background to the 1944 Act, see P. H. J. H. Gosden, *Education in the Second World War: a Study in Policy and Administration*, London, 1976.

46 In November 1942 Butler said that Churchill was 'watching us with some amusement thinking we were squelching about in the mud', but added that if a religious settlement looked feasible, 'he would want the thing done — he was like that': see original Chuter Ede diary, 27 November 1942, BL Add. Mss. 59695, p. 176.

47 Ibid., 21 October 1942, p. 122; minutes of the Lord President's Committee, 18 December 1942, PRO CAB 71/10. Bevin's key role is also highlighted in R. G. Wallace, 'The man behind Butler', the *Times Educational Supplement*, 27 March 1981.

48 See original Chuter Ede diary, 15 October and 1 November 1943, BL Add. Mss. 59697, pp. 34 and 45.

49 '1922 Committee', notes by Butler, 17 March 1943, Butler papers, H61, ff. 208–14; diary notes by Butler, 9 September 1943, Butler papers, G15, f. 92.

50 Kopsch, 'Conservative party and social policy', pp. 261–72; see original Chuter Ede diary, 8 February 1944, BL Add. Mss. 59698, p. 30.

51 V. 398 H. C. Deb., 5 s., c. 1300, 21 March 1944; ibid., c. 755.

52 R. S. Barker, *Education and Politics 1900–1951: a Study of the Labour Party*, Oxford, 1972, pp. 75–80.

53 Diary notes by Butler, 9 September 1943, Butler papers, f. 92.

54 Note by Butler, 25 May 1943, Butler papers, G15, f. 37; Butler to C. Allport, 2 May 1945, Butler papers, G14, f. 107.

55 Butler minute to M. Holmes and R. S. Wood, 6 July 1942, PRO ED 136/351.

56 Note by Butler, 14 September 1942, PRO ED 136/229.

57 Diary notes by Butler, 9 September 1943, Butler papers, G15, f. 90: 'whereas, on religious questions, there is a feeling that it is out-of-date to wrangle'.

58 Addison, op. cit., pp. 239–40.

59 K. O. Morgan, *Labour in Power 1945–1951*, Oxford, 1984, p. 22.

60 Webster, op. cit., p. 44.
61 Addison, op. cit., p. 241.
62 Minutes of the Reconstruction Priorities Committee, 30 July 1943, PRO CAB 87/12.
63 Woolton to Eden, 10 February 1944: Lord Woolton papers, Bodleian Library, Oxford, 15. f. 118.
64 Cited in Webster, op. cit., p. 54.
65 *A National Health Service*, Cmd, 6502, London, 1944, Woolton, *Memoris*, pp. 278–81.
66 V. 398 H. C. Deb., 5 s., cc. 427–32, 16 March 1944.
67 'Report on the Beveridge proposals', January 1943: Florence Horsbrugh, at the time Parliamentary Secretary to the Ministry of Health, was one of only two members of the committee who argued for a more comprehensive health scheme.
68 See especially the speech of Samuel Story, PPS to Horsbrugh between 1939 and 1942, as well as chairman of the Social Services Committee — v. 398 H. C. Deb., 5 s. cc. 504–10, 16 March 1944.
69 Ibid., c. 557, for the comments of Arthur Greenwood. On this topic, see also R. J. Earwicker, 'The labour movement and the creation of the National Health Service 1906–1948', unpublished Ph.D. thesis, University of Birmingham, 1984.
70 H. Eckstein, *The English Health Service*, Massachusetts, 1964, pp. 155–6.
71 Report of meeting with Neotiating Committee, 3 February 1945, PRO MH 77/119.
72 H. Willink, 'As I Remember', unpublished autobiography, 1968, pp. 81–2: Willink papers, Churchill College, Cambridge, Box 1.
73 Webster, op. cit., p. 392.
74 Beveridge to Barrington-Ward, 14 December 1943, cited in Cockett, 'Government, press and politics', p. 231.
75 *Dalton Diary*, 18 July 1944, p. 769: 'I had hoped that, when Woolton had got rid of Employment, Social Security, and Town and Country Planning, the way would be cleared for dealing with a lot of other questions, including many in my field. But we are getting no decisions, and everyone, ministers and officials alike, seems to be dragging back and playing for position.'
76 Woolton, op. cit., pp. 292–5.

6

'Finding one's way in the country'

Any assessment of popular politics during the war must focus on
two themes: the pronounced 'swing to the left' that resulted in
Labour's landslide victory in 1945; and the pattern of political
development at local level, away from Westminster. On the first of
these, Paul Addison has already shown, in general terms, how the
pre-1939 ascendancy of the Conservative party crumbled under the
impact of 'total war', with its demands for 'equality of sacrifice'
and the imposition of sweeping government powers over all aspects
of civilian life. Although it would be easy to exaggerate the degree
of social levelling that resulted, the trend towards egalitarianism
could not be mistaken:

In World War I the dominant ethos was one of traditional parrtriotism,
with the emphasis upon the duty each man owed to his king and
country.... In World War II the prevailing assumption was that the war
was being fought for the benefit of the common people, and that it was
the duty of the upper classes to throw in their lot with those lower down
the social scale. Whenever there was a military setback, or a crisis in war
production, resentment would break out against the 'vested interests',
people who were alleged to be clinging to their privileges at the expense of
the common good.[1]

Manifestations of this new political and intellectual climate
were numerous, and operated with vigour from 1940 onwards.
The progressive intelligentsia found new outlets of expression. J.
B. Prisetley's series of 'Postscripts' on the BBC, urging listeners to
turn their minds to the creation of a brave new world after the war,
was only the most controversial of several examples. Much of the
national press became more receptive to progressive ideas. *The
Times* became an advocate of social reform, and one of the most
successful of wartime dailies was the *Daily Mirror*, whose populist
and abrasive style was based on attacks against Colonel Blimp and

the Old School Tie. The problems of contemporary Britain also found expression in the armed services, with the unprecedented introduction of weekly classes and discussion groups, led by the Army Education Corps and the Army Bureau of Current Affairs. And on top of all this, Hitler's attack on the Soviet Union produced a novel enthusiasm for all things Russian. Entering at a time, in 1941, when it was difficult to see how Britain could win the war, the successful resistance of the Soviet Union naturally produced greater sympathy for the communist system as an effective organising force. Pro-Russian feeling, in other words, was one part of the jig-saw that helps us to explain Labour's 1945 triumph. Certainly, the Home Intelligence division at the Ministry of Information, set up by the government to monitor public morale, found that in nearly every part of the country 'there is a more apparent leaning towards socialism since Russia became an ally'.[2]

But if the idea of the Second World War as a 'people's war' goes far towards explaining changes in public opinion, it arguably does not tell the whole story. 'It is very difficult', Paul Addison has written, 'to believe that the Conservative Party would have won a general election at any point after June 1940.'[3] The fall of Chamberlain, as we have seen, clearly marked a vital first blow against Tory domination, though there are several reasons why too much importance should not be attached to shifting attitudes in the early part of the war. In the first place, Home Intelligence found in 1941 that while there was already a strong feeling in favour of reducing class distinctions, there was also an 'absence of thought along conventional party lines', and as yet few settled opinions about the expected complexion of Britain's first post-war government.[4] And if by 1942 it was reported that two out of five people had changed their political views since the outbreak of war, then the new mood of radicalism must also be set against the immense popularity of the Prime Minister. Why, after all, should the electorate, when given a choice, prefer a Labour alternative whose leader seemed uninspiring and whose rank-and-file continued to resort to internal wrangling? The answer to this question goes to the heart of coalition politics, and leads on directly from the consideration of reconstruction in the last chapter. For the swing to the left can only be fully understood, it will be argued here, in two distinct phases. In the period 1940–42, the Conservatives as the majority party — and the party associated with the 'guilty men'

— suffered in the eyes of the electorate for shortcomings in the nation's war effort. But the Tory malaise only deepened to a point where it became irreversible after 1943, when the Prime Minister shunned the opportunity of implementing far-reaching social change. By its ambiguous attitude to the Beveridge Report in particular, the government threw away its chance to shape and guide public expectations. Churchill, the national hero who 'won the war', was to be the same party leader who 'lost the peace'.

Interpreting wartime trends — 'finding one's way in the country' — was rendered more difficult at the time by the suspension of peacetime rules governing local politics. The major parties were committed throughout to an electoral truce, which in theory outlawed by-election competition; local government elections were suspended; and many political associations in the localities either ceased to function or were severely disrupted. As a result, the most striking developments at this level tended to take place outside the political mainstream. The '1941 Committee' was formed as a cross-party pressure group to press for social change; independent candidates began to challenge and topple government nominees in by-elections; and after 1942 much publicity was accorded to the new Common Wealth party, espousing its unique brand of Christian socialism. Attention given to these groups, however, has tended to obscure what were equally important trends in local politics. The electoral truce, for instance, was never very effective from the outset in preventing local contests between Conservative and Labour supporters, and from 1943 onwards there was an increasingly vigorous return to conventional forms of political activity in many parts of the country. This revival was stimulated, above all, by disputes about the shape of the post-war world; reconstruction, in other words, was the catalyst for party in-fighting locally, just as it was nationally. There was, therefore, little evidence of the war producing lasting agreement among those who sustained the major political parties. And, moreover, the conduct and outcome of by-election contests in the second half of the war were themselves inextricably linked with the wider movement of public opinion. Conservative candidates suffered humiliating by-election defeats after 1942 for one major reason: the electorate had become convinced that the Tory party, from its leadership down to its grass-roots, had no real commitment to what it valued most — a break with the past.

The early years of the war, inevitably, brought great disruption to local politics. Almost immediately after the outbreak of war in 1939 the major parties — following the pattern of the First World War — signed an electoral truce. 'We jointly agree', it began, 'as representatives of the Conservative, Labour and Liberal Parties . . . not to nominate Candidates for the Parliamentary vacancies that now exist, or may occur, against the Candidate nominated by the Party holding the seat at the time of the vacancy occuring.'[5] With major by-election contests ruled out for the duration, or so it seemed, one of the major stimulants to local political activity had thus been removed. The suspension of local government elections, which in many parts of the country had become more overtly party political since the 1920s, had a similar effect.[6] Above all, of course, it was the critical state of the war that disrupted peacetime patterns of local politics. Regional and local organisations throughout the country relied for the most part on the voluntary services of enthusiastic members; they consequently found their operations hampered as members either went away on active service or became absorbed in duties on the home front.

The resulting disruption was particularly noticeable on the Conservative side. With Central Office giving no firm lead, beyond exhorting that things be kept ticking over, many local Tory associations simply closed down until further notice. Several of the party's regional and district associations never met at all between 1940 and 1945; others were convened only spasmodically to deal with routine matters, such as the election of officers.[7] The only exceptions to this pattern were areas where the local organisations had hiterto been exceptionally strong, as in Birmingham, or, where women members were able to maintain a degree of continuity.[8] Labour local associations were similarly affected, again most visibly in areas where organistion had hitherto been relatively weak, for example in Scotland. But in many inner cities — London, Birmingham and Bristol all illustrate the point — Labour's reliance on trade unionists working in 'reserved occupations' permitted a much higher level of activity.[9] As a result, it was the Labour party, though operating nowhere near its own pre-war capacity, which now managed to seize the organisational advantage in local politics.

The emergency of 1940–41 helped to produce, up to a point, a new sense of local co-operation. On many local councils, party stalwarts worked together in order to frustrate the common, external enemy. In Birmingham, for instance, where the Unionist majority bitterly resented the way Labour had backed a Communist-led rent strike in 1939, an agreement was reached giving Labour representation on the council's emergency commitee. Thereafter, inter-party agreement on matters of civil defence was complete.[10] Unanimity about the war effort, however, did not imply the disappearance of pre-existing political tensions. After 1945 Conservatives were frequently to complain that, compared with their own restraint, Labour activists missed no opportunity to proclaim the socialist message. The sensitivity of Tories on this point in the early war years illustrated how quickly the intellectual climate had moved against them. In accusing Labour of 'breaking the truce', Conservatives were often justified, for, as we shall see, there were to be frequent breaches of the electoral truce. On the other hand, it has to be remembered that there was no formal *political* truce; in this sense Tory complaints were invalidated by their own conception of wartime arrangements. 'No time for Politics', ran one local newspaper headline; 'Conservatives engaged in war work'.[11] This refusal to countenance partisan activity continued until late in the war, by which time Labour leaders were openly encouraging local activity. From the outset, in fact, there had been a feeling among Labour leaders that the truce did not extend to all areas of political activity, and that as long as direct party controversy was avoided, there was no reason why local parties should not highlight social problems arising out of the war.[12] By 1941 some local Tories were anxious to find ways of counteracting these 'socialist tactics', though Central Office remained anxious not to jeopardise coalition stability.[13]

An element of party competition was also evident in the first contested by-elections of the war years. Altogether 140 parliamentary seats became vacant for one reason or another during the period; of these, nearly half were filled by a nominee of the incumbent party under the terms of the electoral truce. There were, however, seventy-five contests forced by independent candidates or minor party nominees. Wartime by-elections were, of course, the product of unique, sometimes bizarre, circumstances. Until April 1945 all such contests were fought on the basis of an electoral register drawn up before the war. As a result thousands of young voters were disfranchised, and no account was taken of massive movements of population that might easily distort the social composition of particular constituencies. In addition electioneering itself was naturally curtailed, rendered difficult by physical restrictions such as the black-out and petrol rationing. There remains, moreover, the imponderable element in assessing by-election results of the moral sanction used by the government. The claim that electoral contests damaged national unity and diverted attention from the war against Hitler was commonly made by the government; its effectiveness varied according to the particular circumstances, though, as we shall see, its appeal became less potent after 1942.[14]

In spite of these various factors, wartime by-elections provide an invaluable means of reassessing local politics. In the early war years, between 1939 and 1941, the majority of contests were forced by the British Union of Fascists (BUF), the ILP or the Communist party. Government officials were particulary concerned by the latter's anti-war line, adopted after the Russo-German partition of Poland. Initially, only the ILP evoked anything more than a negligible response when putting up 'peace' candidates, for example at the Stratford by-election in December 1939. With the onset of the Blitz, however, the Communists began to exploit widespread grievances about living conditions. In January 1941 the party convened a 'People's Covention', and large audiences gathered to support the call for a genuine 'People's Government'.[15] At the Dunbarton by-election shortly afterwards, the Communist candidate polled a respectable 15 per cent of the vote after concentrating on grievances such as profiteering, and a Home Intelligence observer reported that 'the Communists succeeded in mobilising more goodwill than was reflected in the actual vote'.[16] As a result, the propaganda war intensified: newspapers were urged to press home the point that the Communist party was essentially defeatist, and wanted to create conditions in which chaos would ensue. Any further development of the Communist threat was forestalled, though, when the Soviet Union's entry into the war produced a dramatic change of line. British Communists now devoted themselves to supporting and encouraging the government's war effort, even to the extent of backing the most hitherto unacceptable of Tory candidates at by-elections. By the summer of 1941, moreover, there was also a new means whereby the electorate might express their frustrations about wartime restrictions and the lack of Allied military success. This was by voting for a fresh breed of independent.

At the Hornsey by-election of May 1941 nearly one-third of the vote went to Noel Pemberton Billing, a maverick independent who toured the constituency in a yellow Rolls-Royce arguing that Germany could be defeated by bombing alone. Billing was soon matched for eccentricity by Reg Hipwell, editor of the magazine *Reveille*, who confessed that his candidature at Scarborough in October 1941 was prompted in large part by his desire for a holiday. Hipwell caused something of a stir by accusing the Conservative candidate, who only had one leg, of shirking military duty, pointing out that the famous pilot Douglas Bader had no legs at all.[17] Military set-backs and production difficulties clearly helped to produce a public mood which the likes of Billing and Hipwell were well placed to exploit, patriotically committed as they were to the war effort in a way that did not apply to the Communists. These 'National' independents quickly sensed that Tory-held seats proffered the most fruitful opportunities. But their limited appeal makes it difficult to interpret the by-elections of 1940–41 as indicative of an irreversible swing to the left. Pemberton Billing, who contested four by-elections in all, polled 24–44 per cent of the vote — a more impressive showing than that of the minor parties hitherto. The imperative of national unity, however, still had a powerful appeal at this stage of the war, and, indeed, in the eight seats the Conservatives defended after Hornsey, their share of the vote was on average 6 per cent higher than in the 1935 general election.[18]

In view of the concentration on the war effort, these early by-elections produced a surprising element of party animosity, notwithstanding the electoral truce. While Chamberlain remained Prime Minister, Labour's rank-and-file, in particular, resented the new nationally imposed agreement. In the Pollock division of Glasgow, a Conservative stronghold, the divisional Labour party was disaffiliated during the spring of 1940 for insisting on sponsoring an independent candidate.[19] After Churchill came to power, the truce was regarded as a symbol of coalition co-operation, but party in-fighting continued to boil over when certain seats became vacant. Home Intelligence noted that at Dunbartonshire in early 1941, 'Labour fought on a Labour Party platform and Conservative co-operation was not apparent either in meetings or in election literature'; the lack of Tory backing for the official nominee, it added, prompted much discussion of the 'unreality of Government unity'.[20] Conversely, the local Labour party in the King's Norton division of Birmingham was disaffiliated in May 1941 for refusing to back the Conservative candidate. The party's annual conference subsequently agreed that discipline must by upheld in the national interest, though a substantial minority accepted an alternative view put by some delegates — that King's Norton had been guilty of nothing more than loyalty to socialism.[21] Tensions in local politics were, thus, becoming more difficult to contain. As the popularity of independent candidates grew throughout 1941, Labour activists became more and more convinced that the electoral truce was denying the party the fruits of anti-Tory sentiment. In the difficult months after Pearl Harbour, when the military position went from bad to worse, this was a feeling that suddenly and alarmingly intensified.

By the spring of 1942 everyday experience of 'total war' had clearly left its mark. Indeed, the Minister of Information's Home Intelligence division, working through observers in all parts of the country, was now finding much evidence of 'home-made socialism'. Only in the south and south-east of England did local officials find little spontaneous political discussion; all other regions commented on definite reactions against vested interests and the 'old gang', and on the feeling that things would have to be different after the war. One contact, working in the north-west, noted a common belief that the nation was 'on the threshold of an entirely new conception of economic and human relationships... in which very large incomes will no longer be tolerated, and the motto Service before Self must come into its own'.[22] But how could such feelings manifest themselves publicly? In view of the constraints of coalition, as well as the urgency of the war in 1942, there were few channels for open discussion along conventional party lines. Instead, sections of the press preferred to concentrate on what became known as 'the movement away from party'. In accounting for this new development, the rise to senior office of Stafford Cripps obviously had a powerful impact, for much of his appeal was based on a reputation for independence from the old party labels. It also became a commonplace of political discussion during this period that the House of Commons was out of touch with public opinion:

elected seven years previously, in 1935, its membership now had an average age of around sixty. As a result, the great majority of those questioned were coming to the opinion that none of the existing parties could fulfil their wishes in the circumstances likely to exist at the end of the war.[23]

The most tangible evidence of a 'movement away from party', however, came with a series of by-election victories for independent candidates in the first half of 1942. At Grantham in March the official Conservative candidate, a former RAF commander, was defeated by the narrow margin of 400 votes after he would pledge himself only to support for the Prime Minister and national unity. His opponent, Denis Kendall, the manager of an armaments factory, described himself as 'Independent yet Churchillian', though it was the popularity of Cripps that he played upon in his campaign, calling for improvements in war production and comprehensive social security.[24] The swing against the Tories was larger still in April when W. J. Brown — a figure of repute as General Secretary of the Civil Service Clerical Association — defeated the chairman of the local Tory association at Rugby. This seat had formerly been held by Chamberlain's Chief Whip, David Margesson, who weighed in on the hustings with the claim that a vote for the independent would satisfy only Hitler. But appeals to national unity now fell on deaf ears, and Brown — campaigning on a platform which stressed his own hatred of the party machines — won by a comfortable margin.[25] On the same day an even more disturbing set back for the government occured on Merseyside, where a local journalist, George Reakes, triumphed at Wallasey. Here the local Tory organisation was extremely weak. By exploiting topical issues such as the need to control prices, Reakes was able to win by 6,000 votes; the Conservative vote fell some 35 per cent.[26]

The immediate context of these results was, of course, readily at hand. Britain's war fortunes had recently reached a new low, especially with the loss of Singapore. As the unpopularity of the government deepened — and Churchill's leadership itself came under fire — a protest vote in a by-election provided an obvious means for electors to express their frustrations. Some political commentators, though, chose to detect wider implications, suggesting a fundamental weakening of traditional party loyalties. Certainly, the atmosphere of 1942 was conducive to new forms of politics. Kendall and Brown now teamed up in parliament with other disaffected back-benchers to promote a 'People's Movement', the only consistent aim of which was to destroy the existing political parties. In May socialists associated with the 1941 Committee issued their own 'Nine Point Manifesto', intended to guide sponsored candidates at future by-elections. And, at the opposite end of the political spectrum, a new British National Party was formed, though without attracting much publicity or support.[27] As Angus Calder writes of this period: 'It was clear to everyone that something extremely odd had happened to British politics, and very few orthodox politicians liked it, whatever it was.'[28]

But it would be wrong to exaggerate the significance of the 'movement away from party'. In the first place, the success of independent candidates served to stimulate a revival of local political feeling, at least to the extent that it stiffened the hostility of Labour's rank-and-file towards the electoral truce. Protest votes for the likes of Brown and Reakes, it was believed, would otherwise be swinging towards Labour. Hence, when Labour's annual conference discussed the situation in May 1942, there was only a very narrow majority in favour of the NEC's resolution to extend the electoral truce.[29] The vote was sufficiently ambiguous to allow continued breaches of the truce by local activists: this applied, in fact, to nearly half of the thirteen by-elections held during 1942. Kendall and Brown had themselves received some backing from local Labour supporters before the party's attitude towards independents began to harden. More serious breaches were already taking place elsewhere, as in the case of Cardiff East, where back in April the local Labour party was extremely reticent about supporting the official government nominee, Sir Percy Grigg, the War Minister.[30] Conern about this trend at Transport House was such that Attlee made a point of sponsoring Grigg on his introduction to the House, and private appeals were made for local parties to 'play the game' at by-elections in order to avoid undermining Labour's credibility as a coalition partner. After the close conference vote, however, the party rank-and-file became more reluctant than ever to be seen endorsing the truce.

Three particular contests in June 1942 highlighted this point. At Llandaff and Barry, the nearest thing yet to an open party contest developed when the government nominee was opposed by an 'Independent Socialist', Ronald Mackay, an Australian-born solicitor.

Mackay resigned from the Labour party in order to contest the seat, and campaigned on a platform of ending the electoral truce, calling a general election and introducing socialist measures such as the conscription of wealth. His Tory opponent, Cyril Lakin, responded by making it clear he was not ashamed of his own party label. The *Daily Express*, fearing an adverse poll, highlighted what it called the 'truce-busting activities' of Mackay, alleging that if he got in it would be due to socialist support in the constituency. Labour's divisional party had, in fact, resisted pressure from the NEC to campaign for the official nominee, choosing instead simply to refrain from interference.[31] In the event, Lakin won the seat comfortably, though the 40 per cent of the poll secured by Mackay clearly represented a substantial proportion of the traditional Labour vote in the division. A spectacular victory by the gossip columnist Tom Driberg in the Maldon by-election two weeks later illustrated the same pattern. Driberg stood on the socialist policies of the 'Nine Point Manifesto', and though he received support from acolytes of the 1941 Committee, the backbone of his campaign was provided — in breach of the truce — by the local Labour party. Coming only days after the loss of Tobruk, Driberg was able to reduce the Tory vote by more than 20 per cent, aided by another government nominee whose only rallying cry was loyalty to Churchill.[32] A few days later at Windsor the divisional Labour party, having declared itself against an independent backed by Kendall and Brown, also refused to campaign for the government, having failed to receive satisfactory assurances from the official Conservative candidate.[33]

Within the space of months, therefore, the so-called 'movement away from party' had helped to revive local political feeling. The success of independents such as Brown and Kendall would, henceforth, be more difficult to repeat now that the existing party machines had gearded themselves up to meet the challenge. In the process, though, fresh pressures had been placed on the electoral truce. With local Labour parties beginning to find new ways of breaking the truce without incurring disciplinary penalties, Attlee and his colleagues faced a new concern: that observation of the truce in name only might jeopardise coalition co-operation in the long term. The situation was prevented from deteriorating further, however, by a fortuitous coincidence. In the second half of 1942 the number of by-election contests fell significantly, and in most of those areas where seats did become vacant, for whatever reason, it was Labour nominees who were returned unopposed. By the time a fresh spate of contests was called in Tory-held seats in early 1943, pressure on the electoral truce had temporarily subsided.

By-election contests in 1942 also led to another development which militated against any lasting influence of a 'movement against party'. This was the recognition by both Conservative and Labour leaders that their local associations could not be allowed to stand idle indefinitely. Early in the year the chairman of Conservative organisation, Sir Douglas Hacking, had resigned, complaining that he found the task of urging forbearance on local associations 'invidious'. His successor, Major Tommy Dugdale, took a more publicly aggressive line, urging local parties to be prepared to contest by-elections anywhere in the country, though his efforts to stimulate a more general revival of party activity in the constituencies came to little.[34] On the Labour side, the NEC was also becoming concerned about the disruption to local activity, and especially about the fall in individual party membership form the pre-war figure of 400,000 to only 235,000. As a result, preparations were made for a new membership and propaganda drive. Although this was to be delayed until 1943, Transport House could take some encouragement from signs of spontaneous development already under way. At Newcastle under Lyme, for example, the adoption of a new parliamentary candidate with strong trade union backing led to a massive increase in membership within a few months.[35] Local Labour groups were still moribund in many areas, but the groundwork was now being laid for a more active revival that was to occur after 1943.

The 'movement away from party' thus proved to be short-lived. Independent successes in the spring of 1942 had reflected, above all, the desire of the electorate to express their dissatisfaction with the war effort. Not only had local political organisations reacted quickly to the challenge, under difficult circumstances, but the improvement in military fortunes at the end of the year also removed the most obvious sources of grievance. The departure of Stafford Cripps from the War Cabinet in November further undermined the possibility of a new centre force emerging in British politics; the idea of a centre party could now safely be dismissed by Hugh Dalton as 'all centre and no circumference'.[36] Even before the removal of Cripps, the People's Movement initiated by W. J. Brown had been dissolved, its sponsors recognising their inability to diminish the power of the party caucuses.[37] Although public approval of the independents had intitially appeared to suggest a growth of non-party views, by early 1943 a majority of those questioned by the British Instsitute of Public Opinion (BIPO) agreed that Britain would go back to its existing party system after the war.[38] Nineteen forty-two had seen the rapid rise and fall of the 'movement away from party'; it was soon to be followed by a stronger force — the movement 'back to party'.

If there was a single decisive moment on the long road to 1945, then it came in the first two months of 1943. Before this time, as we have seen, there was already much evidence of a radical public mood. Indeed, the Conservative vote had fallen in seven of the by-elections held during 1942, whereas support for Laboour was steadily increasing.[39] But the main causes of anti-Tory feeling had been readily apparent: frustrations about the war and restrictions on the home front. Once the tide had turned on the battlefield, the Prime Minister's reputation as national saviour was reinforced, and he now had the opportunity to recover some of the electoral ground lost since the fall of Chamberlain. The swing to the left, in other words, though powerful in the early war years, was by no means irreversible: if Churchill had used the period after 1942 to forge a popular post-war policy, then wartime suspicions about the Conservative party may have been at least partially ovecome. Instead, the Prime Minister paid only lip–service to public concern about reconstruction, and in this sense must bear a large share of personal responsibility for his crushing defeat at the polls in 1945. The desire of the British people to create a better world, though imprecise in many ways, could not be mistaken. But Churchill and his senior colleagues had little faith in the 'New Jerusalem'. Above all, the coolness of Conservative ministers towards the Beveridge plan was to prove profoundly damaging to the party.

Home Intelligence reported from nearly every region of the country that public expectations had been raised by the promise of the Beveridge reforms. This was soon overlaid, however, by 'very real anxiety' that such reforms might never materialise, whether because of government attitudes, 'vested interests' or financial considerations. After the parliamentary debate of February 1943, and Labour's revolt against the procrastination of

Anderson and Kingsley Wood, public anxiety increased. Regional information officers now found that majority opinion deplored what was seen as the shelving of the Report. Public feelings were said to vary from anger to despondency at this 'betrayal': 'Why', it was asked, 'get Beveridge to make a plan at all, if you are going to turn it down?'[40] The government was now squarely blamed for creating a mood of cynicism about the post-war world and, as we shall see, this feeling was to persist and resurface during the remainder of the war. Even after this time, political commentators doubted whether Labour would be the beneficiary: Attlee, for example, was still regarded as an uninspiring leader, and tensions between the political and industrial wings of the movement continued to receive publicity. But signs of Conservative unpopularity now began to multiply. Opinion polls from 1943 onwards generally gave Labour a lead of at least 10 percentage points, though such forecasts were not yet established as reliable guides to voting intentions.[41] Anti-Tory sentiment at by-elections, moreover, now became so pronounced as to be unmistakable.

In April 1943 the government was defeated in the Cheshire constituency of Eddisbury by a nascent political force — Common Wealth. The new party had been created some months earlier from the union of the 1941 Committee and the Forward March movement, led by Sir Richard Acland. Common Wealth's basic rationale was that Britain must adopt socialistic measures in order to win the war: 'Common Ownership', 'Vital Democracy' and 'Morality in Politics' became its principal slogans. Under the guidance of Acland, hitherto a Liberal MP, Common Wealth candidates began to pose a serious threat at by-elections in the spring of 1943. Campaigning on a platform of immediate implementation of the Beveridge Report, 'CW' came close to snatching victory in the safe Conservative seat of North Midlothian, and in several contests bettered the share of the vote achieved by Labour in 1935. At Eddisbury, the party fielded a dashing young pilot, John Loverseed, who had fought in the Battle of Britain. His supporters flooded the area to create an atmosphere of religious revival in this normally placid, rural constituency. By exploiting the government's unpopularity over Beveridge, Loverseed swept to victory.[42]

The significance of Eddisbury lay more in its demonstration of public feeling about reconstruction than in signalling any fundamental change in the party system. Just as the independents had

come and gone in 1942, so it became clear during the course of
1943 that Common Wealth would be hard put to make any lasting
breakthrough. Membership of the new party peaked at around
15,000, and its appeal was mainly in comfortable suburban areas,
among young midddle-class professionals with little tradition of
involvement in politics. After the enthusiasm of the early days,
Common Wealth's share of the vote at by-elections showed a
steady decline, and it was to field only twenty-three candidate at
the 1945 election.[43] Once again, in explaining this, the reaction
of the Labour party was crucial. Although some Labour members
gave active support, there was also widespread suspicion of a new
rival on the political left, especially one with a dominant middle-
class ethos. At Labour's annual conference in 1943, the NEC carried a resolution calling for the proscription of Common Wealth;
the latter, it was argued, undermined party unity by creating a
conflict of loyalty at by-elections.[44] Thereafter, some co-operation
at local level did continue, and 'C.W.' was to achieve two more
major by-election successes. But any long-lasting threat soon evaporated. And the emergence of Common Wealth, moreover, should
not be allowed to overshadow what was equally significant in 1943
— the continuing revival of local party politics.

Throughout 1943 the electoral truce, as before, was ineffective
in preventing partisan controversy. In one of the first by-elections
after Labour's conference, the local party in the Aston division of
Birmingham outlawed any assistance for the Common Wealth
candidate, but at the same time refused to support the Conservative
nominee and opted instead for 'strict neutrality'.[45] Other local
Labour parties went further in flouting the truce by tacitly backing
self-styled independent labour candidates. The most widely publicised example of this came at Bristol Central in February 1943,
where Jennie Lee, wife of Aneurin Bevan, stood against the Conservatives with the support of a group of local Labour councillors.
In spite of pressure from Transport House, the Bristol East Labour
party refused to withdraw recognition for Jennie Lee's campaign,
and promptly found themselves disaffiliated.[46] A similar pattern
was discernible, though with less serious consequences, in the by-
elections later in the year at King's Lynn and Peterborough, where
adopted parliamentary candidates resigned from the Labour party
to contest the seats. At Peterborough, the local party's statement
about how supporters should cast their votes was so ambiguous

that the local press described the eletctoral truce as a dead letter; continued loyalty to the coalition was purely nominal.[47] By the autumn of 1943 Liberal independents were beginning to follow the Labour lead. At Chippenham and Darwen, where Liberals formed the main oppositions, local candidates broke the truce and polled heavily without unseating government representatives, thereby prompting some short-lived speculation about the possibility of a Liberal revivial.[48]

As party feeling gradually came to reassert itself, so it increasingly came to centre on the single issue of reconstruction. By-elections held during 1943 demonstrated that at grass-roots level there was little sense of any emerging consensus between Conservative and Labour forces. Many Tory candidates suffered from their ambivalence towards the type of reforms proposed by Beveridge — Eddisbury was only the clearest of several example in this respect. It was true that Jennie Lee was defeated in Bristol after committing herself to 'every word, letter and comma' in the Report, whereas her opponent, Lady Apsley, refused to make any commitment. This result, however, was conditional by other factors, such as sympathy for the sudden death of Lady Apsley's husband, the sitting MP, and concerted ILP intervention to damage Jennie Lee's campaign.[49] Elsewhere, Major Wise improved Labour's 1935 vote at King's Lynn by 10 per cent after fighting on a 'good Socialist policy'; his Conservative opponent would venture only that it was difficult to say anything about the Beveridge Report for the time being because 'who could say what the value of the pound would be after the war?'[50] In spite of one or two more progressive candidates, the majority of Conservatives coming forward in 1943 had little sympathy for the idea of wholesale social change. One called Beveridge a 'poet's dream'; others more typically took the line that the winning of the war remained paramount and that all contentious political issues must be left until afterwards. It was this line at the Peterborough by-election that prompted Labour's refusal to observe the truce. Sam Bennett, the independent Labour candidate, came close to victory, having based his campaign on the view that 'the Conservative party, with their usual unreadiness, would be found unready for the peace'.[51]

Reconstruction also proved a catalyst for the more general sharpening of local political feeling in 1943. At local government level, for example, the need to produce concrete proposals in preparation for the peace helped to stir old rivalries. The Labour group in Birmingham made reconstruction the central theme of its increasingly bitter attacks on the Unionist majority; this return to acrimonious dabate, after the harmony of the early war years, was by no means an isolated example.[52] Post-war concerns also played a part in prodding back to life the constituency and regional associations. Labour's rank-and-file, disturbed by the Beveridge episode, flooded the party's annual conference in 1943 with resolutions calling for the immediate implementation of a reconstruction programme, as distinct from simply drawing up plans for the future. 'Full socialisation' of the economy, for instance, was urged as the only means of conquering unemployment.[53] On the Conservative side 1943 saw the first tentative signs of organisational revival. Regional councils now agreed that the time had come to counter the 'orgy of Socialist and Communist propaganda', and urged that in the framing of future Conservative policy the emphasis must be placed on the removal of economic controls and the reassertion of private enterprise.[54] There were some signs also of local Tory associations resuming peacetime activities. Spurred into action by the Bristol Central by-election, the local Unionist Association began a major organisational overhaul and published a statement of post-war aims, stressing that full employment could be achieved only by private enterprise and not by the dangerous experiment of nationalisation.[55] But Bristol was still very much the exception. Tory attachment to the notion of a 'political truce' remained deeply embedded, and was seriously shaken only after a new development at the beginning of 1944 — the experience of two crushing, even humiliating, by-election defeats.

The Skipton by-election of January 1944 brought together many of the features of local politics in the second half of the war. The contest was won by a young army officer, Lieutenant Hugh Lawson, standing on the full Common Wealth programme. Lawson's attractive personality and his ability to exploit local grievances — notably farmers' dissatisfaction with government policy — were clearly influential in his victory. Common Wealth also had an organisational advantage, using both full-time workers and numerous young volunteers who flocked to the Yorkshire dales during the Christmas holiday period. At the same time, however, Labour

played a pivotal role. The local party was indignant about the prospect of supporting an elderly Conservative nominee, and flouted
the electoral truce by giving open support to Lawson. 'The hard
core of the vote for Lawson', wrote one observer on the spot, 'came
from Labour, the industrial workers of the wool industry.'[56]
Common Wealth's victory, by the narrow margin of 200 votes,
was made worse for the Tories by the fact that a former Labour
MP had polled 11 per cent of the vote standing as an independent,
having been expelled from the Manchester Labour party for de-
fying the truce. The result, coming during a lull in war news, attracted more press attention than many previous by-elections, and
was difficult not to interpret as a signal of anti-Tory feeling. 'The
old adage: "If you win, praise the Agent; if you lose, blame the
candidate", is being very vigorously applied in this instance', reflected the Labour minister, Chuter Ede. 'This particular candidate', he added, 'seems to have been a typical Yorkshire product.
I imagine the Tory Party will be concerned at their loosening hold
on the agricultural seats.'[57]

The Skipton result did indeed set alarm bells ringing among
senior Conservatives. Shortly afterwards Central Office complained
to the Prime Minister that the Tory party now stood alone in
abiding by the terms of the electoral truce. Appeals to support the
government candidate in order to preserve national unity, it was
noted, had long since lost effect. And whereas independents were
free to make the most expansive promises to the electorate, Conservative candidates were handicapped by the 'lack of a positive
policy on home affairs', and could make only 'vague promises'.
Churchill was, therefore, urged to allow some revision of the rules
governing by-elections. As party feeling had been growing over
recent months, Central Office argued, Tory candidates should be
free to take the offensive by expounding policies consistent with
party principles.[58] The Prime Minister would not go this far,
though he did consent to relaxing the regulation that prevented
cabinet ministers from participating in by-elections. He also attempted, in a move which backfired badly, to intervene personally
in the contest that followed at Brighton. Here divisions in the local
Tory association resulted in independent opposition to the official
nominee. Churchill denounced this 'attempted swindle' by the independent, who nevertheless polled a solid 45 per cent of the vote.
Home Intelligence, moreover, found much local resentment about

the Prime Minister's intervention. 'People interpret the result of the election', it concluded, 'as indicating suspicion of the Government's post-war intentions.'[59] The same lesson could be drawn in February 1944 from what was to be the government's most celebrated by-election defeat of the war — at West Derbyshire.

The West Derbyshire constituency had a long-standing record of almost unbroken representation by the Cavendish family of the Dukes of Devonshire. In January 1944 it was announced that the sitting MP, Henry Hunloke, the Duke's brother-in-law, was to retire. No reason was given, though it transpired that Hunloke, having married the Duke's sister, was having an affair with a married woman, and had been pressurised to give up the 'family seat'. With remarkable speed the Duke's son, the Marquess of Hartington, was adopted as the new candidate, and a writ for the by-election was moved by the Chief Whip, who also happened to be Hartington's uncle. This led to accusations that the Cavendish family was moving quickly to give any interlopers as little time as possible to mount a challenge.[60] Hartington was, however, to be opposed by Charlie White, the only man who had broken the Cavendish hold on the seat in living memory; he resigned as the local Labour candidate to stand as an independent. 'A richly traditional contest ensued', wrote Angus Calder:

On the one hand there was the elegant young marquis, touring the division in a pony and trap and calling out the tenantry to vote in the old way (Hartington knew nothing much about politics, and his remark that he thought the coal mines were already nationalised became legendary...) On the other hand, there was the round-faced, angry White, inflaming the prejudices of the quarrymen and the townspeople. Between them, the jibes flew back and forth. Hartington was so provoked by the slurs which White's supporters cast on his knowledge of farming that he challenged his opponent to a muck-shovelling race on any farm in the constituency. White decline... All this, and the Acland circus too. While Conservative M.P.s flocked down to help Hartington out of his fix... almost all the opposition elements rallied behind White.... The appearance of a Russian-born woman among them attracted breathless interest in the popular press, which increased when the Russian Embassy disavowed her and she turned out to be an experienced trick cyclist.[61]

When the result was announced, White had achieved a spectacular victory, capturing 57 per cent of the vote; the Tory majority of some 5,000 was turned into an independent socialist majority of 4,500. West Derbyshire had clearly provided some light relief for political commentators. This had been further enhanced by the intervention of a third candidate, farm bailiff Robert Goodall, who made only one speech, issued no address and refused to venture out of his remote village to campaign. But it would be wrong to ignore the serious implications of the outcome. West Derbyshire illustrated the extent to which traditional party politics were resurfacing by the beginning of 1944. In what was virtually an open party contest, the electorate had demonstrated their preference for the commitment to welfare reform emphasised by White and his supporters. By contrast, the Conservatives had fielded another candidate out of touch with the public mood; in spite of the Skipton result, Hartington had nothing to offer in the way of post-war policy, and based himself largely on the themes of national unity and support for Churchill.[62] Labour, therefore, had some cause for satisfaction with the West Derbyshire result, though for party leaders this was tempered by the renewed strain placed on the electoral truce. On the NEC, Herbert Morrison now raised the idea of pressing for a resumption of normal party activity in the constituencies, while continuing co-operation at the parliamentary level. Similar schemes to this were, in fact, being devised by local parties, several of whom submitted resolutions to such effect for consideration by the annual conference. But Attlee and Bevin felt that any such scheme would place unbearable strains on cabinet unity, and the party conference, in the event, had to be postponed in order to allow preparations to go ahead for D-Day.[63] When the conference did finally assemble, in December 1944, the electoral truce had ceased to be an issue. By then it was clear that whenever the next election was called, Labour would fight as an independent party.

For Conservatives, of course, the West Derbyshire result was the cause of further consternation. News of the defeat, wrote John Colville, '... caused a pall of the blackest gloom to fall on the P.M.', who had sent a personal message of support praising the political record of the Cavendish family. The Prime Minister, Colville added, was now muttering about the necessity for a general election, arguing that unity was essential if Britain was to complete the task of victory over Hitler.[64] In the following weeks, senior Conservatives were summoned to Downing Street in an effort to make amends. The Chief Whip, James Stuart, was instructed to secure improvements at Central Office and in the constituencies, and for a while the possibility of recalling party agents

Fig 3 Finding one's way in the country

from the services was seriously considered.[65] But, in practice, as the memory of West Derbyshire faded, few concrete measures were taken to overhaul the Conservative machine. Regional and local associations were still sluggish in reviving their activities: by the summer of 1944 many had yet to adopt parliamentary candidates; there were still over 200 agents absent in the forces; and complaints were being made about the lack of clear direction given by national officials.[66] Tory gloom about West Derbyshire was also left behind, moreover, in the wake of new and exciting development on the battlefield. The enormous scale and achievement of the Normandy landings strongly reinforced a feeling which had persisted, in varying degrees, since the summer of 1940: surely Churchill, the great national saviour, could not be beaten at any post-war election?

In a perceptive article written late in 1943 for the journal *Political Quarterly*, Tom Harrisson, the founder of Mass-Observation,

claimed that by-election results and opinion polls provided incontrovertible evidence of a swing to the left in political attitudes.
Among those with whom he came into contact, a distinction was
continually made between the Prime Minister as 'Bulldog of Battle'
and Churchill the party leader who showed little concern for
domestic policy. 'I have no doubt', Harrisson concluded, 'that the
present Conservative Party, even if led by Mr Churchill, will not
accomplish enough of itself to govern again, unless the alternatives
commit suicide.'[67] It is easy to see why contemporary opinion
ignored this lone prediction. The great majority of politicians and
political commentators looked no further than the precedent of
1918, when Lloyd George had swept back to power as 'the man
who won the war'. Churchill's public popularity was at least comparable with that of Lloyd George at the end of the Great War,
and there was little reason to anticipate that the electorate would
vote in preference of Labour's leader, Attlee. It was often assumed
that the left would make gains, but this had to be set against the
Conservative party's 200 plus parliamentary majority; again, this
militated against the likelihood of Churchill actually being defeated.
And if Labour's reputation had been greatly enhanced by participation in government, it could still behave as a party at odds with
itself — a point reinforced by the acrimonious slanging match
between the Minister of Labour and Aneurin Bevan over strike
activity in the spring of 1944. This protracted episode provided
Labour's opponents in the national press with an open invitation,
one which was not spurned, to resume attacks on 'socialist extremism'. Chuter Ede was left to reflect that the party's indiscipline had
'seriously lowered its prestige during the last twelve months'.[68]

What was remarkable about the war years was that Labour
disunity — still evident, if less acute than in peacetime — hardly
mattered to the electorate. By 1944 Labour's weaknesses paled by
comparison with the strongly pronounced tide of anti-Conservative
feeling. The evidence for this, though mounting all the time, was
again easy to ignore. Opinion polls were still in their infancy, and
few yet believed that it was possible to predict accurately the
outcome of a general election on the basis of a small sample of
voters. Similarly, by-election results could be explained away as
the product of protest voting connected with particular wartime
circumstances, unlikely to be repeated in any post-war election.
But those like Harrisson who had regular contact with broad sec-

tions of the electorate were well placed to observe that a major sea-change had taken place in public opinion. The foundations for this shift, as we have seen, were laid by the fall of Chamberlain and the military difficulties of 1940–42, though it was only after the 'turn of the tide' that the trend became irreversible. How far the new public mood reflected a negative image of Conservatism, as distinct from a positive turning towards Labour, remains difficult to disentangle, but Tom Harrisson for one found it difficult to exaggerate the scepticism caused by Churchill's attitude towards the 'New Jerusalem'. Home Intelligence reports during the second half of the war were littered with references to public cynicism about the government's reconstruction programme, even after the appointment of a Minister of Reconstruction. In mid-1944 30–40 per cent of those questioned still felt nothing would come of the Beveridge plan, and trepidation about post-war prospects remained widespread. 'The Government', Home Intelligence reported, 'is variously accused of slowness, vagueness, and making promises which are either beyond its intentions or its powers.'[69]

'Finding one's way in the country' was thus a difficult business in 1944. What was becoming clear by the time Allied troops launched their assault on the Normandy beaches, however, was that a return to two-party politics throughout the country was unavoidable. The effect of the West Derbyshire by-election in this context was vital, for it confirmed what had long been apparent — the ineffectiveness of the electoral truce. Subsequent by-elections, though fewer in number, became *de facto* party contests. In the Rusholme division of Manchester local Labour supporters gave open support to Common Wealth, and at Wolverhampton Bilston in September 1944 Labour activists helped an ILP candidate who came within 350 votes of victory. The Conservative nominee complained that 'the bulk of the Labour party members voted for my opponent . . . and I regret that certain local Labour party leaders advised them to do so.'[70] During the autumn of 1944 there was also a discernible revival of party politics at the local government level; prospects of any serious Liberal revival had been jeopardised by the failure of the various pre-war factions to unite; and the fate of Common Wealth was sealed when Labour's annual conference rejected a request for incorporation as the thin end of a wedge that might lead to Communist affiliation.[71] Common Wealth was to score one further by-election success, at Chelmsford in April 1945, but,

as we shall see, this was primarily another example of the two
major parties lining up against each other in defiance of the electoral truce. The war, therefore, had not produced any lasting sense
of consensus in local politics. Rather, it was the party rank-and-
file, eager to espouse unhindered their very different visions of the
future, who had led the way in what was becoming an increasingly
dominant theme of national politics, particularly after D-Day —
the retreat from coalition.

Notes

1 Addison, *Road to 1945*, p. 131. See also pp. 127–63 for the important
  chapter 'Two cheers for socialism, 1940–42'.
2 'Home-made socialism', Report by Home Intellignece Division, 24
  March 1942: Ministry of Information papers, PRO INF 1/292.
3 Addison, op. cit., p. 162.
4 Home Intelligence Weekly Report, 8–15 January and 26 February–
  March 1941, PRO INF 1/292.
5 Copy in *Labour Party Annual Conference Report*, London, 1940,
  p. 19.
6 J. G. Bulpitt, *Party Politics in English Local Government*, London
  1967, pp. 5–21.
7 See the records of regional and local Conservative associations col-
  lected by Chris Stevens and John Ramsden, with support from what
  was then the Social Science Research Committee (SSRC), in preparation for the volume on the official history of the party since 1940. I am
  grateful to Dr John Ramsden for allowing me to consult these records.
  As an example, the Guildford association, flourishing before the war,
  decided in early September 1939 to suspend operations; a small emergency committee of four was established to oversee development.
8 Management Committee Minutes, 20 November 1941, Birmingham
  Unionist Association: Birmingham Reference Library; *Annual Report
  1941*, Bristol West Unionist Association: Bristol Record Office. In both
  these examples tribute was paid to women's branches for keeping the
  nucleus of organisation in operation.
9 C. Harvie, 'Labour in Scotland during the Second World War', *The
  Historical Journal*, XXVI, 4, 1983, pp. 925–6: Scottish membership,
  measured by constituency, was the lowest of any British region in
  1941. Amongst the many examples of more active local parties, see, for
  instance, Minutes of the General Council, 1940–41, North Lambeth
  Labour party, British Library of Political and Economic Science
  (BLPES) which suggests an organisation campaigning to ensure that
  Labour participation in the coalition secured improvements in areas
  such as shelters, pensions and trade union rights.
10 A. Sutcliffe and R. Smith, *History of Birmingham*, Vol. III, *Birming-*

ham 1939–1970, London, 1974, pp. 24–5.

11 *Durham City Advertiser*, 11 October 1940. In many areas the attitude
that political activity be held in abeyance continued even after the turn
of the tide in the war, e.g. Minutes of Emergency Committee, 11
January 1943, Penryn and Falmouth Unionist Association: Cornwall
Record Office, Truro.

12 'Memorandum on platform propaganda under war conditions now
prevailing', Labour party NEC Organisation Sub-Committee, 16
December 1941; G. R. Shepherd (National Agent) to Bevin, 6 October
1941: Bevin papers, Churchill College, Cambridge, 8/1.

13 E.g. Executive Committee minutes, 28 March 1941, Tynemouth
Conservative Association, SSRC archive. See also records of the
Kennington Conservative association at BLPES, where Central Office
urges that in the interests of national unity even attacks on the integrity
of Chamberlain and Baldwin should not receive any public response.

14 P. Addison, 'By-elections of the Second World War', in C. Cook and J.
Ramsden (eds), *By-Elections in British Politics*, London, 1973, pp.
165–9. For a full description of wartime by-election results, see below,
Appendix II.

15 Calder, *People's War*, pp. 280–4.

16 'Dunbartonshire by-election', Home Intelligence Report, 5 March
1941, PRO INF 1/292.

17 Addison, op. cit., pp. 171–3.

18 Addison, *Road to 1945*, pp. 155–6, notes this point and yet still talks
of a 'statistical harmony between the early war elections and those
which follow'.

19 'The Pollock by-election', May 1940, Typescript Report No. 92:
Mass-Observation Archive, University of Sussex. See also *Yorkshire
Observer*, 30 April 1940.

20 'Dunbartonshire by-election', Home Intelligence Report.

21 *The Times*, 6 May 1941; *Labour Party Annual conference Report*,
London 1941, pp. 123–7.

22 'Home-made socialism', Home Intelligence Report, 24 March 1942,
INF 1/292.

23 'Seventh Report on Sir Stafford Cripps — Political Trends and Post-
War Government', Mass-Observation Typescript Report No. 1443,
26 November 1942.

24 Addison, 'By-Elections', pp. 173–4; *Road to 1945* p. 156.

25 W. J. Brown, *So Far...*, London, 1943, pp. 243–50. Calder, op. cit.,
p. 335, summarises Brown's political attitudes as boiling down 'to
a manic hatred of the party whips and... to a profound belief in the
inalienable right of W. J. Brown to say what he liked, where he liked,
when he liked, and for as long as he liked'.

26 G. Reakes, *Man of the Mersey*, London, 1956, pp. 72–83; Addison,
'By-Elections', pp. 175–6.

27 The activities of the British National Party are noted in a Conservative
Central Office memo, n.d., in Lady Astor's papers: Reading University
Library, MS. 1416/1/1/1625. The party had been formed in January

1942, and its aims included safeguarding the British people against 'alien influence and infiltration'.

28 Calder, op. cit., pp. 335–6.

29 *Labour Party Annual Conference Report*, 1942, pp. 135–40.

30 *Western Mail and South Wales News*, 10 and 13 April 1942.

31 *Barry Herald*, 29 May 1942; *Western Mail*, 30 May 1942; By-Elections, Box 14/F: Mass-Observation Archive; *Daily Express*, 10 June 1942.

32 Tom Driberg, *The Best of Both Worlds*, London, 1953, pp. 181–5; Addison, 'By-Elections', pp. 176–7.

33 *The Windsor, Slough and Eton Express*, 26 June 1942. The Conservative, Mott-Radclyffe, won comfortably with 58 per cent of the vote, though the Independent candidate, Douglas-Home, made a respectable showing with 41 per cent.

34 *Onlooker*, March–July 1942.

35 'Memorandum on condition of party', 25 March 1942, Labour Party NEC minutes; F. Bealey, J. Blondel and W. P. McCann, *Constituency Politics: a Study of Newcastle-under-Lyme*, London, 1965, pp. 89–91.

36 *Dalton Diary*, 6 September 1943, p. 633, citing the view of Sir William Harcourt.

37 A. Calder, 'The Common Wealth party 1942–1954', unpublished D.Phil. thesis, University of Sussex 1967, Vol. I, p. 97.

38 BIPO Survey, April 1942 and January 1943, incorporated in Home Intelligence Reports, INF 1/292.

39 E.g. in the Manchester Clayton contest, Labour's vote increased by nearly 40 per cent.

40 Home Intelligence Weekly Reports, 10 December 1942 an 11 March 1943.

41 *The Economist*, 28 August 1943.

42 Calder, *People's War*, pp. 631–5.

43 'By-Elections in 1943', n.d., Mass-Observation Typescript Report No. 1844; Addison, 'By-Elections', pp. 179–82.

44 *Labour Party Annual Conference Report*, 1943, pp. 18–20 and p. 153.

45 Calder, 'Common Wealth', Vol. I, pp. 129–31 and pp. 168–9; *Birmingham Post*, 2 June 1943. The Conservative vote increased by nearly 4 per cent; Common Wealth polled only 21.6 per cent.

46 *Western Daily Press*, 4 January 1943; minutes of the General Council, 14 February and 21 April 1943, Bristol East Labour party records: Bristol Record Office, 39035/19.

47 *Norfolk News and Weekly Press*, 6 February 1943; *Peterborough Standard*, 22 October 1943. In spite of pressure from party officials, the local party in Peterborough refused to arrange meetings on behalf of the Conservative candidate , Lord Suirdale, and made little secret of their support for the 'independent' — *New Statesman*, 29 October 1943.

48 D. Johnson, *Bars and Barricades*, London, 1952, pp. 229–48; 'Report on Chippenham By-Election', 24 August 1943, Mass-Observation Typescript Report No. 1892.

49 'Bristol By-Election', n.d., Mass-Observation Typescript Report No. 1649; *Chuter Ede Diary*, 19 February 1943, p. 123: 'I hear that McGovern spent a scurrilous hour last Sunday on the I.L.P. Platform in personal denunciation of the Bevans' way of life — their Hyde Park mansion & its luxurious furniture. He inquired why Mrs. Bevan, a childless married woman aged 35 could remain outside the war effort while she drove round in a motor car urging other similarly situated women to join the services or go into the factories. E. Brown said this attack had done great harm to her chances.'

50 *Norfolk News and Weekly Press*, 6 February 1943, for the comment of Lord Fermoy.

51 *Peterborough Standard*, 22 October 1943. Calder, *People's War*, p. 631, notes that the Tory candidate who called Beveridge a 'poet's dream' bowed to public opinion by subsequently calling for immediate implementation, thereby leaving himself open to charges of insincerity.

52 Sutcliffe and Smith, op. cit., pp. 53–4. See also C. Gill, *Plymouth: a New History*, Newton Abbot, 1979, pp. 215–18, for a similar pattern.

53 E.g. Minutes of Mangement Committee, 12 March 1943, North Lambeth Labour Party, BLPES, 1/4; Bealey *et al.*, op. cit., p. 92.

54 E.g. Minutes of the East Mudlands Area Conservative Asssociation, 29 November 1943, SSRC Collection.

55 Minutes of Special Sub-Committee, 12 July 1943, Bristol Unionist Association records: Bristol Record Office, 38036/BCA/la; *Where We Stand and Our Hopes for the Future*, A Statement by the Bristol Unionist Association, n.d. [1943].

56 Kitty Wintringham, *Common Wealth Review*, March 1944, cited in Addison, 'By-Elections', p. 185. For a full description of the Skipton contest, see the appendix in Calder, 'Common Wealth', Vol. II. pp. 231–46.

57 *Chuter Ede Diary*, 9 January 1944, p. 162.

58 Stuart to Churchill (enclosing memo from Central Office), 14 January 1944; Conservative Party archive, Bodleian Library, WHP2, File 1.

59 Calder, *People's War*, p. 637; 'The Brighton By-Election', Home Inteligence Weekly Report, 10 February 1944.

60 *Marchester Guardian*, 31 January 1944.

61 Calder, op. cit., pp. 638–9.

62 'West Derby By-Election', Mass-Observation Typescript Report No. 2036, February 1944.

63 Morrison to Attlee, 9 March 1944: Attlee papers, Bodleian Library, 13/4; *Labour Organiser*, March 1944.

64 *Colville Diary*, 18 February 1944, p. 474.

65 Stuart memo to Churchill, 27 March 1944, PRO PREM 4 64/2; War Cabinet minutes, 28 June 1944, CAB 65/42.

66 Harvie- Watt, *Most of My Life*, pp. 143 and 154.

67 Tom Harrisson, 'Who'll win', *Political Quarterly*, XV, 1944, pp. 21–32.

68 *Chuter Ede Diary*, 12 May 1944, p. 183.

69 'Public feeling about the Beveridge proposals', Home Intelligence

Special Report, 13 May 1944, INF 1/293; Home Intelligence Full Monthly Review, 22 June 1944, INF 1/292.

70 *Midland Counties Express* & *Wolverhamton Chronicle*, 16 and 32 September 1944.

71 On the pattern in local government, see, for example, K. Young, *Local Politics and the Rise of Party*, Leicester, 1975, pp. 171–83, and J. D. Marshall (ed.), *The History of Landcashire County Council 1889 to 1974*, London, 1977, pp. 199–200. *Sylyester Diary*, 21 October 1943, p. 316, reports how the Ernest Brown Liberals had put the whole question of reunion into cold storage.

7

The retreat from coalition

Alongside the debates about reconstruction, Westminster politics in the second half of the war focused on one other major concern — the future of Churchill's government. As ultimate Allied victory became more certain, so speculation intensified about the likely pattern of post-war politics: would the coalition be extended beyond the end of the German war, and, if so, for how long? In 1943 the possibility of prolonging the present administration, primarily in order to tackle the complex problems of international resettlement, was certainly one which exercised the minds of many leading politicians. But at the same time a countervailing tendency was at work. Just as in local politics, the feeling rapidly took hold that an end to the coalition and a complete return to conventional party politics was both desirable and inevitable. This belief, discernible even before the West Derbyshire by-election, became particularly strong after the D-Day landings in June 1944. With victory now in sight, previous imperatives to suspend partisan disagreements in the interests of national unity evaporated, and by the autumn of 1944 it was clear that the chances of post-war co-operation had entirely disappeared. The consequences, as we shall see in this chapter, were twofold. In the first place, long before the coalition finally broke up with Germany's defeat in May 1945, Conservative and Labour politicians alike were taking up entrenched positions and preparing the ground for the forthcoming election. In the War Cabinet, as well as in the Commons, the final eighteen months of the war witnessed an inexorable retreat from coalition. And secondly, there was in turn a marked effect on the government's reconstruction programme. When set against the prevailing political assumptions of the period after 1943, major initiatives, such as the widely acclaimed white paper on employment policy, appear in a new light.

The white paper, like other proposals for reform, should not be too readily depicted as a crowning achievement of wartime consensus. For these measures came at a time when the whole reconstruction process was, if anything, grinding to a halt.

The retreat from coalition began long before D-Day. From early 1943 onwards the configuration of post-war politics became an increasing source of gossip and speculation at Westminster; with the end of the war in sight, at least in Europe if not the Far East, politicians naturally turned their minds more and more to the future. According to Paul Addison, coalition ministers were reticent on this subject, and went through much anguish before deciding that wartime co-operation would have to be abandoned. It is, writes Addison, 'difficult to tell, especially with Attlee and the Labour leaders, whether they differed in their heart of hearts or only because they were compelled to do so by the revival of party feeling on the backbenches and at grassroots'.[1] Party leaders on both sides could certainly not mistake the wishes of their supporters. As we saw in the last chapter, the short-lived 'movement away from party' in 1942 was followed by a very pronounced 'movement back to party' throughout 1943. But if Labour ministers spent time toying with the idea of continuing the coalition after the war, then it will be argued here that they did so not through any lack of partisan commitment or as sign of moving towards the political middle ground. Rather, it was simply through a desire to maximise political advantage. What was more, the greatest reluctance about ending the coalition was to be shown not by Labour ministers but by Churchill and Eden — a reflection of their uncomfortable relationship with the Tory party.

The Prime Minister himself set the ball rolling. During his speech outlining the 'four year plan' in March 1943, he referred to the need when the war ended for a national government 'comprising the best men in all parties who are willing to serve'. This was interpreted by commentators in several ways: as a proposed extension of the coalition on the basis of a 'coupon' election; as a tentative initiative towards the creation of new centre force in British politics; or simply as a warning to Labour that if it repudiated the electoral truce it might lose its leadership, as in 1931. Churchill had used ambiguous language because, as yet, he had no settled opinions, and wanted to keep his options open. 'At present', he told the journalist W. P. Crozier, 'we must leave things to events.'[2] Inevitably, though, the Prime Minister's remarks set tongues wagging. In response, Attlee prepared an equally ambiguous statement to the effect that Labour, until further notice, was not committed to any one particular course of action. But party activists were greatly alarmed by rumours that among Labour leaders Morrison and Dalton in particular were in favour of continuing to work with Churchill. Both men were, indeed, floating the idea of extending the coalition on an agreed programme, with party candidates stressing different aspects of the programme, but again this did not represent any settled thinking. In reality, it was seen simply as one possible way — given the expectation of Churchill sweeping back to power at the end of the war — of maintaining Labour in high office without destroying party unity. Morrison, surprised by the hostile reaction, beat a hasty retreat, and subsequently went out of his way to tell a meeting of lobby journalists that he would live and die with the Labour party.[3] 'The truth was', remarked the Liberal minister Archie Sinclair, 'that [Churchill] hadn't thought it out at all . . . and in fact no one else had gone far in thinking it out'.[4]

By the autumn of 1943 the prospect of extending the coalition was still on the agenda. Hugh Dalton wrote in September:

It would be total lunacy to fight an election, if it could be avoided, against the present Prime Minister while the laurels of victory were upon his brows; . . . therefore, my simple plan was, though it might be quite impossible to execute it, to continue an all-party government, and to screw as much good policy as we could out of our colleagues while it lasted, until such time as we could fight an election and *win it* with a Labour majority.[5]

At the same time, however, with the Allies slowly getting the better of German forces, pressure mounted for a return to conventional party politics. Labour ministers, we have seen, became increasingly annoyed at the way Churchill dragged his feet over reconstruction. When confronted about the 'need for decisions', the Prime Minister gave the impression that he was 'testing out the Labour Ministers to see if they were likely to break away'.[6] Conservatives, for their part, were unhappy about the willingness of their Labour colleagues to publicise controversial post-war ideas. Ironically, it was Herbert Morrison who led the way. In a series of widely publicised speeches, he left behind thoughts of further co-operation by arguing strongly in favour of state planning after the war, attacking those who had rushed to remove controls in 1918 as betrayers of the nation's hopes. This earned not only a stern rebuke from Churchill but also a response in kind from Tory ministers and sections of the press, who identified 'Mr Morrison's Controllers with that dreadful and doleful apparition, the Bureaucrat . . .'.[7]

The impression Morrison helped to create — that entrenched party differences were too great to sustain coalition after the war — rapidly gained ground in 1944. The West Derbyshire by-election, as we saw in the last chapter, was vital in this context, and resulted in a wider recognition by local activists and national leaders alike that a resumption of party politics could not be far off. The Prime Minister now sought to revive Tory organisation, and was urged by Lord Beaverbrook to abandon any thoughts of extending the life of the coalition. Although agreement could be achieved on food and houses, he told Churchill, Conservatives were reluctant to yield to left-wing demands for the nationalisation of banks, transport and coal.[8] On the Labour side, there was a similar hardening of attitudes. By late February the NEC had reached the definite conclusion that Labour should break with Churchill at the end of the European war. To prepare the ground, it was agreed that the next annual conference should be urged to maintain the electoral truce, while simultaneously making clear the party's determination to fight as an independent force at the first election after the defeat of Germany. Hugh Dalton, for all his uncertainty about tactics in 1943, now went along unequivocally with this new approach. After a particularly fruitless and protracted discussion on post-war commercial policy, Dalton lamented that the coalition would never be able to reach firm decisions on many issues, and must inevitably be wound up.[9] Though obviously influenced by grass-roots opinion, it was ideological conviction that ultimatley explained the impatience of Labour ministers. With victory in sight, the necessity for compromise at cabinet level was diminishing all the time, and even Ernest Bevin — never the most partisan minister in strict party terms — was moved to complain to Attlee in May 1944:

The Prime Minister has taken the line that he will not agree to nationalise anything during the war. We must await a general election. Yet it looks as if Max Beaverbrook and all the forces associated with him are attempting to denationalise what we have got; . . . if we cannot, as a coalition, carry any nationalisation of mines, railways or electricity, surely the Party must make its position clear and keep its hand free for the Election.[10]

By mid-1944, therefore, the artificial nature of coalition consensus was becoming ever more apparent. The necessity, indeed desirability, of a return to party politics was now widely accepted, on the front-bench at Westminster as well as in the constituencies. Party leaders, though resuming their traditional rhetoric partly in order to satisfy their followers, had firmed up their position primarily because it was obvious that the coalition had no long-term future. For Labour ministers, the objectives remained consistent. The desire to maximise party advantage and secure policy improvements, evident in thinking about an extension of coalition in 1943, persisted after it was agreed that Labour would fight as an independent force. What had changed, quite simply, were the tactics. In view of Churchill's enormous public prestige, the task now was to delay the calling of an election for as long as possible after Hitler's defeat, in the hope that the Prime Minister's personal appeal would be diminished. Ironically, it was only Churchill among senior ministers who still harboured any doubts about the end of coalition, though, as we shall see, these soon disappeared under the impact of events. Above all, the success of the D-Day landings in Normandy — by opening up the prospect of an early end to hostilities — intensified the growing strains on the coalition, and made it ever more difficult to produce tangible results in domestic policy. This leads us, in turn, to a further and neglected point; the need to recognise that some of the major elements in the government's reconstruction programme were produced at the very time when cross-party agreement was breaking down.

The government's white paper on employment policy, published in the summer of 1944, has frequently been seen as the high-water mark of coalition consensus. Keith Middlemas, for example, has depicted *Employment Policy* as the forerunner of the post-war corporatist economy, pointing to the recognition by government, employers and trade unions of the need to work together in pursuit of a common objective.[11] The white paper clearly represented a move forward from pre-war economic orthodoxy. Before 1939 the Treasury view that additonal employment could not be created in the long term by state interference in the market-driven economy had remained largely unchallenged. But the war, as we have seen, induced major changes in economic management. With Sir William Beveridge promoting the concept of 'full employment' — and threatening a separate report to publicise this idea — the coalition decided to produce its own document, acknowledging that the power of the state in maintaining employment levels had been underestimated in the past. For Keynes and other economic specialists drafted into wartime Whitehall, the publication of the white paper marked a 'revolution' in offical policy-making, a decisive step towards the full employment policies that characterised the welfare state after 1945. Economic historians, however, have recently cast doubt upon this interpretation. The Treasury's acceptance of demand management, for instance, has been shown to be an uneven process: Keynesian techniques were 'on tap' but not 'on top' until at least 1947; and equally, senior Treasury officials continued to believe during the war that traditional methods would ultimately prove most successful in countering unemployment.[12] Here two points will be stressed: that the white paper represented the very limits of coalition consensus; and that the parties were able to support the document only by agreeing to disagree on future policy.

The drafting of the white paper required a series of compromises at every level, from civil servants and economic advisers through to ministers studying the plans on Woolton's Reconstruction Committee. Treasury assumptions came into conflict with the Keynesian propositions of the War Cabinet's Economic Section, and Labour ministers found they met with stern resistance from the new Chancellor, Sir John Anderson, who played a decisive part in government deliberations on this issue.[13] The white paper was accordingly reticent, calling not for full employment but for the creation of conditions necessary for a 'high and stable level of employment', defined at less than 8.5 per cent of the population. More direct management of the economy was envisaged than in the past, especially in relation to public investment, but wartime controls over the economy were to be gradually relaxed and the final document was openly contradictory about the value of deficit finance as a means of countering cyclical depression.[14] Whereas Labour leaders could regard this as a modest advance, Conservative spokesmen were able to claim that unemployment would be more vigorously tackled in future without any fundamental departures in policy. This theme was taken up above all by the Minister of Production, Oliver Lyttelton, a senior figure in the Tory hierarchy; he had, in fact, come very close to replacing Kingsley Wood as Chancellor. The party, he argued, should now accept some 'positive action' by the state, but this must be kept 'down to the minimum, for if the tax-payers' money — and there is no other money available to the State — has to be invested in industry, the State must watch it and control it. It is quite a delusion to draw the inference that because the State in war is highly efficient in industry, that the same applies in peace'. For Tory leaders, unemployment after the war was to be avoided, if not by a return to pre-1939 conditions, then by a heavy reliance on traditional remedies such as the stability of sterling, the expansion of export trade and the encouragement of private enterprise.[15] In this light, the white paper was as important for what it did not say as for what it proposed: it was not clear that *Employment Policy* 'actually represented any single widely held position'.[16]

The ambiguous content of the white paper helped to ensure a satisfactory reception in the House of Commons. Neither side could conceivably oppose the objective of tackling unemployment, especially at a time when national attention focused on momentous events in northern France. But the language of Tory and Labour back-benchers suggested a less than wholesale commitment to the government's plan. On the Conservative side, there had been moves by the Tory Reformers in 1943 to influence the party towards acceptance of state investment in both public and private enterprise, and one of the more widely publicised reports from the Post-War Problems Committee had also called for a vigorous programme of capital expenditure.[17] In the House, Herbert Williams was a lone voice in denouncing what he called 'this miserable document'. Most Tory contributors praised the white paper in the highest terms, complaining only that it had not received the same public attention as other reform proposals.[18] This enthusiasm, however, was clearly double-sided. By 1944 the party had learnt a lesson from the Beveridge episode: electorally, it was vital that reconstruction be publicly embraced. Conservatives, moreover, were satified that, while the white paper provided a suitably ambiguous basis for approaching the post-war economy, it did imply a particular commitment to private enterprise. There were no plans to control private investment, and Anderson caused further

satisfaction by his emphasis on sound budgetary practice.[19] The
employment white paper could, therefore, be given a more cordial
reception than other wartime proposals; something that could not
be said of the reaction on the Labour benches.

Labour MPs were, of course, concerned to push the government's reconstruction programme along as quickly as possible, and
in so far as as the white paper marked a departure in official
thinking it was to be welcomed. But criticism was never far from
the surface. Much has been made of Aneurin Bevan's fierce attack
on the white paper, which he said compromised much of what the
party stood for, though, in fact, doubts were evident among all
sections of Labour opinion. The party's own policy on the employment question, recently worked out by specialist sub-committees,
had divided not on lines of theory but on the question of practical
implementation; what concerned back-benchers was the ambivalence of the white paper about the precise distribution of power
and ultimate responsibility for economic managment.[20] These fears
were summed up in the House by Arthur Greenwood:

> Where we part, as we must part on a matter of this kind, with hon.
> Members opposite is that they do not take the same view of the economic
> life of the country as we do; . . . while we have accepted the recognition by
> the State of a new responsibility which hitherto has been unrecognised and
> unaccepted by the State, we do not believe that the machinery in the White
> Paper will, as it stands now, solve our problems . . . . If the predominant
> motive in industry is to be private gain we can say goodbye to all hopes of
> ending huge-scale unemployment . . . . I still must, on behalf of my hon,
> Friends, re-assert the faith we all hold that the one way is the way we call
> Socialism.[21]

The achievement of the employment white paper was thus
symbolic as much as technical.[22] It enabled the coalition to make a
show of forwarding its reconstrucion programme, though in line
with the rest of wartime social policy it was not part of a progressive strategy. The impact of war had induced some new thinking
among Treasury officials, but at the same time the white paper had
been produced in part to pre-empt more radical demands for full
employment. Because of the need to appeal to both wings of the
coalition, the government's proposals had opted for caution, and
represented the limits of any agreement on economic policy.
Labour regarded the white paper as only a starting point. The
party's own policy document, *Full Employment and Financial*

Policy, made it clear that Labour economists still regarded the major priority as physical control socialist planning — as vindicated by wartime experience — combined with a degree of budgetary demand management.[23] With the exception of the Tory Reformers, most Conservatives had taken comfort from those very sections of the document most criticised by their opponents. It was no surprise that the resultant plan had avoided altogether many key economic issues, such as the future relationship between public and private enterprise. Indeed, ministers had accepted the publication of the white paper only on the strict understanding that the question of the future ownership of industry was in no way prejudiced.[24] The white paper, in other words, was by no means a certain guide to Britain's post-war economy. The battle for the 'mixed economy', with a greatly enhanced role for the state, had yet to be won.

The employment white paper, it must also be remembered, came against a background of rapidly intensifying party hostilities. In the aftermath of D-Day, Labour's NEC agreed to publicise its earlier decision about fighting the next election as an independent force. Under the guiding hand of Attlee, the published statement emphasised the hope that the coalition might be brought to an end with 'dignity and good feeling'.[25] This action followed logically from the view consistently held by Labour leaders. Far from acting reluctantly, Attlee much resented press speculation about the party's intentions, which he felt could be taken for granted. Indeed, it was the Prime Minister alone who had any lingering doubts. 'I have a strong feeling', he remarked privately in September 1944, 'that my work is done. I have no message. I had a message. Now I only say "fight the damned Socialists". I do not believe in this brave new world.'[26] It was, therefore, with a degree of resignation that Churchill told the House of Commons in October that it would be wrong to prolong the life of the government beyond the ending of the German war. Nevertheless, having accepted which way the wind was blowing, the Prime Minister was soon making his own efforts to secure party advantage. Plans were made to galvanise the Tory electoral machine into action, and the Premier prophetically told his son — in an aside which casts doubt on the sincerity of his later offer to extend the coalition – that polling day was likely to be 'about two months from the official collapse of the Germans'.[27] Hence, by the autumn of 1944 the return to party politics had become irreversible. Exactly when an election would take place remained unclear, but the crucial decision to end wartime co-operation had already been taken.

One of the inevitable knock-on effects was that the government's reconstruction programme was left in limbo. *The Economist* summed up the position:

The present session of Parliament, like the war, has reached a late and critical stage. The two are closely connected for, if the best happens in Normandy and on the Eastern Front, the end of fighting in Europe will find the country still unprepared for the rush of new and urgent tasks. This is not because of any lack of preparations. White Papers on Employment Policy, Monetary Policy and National Health . . . have given proofs of hard labour in the departments and the Cabinet — and chance for Parliament to show its paces, with mixed results, in deliberation. It is legislation, however, that counts and it is legislation that is still perilously lacking.[28]

But if time was now running short, then the chances of the coalition redeeming itself in the field of reconstruction were much slimmer than press commentators could have known. For already — around the same time as the final touches were being made to the employment white paper — a series of acrimonious cabinet meetings had ended by effectively putting the lid on further new initiatives. The time for pursuing common objectives had passed.

Sir John Anderson's budget in the spring of 1944 had first alerted the Prime Minister to the level of commitments entered into by the government. In response to a querulous question about how this had happened, given the uncertainty of the post-war financial situation, the Chancellor gave an effective answer: the estimated additional spending — £226 million rising to over £400 million — would occur over a thirty-year period, and on a budget expected to be swollen by greater national income and taxable capacity.[29] Churchill nevertheless returned to this theme in the summer, when he himself was pressed by Lord Woolton about the need for final decisions on social insurance. Without a firm commitment now to the increased expenditure involved, there would be considerable delay in introducing the proposed scheme; such a delay, Woolton added, would be 'most unwelcome to some of my colleagues on the Reconstruction Committee'.[30] The Prime Minister again turned to Anderson, urging him to take the lead in resisting this 'rapid growth of our national burdens'. The Chancellor, after repeating that no fresh commitments had been made since the Beveridge plan had been accepted in principle, pointed out that hard decisions could no longer be avoided. As it presented itself to him, Anderson concluded, 'the issue is whether we take risks on the possibility of reducing taxation or whether we seek postponement of some parts of our schemes.'[31]

Churchill was well aware that Labour ministers would never countenance the latter suggestion. He therefore decided to take the line, urged on him by officials, that nothing could be done about existing commitments except to make the most of them. He did, though, manage to delay the publication of the government's two insurance white papers until after the summer recess, making the disingenuous claim that these would not receive due attention if published at a time of momentous war news.[32] Seen against this background of prevarication, the eventual appearance of the insurance white papers in September 1944 must be treated with caution. In some respects, the new proposals marked an improvement on the original Beveridge plan, but on several central points — notably that of subsistence level payments — the government had clearly retreated. Moreover, the delay in reaching decisions on what amounted to only six contentious points left a strong impression that ministers had spent 'a great part of the past year marking time'.[33] The new white papers attracted very little attention in the Commons, and it was generally recognised that no further action would be taken before an election. Churchill, indeed, had by now returned to the theme of his broadcast in March 1943 — that preliminaty preparation was acceptable, but no controversial measures would be carried before the end of the war. As Lord Beaverbrook told one correspondent: 'Collaboration between the two parties is growing increasingly difficult. As victory draws nearer, the urge for a return to party warfare grows stronger and the stresses and strains of the Coalition become harder to withstand.'[34] Nowhere was this more evident at the end of 1944 than in the troubled area of physical planning.

The arcane problems of town and country planning were brought to the political forefront in the early part of the war by Lord Reith, the energetic founder of the BBC, who had paved the way for the introduction of far-reaching reforms. But under direct pressure from Conservative back-benchers — who regarded talk of 'national

planning' as a euphemism for socialism — Reith had been removed
from office in 1942 and replaced by Churchill's associate, Lord
Portal, who pursued a line of 'masterly procrastination'. He, in
turn, was followed by another Tory loyalist, W. S. Morrison, head
of the new Ministry of Town and Country Planning.[35] Extensive
war damage in many parts of the country inevitably put pressure on
the government to declare its future plans for physical rebuilding.
But, by 1943, ministers were still unable to agree on how best to
respond to a series of weighty offiical reports published over
recent years. In September the Prime Minister was urged by some of
his advisers that decisions were now imperative, on the grounds
that the work of the new department was fundamental to all
physical reconstruction. The ministry, Churchill was told, 'must be
well ahead of its task and the necessary legislation for the purpose
must have been passed before hostilities cease'.[36] The great sticking
point was how to frame any such legislation. It was generally
agreed that effective planning of resources required increased state
control over the use of land. The degree to which development
rights might be acquired, however, and compensation paid to
dispossessed owners — the major themes of the 1942 Uthwatt
Report — occasioned both major technical difficulties and acute
political controversy. 'Shanks' Morrison was not personally prepared to endorse the Uthwatt Report in full, and spent much of his
early period in office attempting without success to find an acceptable alternative.[37] Hence, it was not until the summer of 1944 that
the government finally declared its hand, introducing a white paper
on land use and a limited bill concerned with rebuilding.

   Morrison's white paper, *The Control of Land Use*, accepted the
principle of using land in the best interests of the community. But it
ruled out the Uthwatt recommendation that the state should
acquire development rights in all undeveloped land. This conclusion had been reached only after considerable debate — mostly
along party lines — among senior ministers. 'We Conservatives',
noted one, 'got as far as coming to the conclusion ... that the
Uthwatt proposal was a bad one.'[38] Morrison himself was satisfied
that his scheme had side-stepped more radical possibilities. Whereas
the Uthwatt plan ultimately implied the disruption of traditional
patterns of land ownership, 'some such scheme as I propose', he
told one colleague, 'far from hastening land nationalisation, would
defer it at least for a generation.'[39] The controversial nature of the

white paper was such that it was decided to avoid any full-scale parliamentary discussion. Instead, attention was directed towards the new Town and Country bill, published simultaneously. This concerned itself only with the particular problem of how planning authorities were to acquire land necessary for reconstruction as a result of war damage. Again, though, there had been great difficulties in reaching the legislative stage. Shortly after the Normandy landings, Churchill had to spend much time and energy persuading the Minister of Economic Warfare, Lord Selborne, not to carry out his threat of resignation. The new bill, Selborne claimed, cut 'fundamentally at the rights of property and disregards equity between the State and the individual'; compromise was unacceptable, he added, because on this there existed 'a deep cleavage between the Conservative and Socialist view'.[40]

In the event Selborne, not wishing to embarrass the Prime Minister as the battle raged in northern France, reluctantly agreed to stay in office. But his reference to irreconcilable party differences was borne out when Morrison's bill reached the House of Commons. Although the second reading could hardly be opposed, given the urgency of events on the continent, Conservatives made it very clear that they viewed the measure as an invasion of property rights. Labour MPs conversely, attacked the bill for failing to adopt the principle of national planning, and Arthur Greenwood even called for its withdrawal. Indeed, only ten Labour back-benchers voted for the bill, with the great majority abstaining.[41] When the bill reached its final stages in the autumn, tempers flared. Tory MPs sought to move an amendment designed to weaken powers of compulsory purchase; this led to Labour accusations that the minister had been 'led astray by the 1922 Committee'.[42] The greatest problems, however, centred on the proposed compensation clauses: party feelings on this part of the bill ran so high that Churchill feared for the continuation of the coalition. Chuter Ede was told by William Whiteley, the Labour party's chief whip, that

the Tories went to the P.M. and threatened trouble. It looked as if the Govt. might collapse while the P.M. was in Russia. Naturally the P.M. thought this would have a very bad effect abroad. The Labour Ministers said, however, that they had given way enough on this measure. A serious crisis arose and had not yet been overcome.... Whiteley said he had strongly pressed on Attlee that if, before the end of the war, a break came, it had better come on the land issue than on any other.[43]

For a while there was a real danger that Tory MPs would vote *en masse* against the compensation clauses, especially after Sir John Anderson made a poor showing at the 1922 Committee.[44] James Stuart, the Chief Whip, told Churchill that 'the majority of Conservatives are in disagreement with the government', and that his best hope was for abstentions rather than outright hostile votes.[45] Faced with this situation, Morrison hastily devised various concessions, allowing the payment of increased levels of compensation and giving assurances that the scheme would be applicable only in certain well-defined cases. This was sufficient to do the trick: on an amendment to fix prices for compensation at levels which reflected increased land values since 1939, only fifty-six Tory backbenchers went into the opposition lobby, leaving the government with a comfortable majority. The crisis over town and country planning was thus averted, though neither side was left with any feeling of satisfaction. Speaking for Labour, Arthur Greenwood made it clear that the compensation concessions were the final straw, and that if any further modifications were made, the party would vote outright against the bill on the third reading. Any further concessions, concluded *The Times*, would 'break the Bill and the Coalition too'.[46]

Ultimately, the Town and Country Planning Bill was an accurate reflection of the nature of coalition politics as the war drew to a close. Ministers were much criticised for their long delay in acting. Many observers felt that any major initiatives should have been produced early in the war when partisan disagreement was least evident; by 1944 the atmosphere had changed to such an extent that concerted action on physical planning was no longer viable. The reality was that, having exhausted other policy options, the Prime Minister was by now left with contentious issues upon which agreement remained elusive. It came as no surprise that the King's Speech, opening the new parliamentary session at the end of 1944, promised no more than the introduction of a limited number of social and economic reforms as 'opportunity served'. The return to party politics had become so well established that open disagreement was also developing, for the first time since 1940, in the field of foreign policy. In particular, the controversial use of British forces in Greece provoked outrage on the left, and resulted in a strongly supported Labour amendment attacking the government for encouraging the suppression of 'those popular movements which have vigorously assisted in the defeat of the enemy'.[47] The end of the war, and of Churchill's government, was clearly in sight.

The final months of coalition in 1945 produced little of substance. Attlee, in his capacity as Lord President, became so frustrated with the drift of events on the home front that he wrote an uncharacteristically bitter — and lengthy — letter of complaint to the Prime Minister. This not only accused Churchill of wasting time in cabinet but also attacked Beaverbrook and Bracken for allegedly blocking measures agreed outside their remit in cabinet committees. 'Instead of assuming that agreement having been reached, there is a prima facie case for the proposal, it is assumed that it is due to the malevolent intrigues of socialist Ministers who have beguiled their weak Conservative colleagues.'[48] Clearly, Attlee would not have written in this vein had the parting of the ways not been far off. The Prime Minister, predictably, was furious. He eventually, and reluctantly, accepted his wife's advice not to send a blistering reply.[49] But there was no indication that the episode did anything to shift Churchill on policy matters. Indeed, during February 1945 he insisted on reaffirming the principle that no measures dealing with controversial subjects be introduced unless approved at the highest level. He also took the opportunity to complain that a particular bill, dealing with requisitioned land and war works, had been introduced into parliament without prior submission to the War Cabinet, even though it had gone through the normal channel of the Lord President's Committee.[50]

The likelihood of any far-reaching new initiatives was thus remote. In addition to measures aimed at easing the transition from war to peace, notably demobilisation, the coalition did, however, manage to carry two important items during its final weeks in office. The first of these was Hugh Dalton's Distribution of Industry Bill, which sought to introduce greater government powers over the post-war control of industrial location. This reform had met with stern opposition in cabinet, primarily form Oliver Lyttelton and Sir Andrew Duncan who — as Dalton put it — 'sit side by side just opposite me, looking like a pair of very sinister capitalists, whispering to one another and suspecting socialism everywhere'.[51] Press commentators attached only limited importance to the new legislation. *The Economist*, for example, argued that, in essence, the measure was the old special areas legislation writ large, and as

such was still a long way from 'regulating the nation-wide
distribution of industry'.[52] Moreover, although the bill was
hurriedly passed into law at Dalton's insistence, there was .no
guarantee that it would be taken up by a future Churchill
administration as Labour ministers intended. Tory industrialists,
while agreeing not to divide the coalition at this late stage, did, in
fact, call for the rejection of the bill on the grounds that it
threatened private enterprise.[53] The second major item of legislation, the introduction of family allowances, had a wider measure
of cross-party support, though Conservative opinion was receptive
only after the Treasury set the level of allowances lower than
initially proposed in the Beveridge Report.[54] Once again, the Prime
Minister proved an uncertain friend of reform, having to be dis-
suaded by Lord Woolton from dropping the bill when agreement
proved difficult to reach on the issue of duplication of benefit.[55].

To set against these two reforms, there were several areas of
policy — notably in the economic and industrial field — where
cabinet discussions produced stalemate early in 1945. The future
ownership and control of industry remained particularly contentious. Tory ministers on the Reconstruction Committee, led by Rab
Butler, refused to countenance the reorganisation of the electricity
industry into a public corporation. Butler told Oliver Lyttelton that
he objected 'violently' to a measure that would treat private
investors in the electrical companies unfairly and remove all 'responsibility and incentive'.[56] The pattern was repeated when
Morrison pressed the Labour case for nationalisation in other
major industries. And the revival of old political antagonisms was
vividly illustrated by renewed discussion of revising the 1927 Trade
Disputes Act. Having accepted Churchill's injunction earlier in the
war that this topic could threaten national unity, the TUC was
hopeful of a more sympathetic hearing with victory so clearly in
sight. Instead, the Prime Minister reiterated that any amendment
was out of the question before a general election. As *The Economist*
observed: 'Both sides regard it as a symbol — one of victory for the
Conservatives and one of defeat for Labour . . . . The Conservatives
would never voluntarily agree to amend the Act, and such a motion
would be overwhelmingly defeated in the House of Commons, thus
forcing the withdrawal of Labour Ministers.'[57]

At the same time, cross-party agreement about medical reform
was breaking down. In March 1945 Lord Woolton reported to

Churchill that negotiations with the various interested parties had produced the outline of fresh plans for a national health service, different in certain important respects from the 1944 white paper.[58] In the Commons, however, the Minister of Health proved highly elusive when questioned about his negotiations. From the Labour benches Edith Summerskill, a leading light in the Socialist Medical Association, bitterly denounced Willink for refusing to confirm that he intended to drop the idea of introducing a salaried medical service in the new health centres. The minister's assurances that any changes to the white paper were cosmetic did not go down well: Labour speakers suspected a repeat of the climb-down to medical opinion seen in setting up the 1911 insurance scheme, and made it clear that a future Labour government would not be bound by possible changes to the 1944 plan.[59] The position of stalemate reached by the final months of the war was also reflected in the government's white paper on local government, published at the beginning of 1945. The war had clearly demonstrated that many local authorities were too small to deal with the increased burdens placed upon them, for example in the area of health, and that the rating system was unlikely to be productive enough to provide authorities with adequate resources in the future. The white paper, however, consciously avoided these controversial themes. In spite of the fact that reform of the social services would ultimately depend on the efficiency of local government, the government would go on further than promising to extend existing schemes for revising local boundaries and functions.[60]

'The coalition', observed *The Economist* in March 1945, 'is getting more and more threadbare.... The delay in completing social insurance plans; the failure to reach agreement on land values, without which no town planning is possible; the housing muddle; the coal calamity — these are the fruits of coalition in domestic affairs.'[61] In these circumstances, and with personal relations inside the War Cabinet deteriorating, party leaders began preparing the ground for the inevitable electoral contest ahead. The Prime Minister, speaking to the Conservative party conference about future priorities, attacked easy promises of a 'cheap-jack Utopia', and described nationalisation as a system 'borrowed from foreign lands and alien minds' — a theme he was to pursue in the subsequent campaign.[62] He also made an unexpected appeal to men of 'every party and no party' to join him in a re-formed national administration; an appeal that displeased Tory delegates anxious to resume the party fight. In practice, Churchill's appeal smacked of an attempt to secure party advantage: either by placing the onus for leaving the coalition on Labour ministers or by embarrassing those such as Bevin still rumoured to favour continued co-operation. Bevin, as we have seen, had long ago rejected any such possibility, and his response was to make the sharpest public attack on the Tory record by any Labour minister since 1940. The Conservatives, he claimed, were already resorting to dirty tricks because they were afraid to face the electorate on their policies alone. 'The thing that stung the P.M. most', Bevin claimed afterwards, was the declaration 'that this was not a one man Govt. or a one man war.'[63] Government ministers were to remain in office for another six weeks yet, but the implications of this clash were obvious: the odour of dissolution was in the air.

After the news of Germany's final surrender and Britain's victory celebrations in early May, attention at Westminster soon turned to one pressing question — when would a general election be called? Most Conservatives favoured a contest in June, assuming thereby that this would allow the party to capitalise on Churchill's popularity as war leader. Thinking along similar lines about the 'Churchill factor', many Labour supporters favoured October; this could be publicly justified in terms of allowing the majority of servicemen to return home and enabling the electoral register to be updated fully. In view of the sharp exchanges between leading ministers over recent months, and, indeed, taking into account the whole pattern of political development since 1943, doubt must be cast on the seriousness of discussions that took place after V-E Day. On 11 May Churchill told Labour ministers he had not yet made up his mind about an election, and the following week he offered his colleagues a choice: either an extension of the government until the end of the Pacific War, or else an immediate election. Some Labour leaders believed that continued co-operation might serve a dual purpose: facilitating the settlement of international problems left by the war, but at the same time delaying an election and so diminishing Churchill's reputation. For this reason, Attlee inserted into the text of the Prime Minister's offer the proviso that in the interim the government would do its best to act upon the social insurance and employment white papers. But when the NEC formally considered the idea, Herbert Morrison took the lead in arguing that the party conference, now gathering at Blackpool, would never agree to extend the coalition. The parliamentary party was reported to be of like mind. On 21 May Labour's conference, accordingly, took the decisive step in breaking up the government, voting by an overwhelming majority not to take up Churchill's offer of further co-operation.[64]

It would be misleading, however, to think that the ending of the coalition pointed to any serious split between Labour leaders and the rank-and-file. Attlee and Bevin did not, as some claim, have to be hauled out of coalition 'by the scruffs of their necks'. Their main anxiety was simply about the tactical question of when an election should be called. As we have seen, Labour ministers had consistently embraced the return to party politics, and had no intention of going back on the decision to fight as an independent force. The point at issue was the tricky one of at what time an electoral contest would best suit Labour prospects, given the widely accepted view that Churchill would be unbeatable. The Prime Minister, it might be surmised, had made his offer to continue the coalition in the knowledge that it was unlikely to be accepted. His main concern by May 1945, like his Labour counterparts, was with maximising chances of electoral success, for if his offer were turned down, then the way would lie open for a contest with images of Britain's glorious victory still fresh in the mind. When news came through from Blackpool that continuing until the end of the Pacific War was unacceptable to conference delegates, Churchill and his senior advisers were satisfied that they had won what amounted to the first round of the election campaign, placing the onus on Labour for breaking up the government and leaving them open to the charge of preferring faction to unity at a time when international dangers still remained acute.[65] Two days later, on 23 May, the Prime Minister drove to Buckingham Palace and tendered his resignation. Churchill's wartime coalition was over; the 1945 election had begun.

Notes

1 Addison, *Road to 1945*, p. 252.
2 Interview with the Prime Minister, 26 March 1943 — Taylor (ed.), *Off the Record*, p. 346.

3 *Dalton Diary*, 26 March, 7 April and 24 May 1943, pp. 571, 576 and 595–6; interview with Morrison, 28 May 1943 — Taylor, op. cit., pp. 360–1; *Channon Diary*, 26 March 1943, pp. 353–4.

4 Interview with Sinclair, 25 March 1943 — Taylor, op, cit., p. 340.

5 *Dalton Diary*, 6 September 1943, pp. 632–3.

6 *Chuter Ede Diary*, 15 October 1943, p. 147.

7 *Daily Mail*, 3 October 1943. At a recent meeting of the Conservative party Central Council, the outspoken back-bencher Herbert Williams had attacked the composition of the government on the grounds that no senior Tories were responsible for economic policy now that Kingsley Wood had gone. 'This', reported Rab Butler, 'had greatly excited the Conference, who were very nervous of Herbert Morrison' — *Chuter Ede Diary*, 7 October 1943, p. 147.

8 Beaverbrook memo to Churchill, 4 February 1944, cited in Taylor, *Beaverbrook*, pp. 553–4.

9 *Dalton Diary*, 27 April 1944, pp. 739–40.

10 Bevin to Attlee, 18 May 1944, cited in Bullock, *Ernest Bevin*, p. 315.

11 Middlemas, *Power, Competition and the State*, esp. pp. 90–2.

12 Booth, ' "Keynesian Revolution" in economic policy-making', *Economic History Review*, XXXVI, 1, 1983, pp. 103–23; G. C. Peden, 'Sir Richard Hopkins and the "Keynesian Revolution" in employment policy 1929–45', ibid., 2, 1983, pp. 281–96.

13 Addison, op. cit., pp. 243–4; Butler, *Art of the Possible*, p. 125.

14 *Employmemt policy*, Cmd, 6527, 1944. See also Harris, *William Beveridge*, pp. 424–48.

15 Oliver Lyttelton, *Seven Points of Conservative Policy*, London, 1944.

16 R. Macleod, 'The development of full employment policy 1938–1945', unpublished D.Phil thesis, University of Oxford, 1978, Chapter 3.

17 Hugh Molson, 'The Tory Reform Committee', *New English Review*, July 1945, pp. 247–8; NUCUA, Central Committee on Post-War Reconstruction, *Work: the Future of Industry*, interim report by the sub-committee on industry, 1944.

18 Williams — V. 401 H. C. Deb., 5s., c. 533, 23 June 1944. See also the reaction of the Tory industrialist Arnold Gridley — ibid., cc. 435–43, 22 June 1944.

19 Ibid., c. 411.

20 M. Kemp, 'The left and the debate over Labour party policy, 1943–50', unpublished Ph.D. thesis, University of Cambridge, 1985, pp. 88–97.

21 V. 401 H. C. Deb., 5s., cc. 363–5, 22 June 1944.

22 Lee, *The Churchill Coalition*, pp. 115–16 and 136–7. It has also been shown that although both major industrialists and trade unionists agreed with the objective of full employment, neither side was prepared to give up previously held positions in order to achieve the agreed aim — R. Macleod, 'The promise of full employment', in H. L. Smith (ed.), *War and Social Change: British Society in the Second World War*, Manchester, 1986, pp. 92–3.

23 S. Brooke, 'Revisionists and fundamentalists: the Labour party and

economic policy during the Second World War', *The Historical Journal*, 1, 1989, pp. 157–75. See also Stephen Brooke's *Labour's War*, Oxford, forthcoming.

24 Reconstruction Committee minutes, 8 May 1944, PRO CAB 87/5.

25 Harris, *Attlee*, 324–5. See also *Dalton Diary*, 22 August 1944, pp. 779–80, where in a prophetic assessment about the ending of coalition, Attlee stated that 'after the German surrender we shall all be too busy for a little while to think about this, but that a moment will come when the P.M. will say to him that he hopes, having gone through the war in Europe together, we can go on together through a general election on an agreed programme. Attlee would then reply that he is afraid that this is impossible and that, when the general election comes — and we should do nothing to hasten it — we must offer the country the choice between two alternative programmes.'

26 Moran, *Struggle for Survival*, 20 September 1944, p. 205.

27 Prime Minister to Randolph Churchill, 23 November 1944, cited in Gilbert, *Road to Victory*, p. 1072. See also *Amery Diary*, 4 September 1944, p. 998, which suggests from Churchill's conversations with Eden that he was clearly thinking about an election to follow on immediatley from Germany's surrender.

28 *The Economist*, 12 August 1944.

29 Churchill to Anderson, 5 May 1944; Lord Cherwell minute to Churchill (summarising Anderson's response), PRO PREM 4 16/4.

30 Woolton to Churchill, 27 June 1944, PREM 4 89/5.

31 Anderson minute to Churchill, 27 June 1944, PREM 4 89/5. On the likely course of future developments under a post-war Churchill administration, see 'post-war Financial Commitments', memorandum by the Chancellor of the Exchequer, 28 June 1944, CAB 66/52.

32 P. L. Rowan minute to Churchill, 4 July 1944, PREM 4 89/5; War Cabinet minutes, 4 July 1944, CAB 65/43.

33 *The Times*, 3 October 1944.

34 Beaverbrook to A. A. Berle, 31 August 1944, cited in Taylor, op. cit., p. 560.

35 Addison, op. cit., pp. 174–8; W. Ashworth, *The Genesis of Modern British Town Planning*, London, 1954, pp. 224–37.

36 J. H. Peck minute to Churchill 29 September 1943, PREM 4 92/9.

37 Morrison to Woolton, 17 November 1943, copy in Beaverbrook papers, HLRO, D/181.

38 D. Maxwell Fyfe, *Political Advanture: the Memoris of the Earl of Kilmuir*, London, 1964, p. 75.

39 Morrison to Beaverbrook, 19 April 1944, Beaverbrook papers, D/181.

40 Selborne to Churchill, 24 May 1944; Cranborne to Selborne, 18 June 1944: 3rd Earl Selborne papers, Bodleian Library, Oxford, MS. Eng. Hist. c. 981, ff. 6–8.

41 V. 401 H. C. Deb., 5s., cc. 1747–1854, 11–12 July 1944.

42 H. Kopsch, 'Conservative party and social policy', pp. 346–51.

43 *Chuter Ede Diary*, 10 October 1944, p. 191.

44 *Dalton Diary*, 22–23 October 1944, pp. 796–7: '[Beaverbrook] says

that Anderson made a complete mess of it when he met the 1922
Committee . . . . Herbert Williams spoke to him very roughly and
rudely at the meeting, and asked him who he thought he was and how
he managed to get where he was. Anderson had made the great mistake
of thumping the table at these people and they wouldn't stand it.'

45 Stuart minute to Churchill, 23 October 1944, PREM 4 92/8.
46 *The Times*, 25 October 1944.
47 On the whole Greek debate, see Bullock, op. cit., pp. 340–7.
48 Attlee to Churchill, cited in Harris, op. cit., pp. 241–3.
49 *Colville Diary*, 20–21 January 1945, pp. 554–5.
50 War Cabinet minutes, 22 February 1945, PRO CAB 65/45; Sir
    Edward Bridges memo to Churchill, 22 February 1945, PRO PREM 4
    6/5.
51 *Dalton Diary*, 31 October 1944, p. 802. On this measure, see also
    Pimlott, *Hugh Dalton*, pp. 400–7.
52 *The Economist*, 3 March 1945.
53 V. 409 H. C. Deb., 5s., cc. 868–75, 21 March 1945.
54 The fullest treatment of this issue remains J. MacNicol, *The Movement
    for Family Allowances 1918–1945*, London, 1980.
55 Note by Lord Woolton, n.d. (1945), Beaverbrook papers, D/147.
56 Butler to Lyttelton, 6 February 1945, Butler papers, G17, f. 96;
    Reconstruction Committee minutes, 9 April 1945, PRO CAB 87/10.
57 *The Economist*, 24 March 1945.
58 Woolton to Churchill, 26 March 1945, PRO PREM 4 36/3; Willink,
    'As I Remember', pp. 81–2.
59 E.g. V. 410 H. C. Deb., 5s., cc. 1096–1100, 26 April 1945.
60 *Local Government in England and Wales during the Period of
    Reconstruction*, Cmd. 6579, 1945.
61 *The Economist*, 24 March 1945.
62 *The Times*, 16 March 1945, for the full text of Churchill's speech.
63 Bullock, op. cit., pp. 366–70; *Chuter Ede Diary*, 11 April 1945, pp.
    212–13. Bevin also told Dalton: 'He's all right as a National leader,
    but when he turns into the leader of the Tory Party, you can't trust him
    an inch. He just becomes a crook' — *Dalton Diary*, 19 April 1945,
    p. 852.
64 Bullock, op. cit., pp. 375–7; Harris, op. cit., pp. 248–51.
65 *Colville Diary*, 21–23 May 1945, pp. 601–2.

8

Victory

Why did the Labour party sweep to power at the 1945 election? And what was the significance of the election in a longer term historical perspective? This chapter sets out to re-examine the period between the ending of Churchill's coalition and the announcement of Labour's landslide victory in late July. Two major themes have tended to dominate the historiography of the general election. In the first place, the result has been attributed primarily to Labour's improved wartime performance, notably because of its share in government since 1940. Secondly, historians have tended to play down differences between the main participants, arguing that the election confirmed the emergence of consensus politics during the war. In this line of thinking, the lasting importance of 1945 was that it opened up an era of much closer party co-operation in British politics, centring on agreement on the fundamentals of a welfare state and mixed economy. Both these general lines of thinking will be challenged here. On the first point, though the 1945 result must, of course, be set against the back-ground of Labour's increased wartime popularity, a complementary and neglected point needs to be brought out — that the Prime Minister bore a large burden of personal responsibility for the poor performance of the Tory party. If the 'people's war' had made a Labour victory certain by the time of Germany's surrender, then Churchill, it will be argued, made matters worse by his disastrous handling of the election campaign. More important, it will be shown that most contemporaries did not regard the election as the harbinger of a new consensus. Conversely, it was a campaign marked by profound and often bitterly expressed disagreements. And in spite of the artificial posturing that characterises all elections, the divisions on the issue of public versus private provision, above all, reflected a recognition that the outcome would be vital in determining the shape of post-war society. The 1945 election — the campaign, the major issues, the result — was to be crucial in the forging of Britain's post-war settlement.

After his resignation as head of the coalition on 23 May, Churchill returned later the same day to Buckingham Palace, where the King invited him to form a temporary administration pending the election. Parliament was to be dissolved in mid-June, leaving three weeks before polling day on 5 July; in order to allow service votes from around the world to be counted, however, the result would not be known until the end of the month. In the meantime the Prime Minister, deprived of Labour support, set about devising a new team, his task complicated by the customary awkwardness of Beaverbrook and Bracken. Once their needs had been met, Churchill was in a position to announce the full list of what became known as the 'caretaker' government. This short-lived administration, in office for only a matters of weeks, has generally been regarded as a minor interlude, devoid of any real political significance. 'The new government', claims Paul Addison, 'had the air of a light-hearted revue by Noel Coward', reflected, for example, in Brendan Bracken's eventual appointment as First Lord of the Admiralty.[1] But for many contemporaries in politics the caretaker government was not simply a stop-gap; rather, it was a good guide to the probable shape of the Tory administration that most commentators still expected to result from the forthcoming election. As Lord Winterton later remarked: 'No doubt, if the Conservatives had won the election, it would have continued much as it was in composition.'[2] What, then, did the composition of the new government suggest about post-war politics and policy-making?

There would, it goes without saying, have been some changes among the caretaker office-holders in the event of a Churchill victory in 1945. If only for tactical reasons, the Prime Minister wanted to convey the impression that he was primarily filling posts 'deserted' by Labour ministers. But, on the whole, the personnal of the new government represented the sum of talent available to any Conservative administration at the end of the war, notwithstanding the inclusion of a few National Liberals and non-party functionaries. And in this context, the sixteen-strong cabinet promised little in the way of an innovative, progressive domestic policy in the post-war period. Economic policy would clearly be dominated by the cautious Chancellor, John Anderson, and to a lesser extent by Oliver Lyttelton, who combined the posts of Trade and Production. On social policy questions, co-ordination was to be provided by Lord Woolton, who continued with his reconstruction duties as Lord President of the Council. Those most readily identified with social reform, however, were not promoted in any systematic way. Rab Butler's skills of conciliation, so evident in the framing of the 1944 Education Act, were now to be deployed at the Ministry of Labour, a post which, incidentally, kept him apart from Woolton, with whom he had increasingly differed over reconstruction.[3] Harold Macmillan entered the cabinet for the first time, but as Air Minister, and the Tory Reformers had to settle for a few junior ministerial posts. In the meantime, key domestic posts such as National Insurance and Education were entrusted to the likes of Hore-Belisha and Richard Law, the latter allegedly promoted in order to remove him from Beaverbrook's sphere of influence.[4] In completing his team, Churchill even found it necessary to recall some of the 'old gang', including, for example, Viscount Simon, who became Lord Chancellor. Overall, far from giving a forward-looking impression, the government appeared as something of a throwback to the past. Family connections, Oliver Lyttelton noted, were still valuable in the Tory party, with the new government containing two sons of Prime Ministers, one grandson of a Prime Minister and several others related to former ministers.[5]

The chief task of the caretaker administration was, of course, simply to provide stability and authority in the run-up to the July election. Such indications as there were from cabinet discussions about future policy, however, suggest that in the aftermath of coalition, Conservatives did not regard themselves as being bound by wartime proposals. The details of economic policy, to take one important example, remained to be spelt out openly during the election campaign, but this did not prevent sharp exchanges when the House of Commons reassembled, both over the fate of wartime controls and the future ownership of industry. On 29 May the Minister of Fuel and Power, Gwilym Lloyd George, announced on behalf of the government that 'the working, treatment and disposal of coal should continue to be conducted by private enterprise, provided these are planned in accordance with the national need...'. Emphasis in the minister's statement on private enterprise had been insisted upon by the Conservative chairman, Ralph Assheton; he, in turn, had been pressurised by party activists who were reluctant to accept the proposal for a new central authority charged with the task of increasing coal production.[6] Lloyd George's declaration, which foreshadowed legislation that was projected for introduction in the early stages of a new parliament, was bitterly attacked on the Labour benches. The Conservatives were relying primarily, it was argued, on the voluntary amalgamation of pits where necessary to promote efficiency. In Labour eyes, this was a discredited pre-war solution. The policy, moreover, was a deliberate attempt to forestall the only mechanism which Labour felt could impove this and other sectors of the economy — nationalisation. Indeed, for many on the left, coal policy was only one ominous sign of the economic intentions of a future Churchill government; others included relaxation over the control of capital issues, reducing the period for extending emergency powers from two years to six months and attempts to emasculate Dalton's Distribution of Industry Bill.[7]

The approach of the caretaker cabinet to social questions also illustrated how sharply divergent interpretations could now be given to agreed coalition commitments. Beveridge's scheme for social security was one which both parties were to present to the electorate, but the Prime Minister's sullen attitude suggested he had not given up attempts to tailor the 1944 white papers more in accordance with Tory preferences. In inviting Hore-Belisha to become Minister of National Insurance, Churchill remarked that he 'attached great importance to this office, particularly from an electoral point of view. The scheme wanted humanising and purging of its present traces of socialism.'[8] On the planning questions that had beset the later stages of the coalition, caretaker ministers decided that priority must be given to tackling the problem of immediate housing shortages. When it came to the wider issues of physical planning, compensation and betterment, Conservatives remained conspicuously silent. And knowledge of cabinet discussions about medical reform would also have confirmed the suspicions of those alarmed by Willink's modification of the 1944 health service scheme. The Minister of Health now persuaded his colleagues to accept a revised plan, one he said differing from its predecessor in its determination to protect more fully 'freedom of choice for the patient, professional freedom for the doctors and . . . the autonomy of the voluntary hospitals'.[9] In mid-June approval was given for the preparation of draft legislation along these lines, but at the last moment Churchill decided that any announcement about the new proposals would provide ammunition for the opposition to claim that coalition promises were being betrayed. 'Infinite regress', which had characterised medical reform for much of the war, remained the order of the day. Willink was left to lament:

I had prepared a Health Service scheme more agreeable to Conservatives and to the medical profession than that of February 1944: I had obtained Cabinet approval for it: I had all arrangements made for a speech describing it: at the last minute the Prime Minister decided that it would lose rather than gain votes in the following General Election. My White Paper, though printed, was never published, and I had to cancel the arrangements for my speech, because — as the Prime Minister himself told me — Beaverbrook thought it inexpedient.[10]

Lord Beaverbrook certainly loomed large in the 1945 election campaign. The campaign proper was started by the Prime Minister on 4 June, delivering the first of a series of radio broadcasts allocated to each party. Churchill's fierce and sustained polemic against his labour opponents — including the notorious claim that the introduction of socialism in Britain would require 'some form of Gestapo' — demonstrated, above all else, his own lack of any positive vision for the future. Attlee refused to be provoked in replying for Labour, though he did make the unfounded accusation that Beaverbrook was behind the ferocity of the language. Churchill, in fact, had worked at length on the speech himself, ignoring his wife's advice to omit any reference to the Gestapo, which, she pointed out, was extremely tasteless at a time when the full extent of Nazi atrocities was becoming known.[11] In private, some Labour partisans were delighted with Prime Minister's speech. One back-bencher claimed that it had 'given us 50 seats'. Press commentators on the whole agreed that Churchill had been unnecessarily provocative in attacking those who until recently had been loyal colleagues. Mass-Observation also found from its surveys of public opinion that the speech had caused great disillusionment, compounding the aggravation of an electorate already suffering from war weariness.[12] Whatever the electoral consequences of the 'Gestapo speech', it certainly set the tone for the month-long campaign the followed. Herbert Morrison for the Labour party, in a sly reference to Churchill's bathing habits, attacked Beaverbrook and Bracken as the 'Companions of the Bath', the culprits who had forced an unwanted election; the *Daily Express* responded by claiming that Labour had run away from its duty to see through the war in the Far East.[13] The conduct of the campaign, far from being consensual, soon developed into one of the bitterest in living memory.

Bickering over who was responsible for calling the election continued to occupy the front pages for nearly two weeks. When this argument did subside, it was replaced by a personal clash between two of the major coalition antagonists, Beaverbrook and Bevin. 'Lord Beaverbrook is apparently the guiding spirit of the Conservative campaign', wrote *The Economist*. 'In the last few days he has been giving his audiences the impression that if it were not for Mr Bevin's labour controls, there would be unlimited housing, food and clothing by tomorrow morning.... Mr Bevin, on his side, has also been hitting hard, and without any respect for persons.'[14] By this stage, there were signs that the Conservative campaign lacked any real central theme or unity. In the second of his broadcast speeches, the Prime Minister took the advice of his daughter by reviving discussion of his four year plan, but newspaper commentators remained sceptical of the idea that the Tories had suddenly become fired with enthusiasm for social reform.[15] The only clear direction, in consequence, was that provided by the truculence of Beaverbrook and Bracken, but their outspoken interventions on future economic policy showed clear signs of being counter-productive. In North Paddington — where Bracken was to lose his seat — scaremongering speeches aroused such passions that a fire bomb exploded at the Tory party headquarters, and towards the end of a campaign Bracken's car window was broken as he left a meeting.[16]

In comparison with the Conservative party, the Labour campaign was both carefully orchestrated and purposefully conducted. With Morrison providing a firm guiding hand as chairman of the campaign committee, the Labour movement showed a rare degree of unanimity in espousing the party's manifesto. The Labour left, having failed to move party leaders towards more radical policies during the life of the coalition, now had little choice but to throw their whole weight behind the official campaign. The likes of Bevan and Shinwell could also satisfy themselves that there would be no repeat of the 1931 'betrayal', and that, whatever their differences on individual points, the party programme did at least represent an important first step toward socialism.[17] By mid-June some observers sensed the potential importance of the way the campaign was unfolding. John Colville, the Prime Minister's secretary, confided in his diary that Beaverbrook and Bracken were firing 'vast salvos which mostly . . . miss their mark. Labour propaganda is a great deal better and is launched on a rising market. Without Winston's personal prestige the Tories would not have a chance.'[18]

The Prime Minister, in fact, was himself beginning to sense which way the wind was blowing. On 22 June he confided to his doctor that 'I am worried about this damned election. I have no message for them now.'[19] Aside from confirming the bankruptcy of Conservative policy, this revelation also pointed to a growing sense of desperation on Churchill's part. Herein lies part of the explanation for his role in prolonging, until the very end of the campaign, the so-called 'Laski episode'. Professor Laski, at the time acting as chairman of the Labour party, had spent much of the war denouncing what he saw as Attlee's tame and ineffective leadership. After the Labour leader had accepted Churchill's invitation to join him in attending the forthcoming Potsdam conference, Laski claimed that Attlee's presence could not bind the party to any specific foreign policy commitments. The Beaverbrook press quickly picked up on this, alleging that the chairman of the NEC was dictating terms to the Parliamentary Labour Party, and that this, in turn, was a threat to the sovereignty of parliament. With encouragement from Downing Street, many Conservatives now launched a familiar style 'red scare' — with some barely concealed anti-Semitic overtones — to the effect that Laski represented a threat to the British party system.[20] But the impact of the campaign was negligible. Hugh Dalton noted that the Laski episode was unlikely to lose Labour many votes, and Mass-Observation confirmed that the 'Churchill–Attlee–Laski incident isn't taken very seriously because people realise that it is just an election stunt to catch votes.'[21] The significance of the whole affair was rather twofold: it highlighted once more the defensiveness and lack of serious content in the Conservative programme in 1945; and it ensured that the campaign ended, just as it had begun, on a note of bitterness.

The bitterness of the campaign made it increasingly difficult to discern exactly what was at stake in 1945. With the two main parties having worked together for five years, and now inevitably addressing many of the same themes, political commentators found it easy to play up the element of bipartisanship in Conservative and Labour policy. This was particularly true in the case of those national newspapers, notably *The Times*, that had battled against the odds to push the Tory party towards embracing progressive welfare reform. Clearly, on foreign policy, the experience of fighting to defeat Nazi Germany had resulted in the emergence of similar priorities, though, for many on the Labour left, the prospect of a distinctive 'socialist foreign policy' remained a banner around which to unite.[22] The Conservatives, moreover, seeking to exploit Churchill's experience on the world stage when compared with Attlee, placed an altogether greater emphasis on overseas policy in their campaign. 'Mr Churchill', wrote the historians of the pioneering Nuffield election study, 'was thinking in terms of the dangers that still lay ahead both in the Japanese War and in post-war Europe. The Labour Party was thinking in terms of victory won and the deserts of those who had won it.'[23] Nor, on the latter theme of domestic policy, does a close scrutiny of party policies suggest any genuine meeting of minds.

Churchill's intentions for the Beveridge scheme have already been noted. By contrast, Labour's manifesto commitment was to a more far-reaching national insurance scheme based upon reinstating the principle of subsistence level payments. Indeed, it was along such lines that Attlee's government first introduced the scheme in office, though it was soon overtaken by unforeseen financial pressures.[24] Housing and town planning was an area of more obvious partisan disagreement. Whereas Labour committed itself to the Uthwatt Report as the best means of ensuring effective long-term planning of the physical environment, Conservative election literature – in line with the policy of the caretaker government — avoided altogether the wider issues at stake.[25] In addition, medical reform provided a clear illustration of how the parties could make similar election commitments while meaning in practice very different things. Labour candidates throughout the campaign emphasised their belief that a free and comprehensive health service was a central component of any new welfare system. The Tory manifesto, however, threw its weight behind the essence of Willink's scheme, which, by playing up the need for 'thriving voluntary hospitals' and the importance of private practice, clearly fell short of the 1944 white paper.[26] This approach suggested less a wholesale extension of state welfare, a move towards the New Jerusalem, but rather a gradual extension of pre-war services, allowing private provision to remain paramount. Lord Woolton, having tried to reconcile differences on this issue as Minister of Reconstruction, later commented on his certainty that the working out of the new health service 'would be very different under a Conservative government from what it would be under a socialist Government'.[27]

In the area of economic and industrial policy, party divisions were both more profound and more publicly visible. Indeed, Attlee had told Churchill that a breakup of the coalition was unavoidable because it was on 'the reconstruction of the economic life of the country that Party differences are most acute'.[28] Labour's campaign committee agreed early on, in the spring of 1945, that the central election issue should be 'the basic, clear cut one of Public versus Private Enterprise'. Hence the Party's manifesto, *Let Us Face the Future*, had as its core the detailed policies hammered out by Labour economists during the war, combining physical control socialist planning with Keynesian-style demand management. Labour was now proposing, among other things, a wide and growing field for public expenditure, the maintenance of purchasing power and the establishment of a National Investment Board to establish priorities in the use of capital goods, and the nationalisation of a whole range of key industries.[29] The Conservative approach, by contrast, was to stress that private enterprise was the 'life-blood' of the industrial system; state intervention should, therefore, be contemplated only where absolutely necessary. On these grounds, nationalisation was dismissed as a dangerous and alien experiment, and the early abolition of wartime economic controls was regarded as essential. The maintenance of high levels of employment, it was argued, could be achieved only by the restoration of Britain's depleted export trade, 'sound' financial methods and the progressive reduction of onerous levels of wartime taxation.[30]

This is not to suggest that electors in 1945 were being offered a straight choice between 'socialism' and 'free enterprise'. But if, as some historians have subsequently claimed, both sides accepted

that in practice they would have to operate within a mixed economy — combining public and private sectors — then both the
form and ultimate purpose of such an economy had yet to be determined, and remained the subject of intense disagreement. Because
of its various traditions and internal tensions, the Labour party's
objectives remained difficult to define with precision. In so far
as left and right were agreed on future strategy, it was to work
towards the creation of a 'Socialist Commonwealth' — itself an
ill-defined concept — though in the short term all could unite
behind the idea of a 'people's peace'; a post-war settlement that
would serve the interests of working people instead of the 'Czars
of Big Business'. Whatever the ambiguities of Labour's programme, however, its whole thrust was very different from that on offer
in the Conservative campaign. Sir John Anderson, Churchill's chief
spokesman on economic matters during the campaign, continued
to be purposefully vague on the question of how full employment
would be achieved, in spite of the pledge made in the 1944 white
paper. He would not commit himself, for example, on the thorny
subject of tackling fluctuations in spending, on whether priorities
would be imposed in the use of capital goods or how, as Chancellor, he would set about modernising industries shown to be
inefficient in the hands of pre-war owners. In spite of pressure
from Tory Reformers and the party Sub-Committee on Industry,
the Conservative party, on the whole, remained wedded to pre-
1939 methods of dealing with the economy. This, in turn, had
wider ramifications. Tory election literature made much of the
claim that 'unless a sound and flourishing economy can be established, there is no possibility of full employment, improved conditions or the carrying out of plans for social betterment.'[31] The
implications of this for post-war domestic policy were clear: unless
a future Churchill government succeeded in restoring a flourishing
private enterprise economy, welfare reform would have to wait.

The campaign as fought by rival candidates in various parts of
the country reinforces this view of the election. Most Conservatives
could not resist playing up the personal qualities of the Prime
Minister, casting doubt on the ability of Attlee to play any sort of
leading role on the international stage. Labour candidates, on the
other hand, deliberately chose to pin their hopes on discussion of
welfare questions and the need for an efficient, planned economy.
On the Conservative side, Tory Reformers struck a progressive

note in urging the introduction of Keynesian-type fiscal measures.[32] But such calls were exceptional. The majority of Conservatives came out instead as unashamed advocates of free enterprise capitalism, calling for the swift removal of economic controls and reiterating that 'without national prosperity any form of what is known as "social security" is impracticable'.[33] Mass-Observation found from its detailed study of constituencies in London that the electorate came to see the most fundamental issue as that of 'socialisation versus private enterprise', with the most acrid arguments usually centring on this theme. Whereas large numbers of Labour candidates started their election addresses with the need to control and plan the economy as it had been in wartime, many Conservatives were both confused and defensive about economic issues. When asked how his party would achieve full employment, the Tory candidate in Reading could reply only that, if necessary, 'we shall build battleships, tow them out to sea, sink them, and come back and build some more'.[34] Here, then, was what the 1945 campaign was really about: a greatly enhanced role for the state, in both the economy and society more generally, was by no means inevitable when the nation went to the polls. 'The question electors have to decide', concluded one Laour candidate on the eve of polling day, 'is whether this country, in peace as in war, is to be governed on the principle that public welfare must come before private interest'.[35]

By the time the campaigning came to end, politicians and press commentators were still divided about the most likely outcome. Forecasts about the probable result were inevitably coloured by perceptions of Churchill's unassailable reputation as war leader, and by the size of the existing Tory majority, standing at over 200 parliamentary seats. Against this background, most Conservatives remained confident of victory, and Central Office — basing its figures on reports from party agents — was originally thinking in terms of maintaining a three-figure majority.[36] Lord Winterton later reflected that he spoke to only two senior party figures who predicted defeat; one of them was the Duke of Devonshire, who had experienced the mood of the electorate first hand in the West Derbyshire by-election.[37] Labour leaders were equally reticent about predicting Churchill's demise. Attlee and Morrison thought the best that could be hoped for was to reduce the Tory majority to about forty seats; Hugh Dalton was even more pessimistic, though he later claimed otherwise in his memoirs.[38] To set against this, newspaper opinion was generally agreed that Labour had come out better from campaign exchanges, and opinion poll evidence still showed Labour in the lead, though with the Tories closing the gap.[39] As a recent innovation, however, the polls were not regarded as accurate indicators, and recent by-elections seemed equally difficult to interpret. Although the Tories had suffered a crushing defeat at the hands of Common Wealth in Chelmsford, on the same day Labour had been defeated by the Scottish Nationalists at Motherwell. Labour activists had, of course, been boosted by signs of a swing to the left during the campaign, whereas Conservatives had been thrown on the defensive by the amount of 'left-wing nonsense' to which the electorate were subjected.[40] But if there was a common view on polling day, it was still that Churchill — the 'man who won the war' — would be returned as Prime Minister, even if with a much reduced majority.

In these circumstances, the scale of Labour's victory came as a complete surprise. When the results finally began to come through at the end of July, it soon became clear that there had been a landslide: the Labour party had swept to a decisive victory, and Churchill had been crushingly rejected. Altogether, Labour won 393 seats, capturing nearly 48 per cent of the vote; the Conservative party was reduced to 213, with the Liberals returning only twelve MPs. As news spread that more than thirty members of the caretaker government had been defeated, those on the Labour side found it difficult to conceal their sense of surprise and elation. 'This is as great as 1906', wrote Chuter Ede, betraying his Liberal past. 'I warned Butler more than once', he added, 'that one day the nation ... would swing violently left. I had expected it to be at the election following this but the hatred of the Tories has been so great that they have been swept out of office by a tidal wave. This is one of the unique occasions in British history — a Red Letter day in the best sense of that term.'[41] Conservatives reacted rather differently. Churchill, after going to the Palace to resign, remarked memorably in reply to his wife's claim about the result being a blessing in disguise that if so it was very effectively disguised. One back-bencher, beginning the search for scapegoats that was to preoccupy the party for many months to come, spoke of his shame at his fellow countrymen in swallowing left-wing propaganda, and lamented that the House of Commons would now be filled with 'half-baked young men — mainly from the RAF so far as I can make out'.[42]

Certainly, in accounting for Labour's victory the service vote was of considerable importance. Over 1.5 million votes by those in the forces were counted separately after arriving from various parts of the world, making it easy to distinguish an overall pattern of support for Labour. Other particular forces at work could also be detected. Large numbers of new voters, for instance, now came on to an electoral register that had become badly out of date, and it was later calculated that some 60 per cent of these voters, many of them young, voted to put Attlee into Downing Street.[43] Equally important, Labour made significant gains among skilled workers and lower middle-class voters, many of whom had no previous pattern of support for the party. At the same time, advances were made in many rural constituencies.[44] The biggest breakthrough, however, came in urban Britain. Labour gains were most marked

Fig 4 'Make way!'

in the major conurbations, though variations upon the average swing of 12 per cent tended to follow the party's pattern of organisational strength and weakness. Scotland, for example, the area with the lowest regional swing overall, was a part of the country where Labour had struggled to improve its organisation throughout the war years.[45] By contrast, the flexibility of the party machine helped to produe a pronounced Labour surge in London and Birmingham; the latter, Britain's second city, experienced a remarkable 23 per cent swing away from the Conservatives. While Unionist organisation had rusted under the impact of war and the death of Neville Chamberlain, Labour branches had gradually expanded in co-operation with the trade union and shop stewards' movements. Much to the surprise of commentators, not to mention local party workers, Labour was rewarded with ten of Birmingham's thirteen seats.[46]

Party organisation was, therefore, one piece in the jigsaw that explains the 1945 result. The Conservative machine was clearly well below its peacetime level of efficiency. Although Labour was far from its own pre-war level of activity, by maintaining some degree of presence in many parts of the country, it had nevertheless seized a valuable advantage. But organisational factors in the final analysis account only for the *scale* of Labour's victory. The underlying causes of the landslide, as we have seen, lay much earlier in the war, and had little to do with how the campaign was fought in 1945. Indeed, one opinion poll found that 84 per cent of those questioned had already made up their minds how to vote before nomination day, and if anything the final weeks saw a small drift back to the Conservatives, notwithstanding Churchill's infamous 'Gestapo' blunder.[47] The first crucial shift in the public mood, we must rememeber, had occurred back in 1940, and coincided with the destruction of the power vested in the pre-war Conservative elite. This, in turn, had been compounded by the social experience of a 'people's war', and produced a trend that became irredeemable after the government prevaricated over reconstruction from early 1943 onwards. The net effect was to make Labour popular to a degree unimaginable at the outbreak of war. Attlee and other coalition ministers had succeeded in making Labour both the patriotic party and the party most likely to deliver on welfare reform. 'There was a place', David Howell has written, 'for a party that could give realistic answers to practical problems, but there was also a reservoir of idealism, a readiness to experiment . . . "bread and butter plus a dream". That was the secret of 1945.'[48]

But if the Labour party came of age in 1945, reflecting the mood of the electorate in a way it has rarely done before or since, then it must also be recognised — following the old adage that it is governments which lose elections — that the Conservative party helped to dig its own grave. In the following months Conservative supporters spent much time apportioning blame for the defeat: the two most frequently mentioned culprits were Lord Beaverbrook, for his part in the campaign; and Neville Chamberlain, the 'man of Munich'. 'It was not Churchill who lost the 1945 election', Harold Macmillan subsequently claimed, 'it was the ghost of Neville Chamberlain.'[49] In spite of his war record, however, there were several ways in which Churchill as much as Chamberlain had contributed to the malaise of wartime Conservatism. He had refused to give any strong lead in domestic policy; had neglected the party machine in a way that would have shocked his predecessor; and had scored an own goal in 1945 by inadvertently building up Attlee's reputation, through prolonged pursuit of the Laski affair. Above all, he had seriously underestimated the desire of the electorate for the creation of a New Jerusalem. As one press commentator put it: 'With the exception of one single broadcast more than two years ago, Mr Churchill has been consistently contemptuous toward the need for reform.'[50] This is not to suggest that with different presentation the Tories could have achieved victory in 1945; the swing to the left was clearly unstoppable by the time of the election. But, as Anthony Eden concluded, a clearer and more positive programme might at least have reduced the Labour majority. Rab Butler, who had spent so much time trying to force the party to recognise the domestic consequences of the war, summed this all up by reflecting that the Conservatives would have fared much better if affirmation of post-war policies had not taken such a poor third place behind the exploitation of Churchill's record as war leader and vitriolic attacks on the opposition. 'It was sad', he added, 'that the work done by the Post-War Problems Committee played so little part in the formulation of our Conservative campaign, and that the conduct of the election swept away much of the idealism which we wanted to instil and which emerged only in the 1945–51 period in opposition.'[51]

Butler's verdict on the shift in Conservative thinking which took place *after* 1945 points us towards a central conclusion of this study — the danger of exaggerating, with the benefit of hindsight, the impact of the war on British politics and policy-making. In the first place, we have seen that the Churchill government made only faltering steps towards the creation of a New Jerusalem. The experience of 'total war', and intense agitation from a variety of sources, did prompt government departments to formulate a whole host of new proposals. In some cases, such as education and employment policy, this led to the endorsement of ideas which had been resisted in Whitehall before 1939. But the new agenda produced few tangible results before the end of the war. Individual departments continued to operate separately in accordance with their own particular interests, and some of the policies put forward were designed, in part, to forestall the possibility of more radical reform at a later stage. There was, moreover, no guarantee that formulated plans would lead to the introduction of legislation, even after the government was spurred into greater activity by its mishandling of the Beveridge Report. In spite of all the public attention focused on the reconstruction theme after 1942, only two major measures — the Education Act and the new system of family allowances — had, in fact, reached the statute book before Churchill ceased to be Prime Minister.

The nature of the coalition was, as we have seen, vital in determining such an outcome. In a private conversation with the Minister of Reconstruction in 1944, Rab Butler drew an important distinction between public perceptions — which increasingly identified Labour as the party of social progress — and actual policy-making, where he rejected the assumption that Conservative ministers had been overshadowed by their Labour counterparts. The Beveridge Report, Butler noted, had been modified in such a way that the government scheme avoided the subsistence principle, and the proposed reforms in town and country planning had ultimately given more satisfaction to Conservatives than to Labour supporters.[52] He might also have mentioned the ambiguities of the employment white paper and the concessions which resulted from Willink's negotiations on the health service. In effect, the balance of coalition forces had produced a series of compromises tilted towards Conservative orthodoxy. In most areas of policy, the difficulty of arriving at these compromises was such that the coalition was unable to go beyond the publication of a white paper; any further action was regarded as a question of partisan disagreement. The precise lines upon which domestic policy might proceed were thus left deliberately unclear by the coalition: such matters could be determined only by the verdict of the electorate and by the aspirations of the first post-war government.

This leads us directly to a second element implicit in the argument here — the war had not initiated a process of genuine convergence between the parties on domestic policy. Notions of a political consensus, defined as an unprecedented level of agreement, are misleading in two respects. In policy terms, it has been argued throughout that the war produced only temporary, artificial agreement. There were, moreover, some fundamental underlying differences of ideology. The manner in which reconstruction policy was interpreted on the back-benches and outside Westminster gives little credence to the idea that Conservative and Labour supporters were coming to share long-term objectives. Apart from the recognition that various social questions would have to be faced, the parties were in many ways as far apart as they had been before the war. The Labour party had endorsed coalition proposals largely for tactical purposes: the first two years of coalition had shown the futility of pressing the party's own policies too openly; and the expectation that Churchill would be returned to power made it expedient to concentrate on pushing the Conservatives towards reform before the war came to an end. But Labour's agenda remained distinctive. Although the party relied heavily on reformers such as Beveridge to provide a rationale for future policy, politically there were several respects in which Labour was set apart. Above all, it embraced a positive vision of the welfare state; one in which the powers of the state would be extended and used as an instrument for redressing social and economic inequality.

The impact of the war on Labour thinking, and the limitations of wartime consensus, were brought together in a lengthy letter written by Clement Attlee to Harold Laski in 1944. Responding to the charge that Labour leaders had 'sold the pass' to their Tory colleagues, and moved to the political middle ground, Attlee wrote:

Whether the postwar government is Conservative or Labour it will inevitably have to work in a mixed economy. If it is a Labour government it will be a mixed economy developing towards socialism. If a Conservative government it will be an economy seeking to retain as much as possible of private enterprise. But both governments will have to work with the world and the country as it exists. There are limits to the extent to which the clock can be put forward or back. . . . What then should be our tactics? For myself I should on the practical side argue for our programme on the basis that the acceptance of abundance, of full employment, and of social security require the transfer to public ownership of certain major economic resources and the planned control in the public interest of many other economic activities. I should further argue that our planning must now be based on a far greater economic equality than obtained in the prewar period and that we have demonstrated in this war that this can be obtained. . . . I am sorry that you suggest that I am verging towards MacDonaldism. As you have so well pointed out, I have neither the personality nor the distinction to tempt me to think that I should have any value apart from the party which I serve. I hope you will also believe that because I am face to face every day with the practical problems of government I am nonetheless firm in my Socialist faith and that I have not the slightest desire to depart from it.[53]

The Conservative party, from its leader downwards, spoke in a very different language. Churchill had barely disguised his contempt for the Beveridge school of idealism, and the brief experience of the caretaker government indicated a predilection for retreating from coalition initiatives. The vision of the future for Tories in 1945, including those who had sought unsuccessfully to push the party in a new direction, had little in common with the ideological concerns of Attlee and his colleagues. Rather, Conservative opinion remained wedded to pragmatism: in view of wartime developments, an extension of state power would have to be accepted, but only on a piecemeal basis as before 1939, and without challenging the sanctity of private over public provision. The belief that Churchill's pre-eminence as war leader would secure a post-war Conservative government, despite the discouraging trend of by-election results, was again a crucial consideration. In the expectation of electoral victory, there was little incentive for Conservatives to contemplate any major change of course on economic and social issues. The belief that the party's political domination would continue undisturbed was shattered only at the end of the war by the crushing electoral defeat outlined in this chapter. The profound shock of Labour's overwhelming victory, in other words, was to be of greater importance than the experience of war in shifting the Tories towards a more fundamental reassessment of domestic policy. In order to understand more fully the creation of the welfare state, the mixed economy and the emergence of 'Butskellism' in British politics, greater attention has to be focused on the road *from* 1945, on events which followed — rather than preceded — the ending of the wartime coalition.

Notes

1 Addison, *Road to 1945*, pp. 257–8. On the formation of the cabinet, see *Colville Diary*, 24 May 1945, p. 602.
2 Winterton, *Orders of the Day*, p. 313.
3 A. Howard, *RAB*, pp. 146–7.
4 *The Economist*, 2 June 1945.
5 Oliver Lyttelton, *The Memoirs of Lord Chandos*, London, 1962, pp. 324–5.
6 V. 411 H. C. Deb., 5 s., cc. 87–8, 29 May 1945; R. Assheton to T. L. Rowan, 28 May 1945, PRO PREM 4 9/6.
7 M. Kemp, 'The left and Labour party policy', p. 130.
8 Minney, *Private Papers of Hore-Belisha*, p. 229.
9 Woolton minute to the Prime Minister, 1 June 1945, PRO PREM 4 36/3; 'Memorandum by the Minsiter of Health and Secretary of State for Scotland', Cabinet minutes, 15 June 1945, CAB 65/53.
10 Willink, 'As I Remember', pp. 81–2; Webster, *Health Services Since the War*, pp. 67–75.
11 Mary Soames, *Clementine Churchill*, p. 382.
12 *Chuter Ede Diary*, 5 June 1945, p. 222; Mass-Observation Typescript Report No. 2268, 'The General Election, June–July 1945', October 1945, p. 4.
13 *Channon Diary*, 6 June 1945, p. 408; *Daily Express*, 8 June 1945.
14 *The Economist*, 16 June 1945.
15 M. Gilbert, *Winston S. Churchill*, Vol. VIII, *Never Despair 1945–1965*, London, 1988, pp. 39–40. On press comment, see, for example, *The Manchester Guardian*, cited in R. Kee, *1945: the World We Fought For*, London, 1985, p. 224.
16 Lysaght, *Brendan Bracken*, p. 251.
17 Donoughue and Jones, *Herbert Morrison*, pp. 331–5; Kemp, 'The left and Labour party policy', pp. 128–9.
18 *Colville Diary*, 18 June 1945, P. 607: 'Even with him I am not sanguine of their prospects, though most of their leaders are confident of a good majority . . . . The main Conservative advantage is the prevailing good humour of the people and the accepted point that Attlee would be a sorry successor to Winston at the meeting of the Big Three and in the counsels of the Nations.'
19 Moran, *The Struggle for Survival*, p. 276.
20 H. Pelling, 'The 1945 general election reconsidered', *The Historical Journal*, XXIII, 2, 1980, pp. 403 ff.; Harris, *Attlee*, pp. 259–61.

21 Mass-Observation Report, 'The General Election', p. 85. *Dalton Diary*, July 1945, p. 357, comments on the further fuss which developed 'as to whether the little fool said that in any circumstances we should "use violence" — I always find it rather comic that this contingency should be discussed by this puny, short-sighted, weak-hearted, rabbinical-looking little chap!'

22 J. Schneer, 'The Labour left and the general election of 1945', in J. M. W. Bean (ed.), *The Political Culture of Modern Britain*, London, 1987, pp. 264–9.

23 R. B. McCallum and A. Readman, *The British General Election of 1945*, London, 1947, p. 48.

24 J. Hess, 'The social policy of the Attlee government', in Mommsen (ed.), *Emergence of the Welfare State*, pp. 300–6.

25 *The Times*, 28 June 1945, commented that this was the most obvious lacuna in Conservative policy: the failure to recognise the need for a final settlement of the problem of compensation and betterment, which continued to frustrate effective public use of the land.

26 Conservative Party, *Mr Churchill's Declaration of Policy to the Electorate*, London, 1945. See also Willink's election speech in Reading, delivered on 12 April 1945; Willink papers, Box 2.

27 Woolton, *Memoris*, p. 282.

28 Attlee to Churchill, 21 May 1945, cited in Attlee, *As It Happened*, London, 1945, p. 137.

29 Labour Party, *Let Us Face the Future*, London, 1945.

30 NUCUA, *General Election 1945: Notes for Speakers and Workers*, London, 1945, p. 13.

31 Ibid.; *The Times*, 22 and 28 June, 1945.

32 Rab Butler also claimed that there was now the opportunity for carrying out 'the greatest Social reform programme in our country's history' — cited in McCallum and Readman, op. cit., p. 115

33 On this and the constituency campaigns generally, see the original 1945 election addresses, held at Nuffield College, Oxford.

34 Ian Mikardo, *Back-Bencher*, Londor, 1988, p. 83. As another typical example of the Conservative approach, see 'Address to the electors of the Penryn and Falmouth Division', Maurice Petherick MP, Cornwall Record Office, DDX551/15.

35 *The Western Morning News*, 5 July 1945, for the comment of one of the Labour candidates in Devon.

36 'Agents' electoral forecasts 1945', Conservative party archive, Bodleian Library, CC04/2/61.

37 Winteron, op. cit., p. 313.

38 *Colville Diary*, 26 July 1945, p. 611; Donoughue and Jones, op. cit., p. 338; *Dalton Diary*, July 1945, p. 360; Dalton, *Fateful years*, p. 466.

39 Addison, op. cit., p. 226, notes that the Labour lead in the Gallup polls fell from 16 per cent on 28 May to 6 per cent on 4 July.

40 *Chuter Ede Diary*, 1 and 12 June 1945, pp. 221–3; Headlam diary, 21 June and 3–4 July 1945, D/He 41.

41 *Chuter Ede Diary*, 26 July 1945, p. 227.

42 Headlam diary, 26 July 1945, D/He 41.
43 D. Butler and D. Stokes, *Political Change in Britain*, London, 1969, p. 54.
44 On this, see J. Bonham, *The Middle Class Vote*, London, 1954.
45 Harvie, 'Labour in Scotland', pp. 437–42.
46 See R. Hastings, 'The labour movement in Birmingham 1927–45', unpublished M.A. thesis, University of Birmingham, 1959.
47 McCallum and Readman, op. cit., p. 296.
48 D. Howell, *British Social Democracy*, London, 1976, p. 132.
49 H. Macmillan, *Tides of Fortune 1945–1955*, London, 1979, p. 313.
50 *The Economist*, 28 July 1945: 'One of the most significant of all the individual results was the 10,000 votes polled against Mr Churchill in his own constituency by a totally unknown . . . outsider. If this is the hour of Mr Churchill's departure, let tribute be sincerely paid, once again, to the matchless moral services he rendered to the nation and to the world in 1940 and 1941. But as a political leader, the epitaph on him must be that Lord Baldwin would have done much better.'
51 Rhodes James, *Athony Eden*, p. 310; Butler, *Art of the Possible*, p. 128.
52 Butler to Woolton, 13 September 44, Woolton papers, 16, f. 9.
53 Cited in Harris, op. cit., p. 254.

Epilogue

Britain's post-war settlement was forged between 1945 and 1947. According to the accepted line of thinking, the new Labour government, by introducing a mixed economy and welfare state, was for the most part completing changes set in motion during the war. The new consensus, writes Paul Addison, 'fell like a branch of ripe plums into the lap of Mr Attlee'. The era of 'Butskellism', with its origins stretching back to the days after Dunkirk, was henceforth to characterise British politics for a generation to come; many would say at least until the 1970s.[1] Certainly, in assessing the record of the post-war Labour government, historians are agreed that Attlee's party made only limited advances towards its stated aim in 1945 — the creation of a socialist commonwealth. In some policy areas, continuity with wartime practice was undeniable. Under Ernest Bevin, for example, the surprising choice as Foreign Secretary, hopes of a 'socialist foreign policy' soon disappeared as the Cold War got under way, much to the dismay of many Labour activists.[2] But in domestic policy, it will be argued here, the story was different. As this study has sought to show, party political consensus — the concept of a historically unusual level of agreement — was by no means complete at the end of the war. The coalition had been unable, because of ideological differences, to proceed far with its reconstruction programme, and a brief survey of Labour's policy in office after 1945 suggests that several important departures were made from wartime orthodoxy. Attlee's powerful cabinet — which included Hugh Dalton at the Treasury, Herbert Morrison as Lord President and Aneurin Bevan at the Ministry of Health — wasted no time in setting out to implement the party's radical programme, encountering considerable resistance in the process from the new Conservative opposition.

The central theme of Labour's approach was the desire to benefit working people. In July 1945 the government faced a daunting economic position; what Keynes termed a 'financial Dunkirk'. British exports and assets abroad had fallen drastically during the war, and shortly after the ending of hostilities in the Far East, the Americans abruptly terminated the Lend-Lease arrangements upon which Britain had become so reliant. These circumstances dictated obvious economic priorities: the raising of domestic investment; improved productivity; and the recovery of lost export markets, in order to redress the huge balance of payments deficit. At the same time, though, the cabinet never lost sight of its desire to maintain full employment, while also pushing ahead with welfare reforms. Aided by a massive new loan from the United States, Dalton as Chancellor of the Exchequer opted for a budgetary policy with a strong social component. Food subsidies, for example, were kept at a high level in order to keep down living costs, and taxation policy — in spite of complaints from the Conservative opposition — was refined to benefit lower wage earners. This did not make the deep inroads into poverty believed at the time, though it did lead to an uprecedented redistribution of income. Dalton was also determined to avoid any repeat of the post-war slump experienced after the First World War. Within eighteen months, the demobilisation of millions of service personnel had been completed without pushing up the numbers out of work, and, with the exception of a short period in 1947, unemployment was kept below 2 per cent. Although this achievement owed much to the recovery of world markets, ministers clearly played their part. In particular, the Board of Trade vigorously promoted regional initiatives by taking up the powers of the 1945 Distribution of Industry Act — a measure from which Conservative industrialists had openly dissented. Through all the economic problems to come, Labour's most powerful claim on the loyalty of working-class voters was that it was 'the party of full employment, the party which had exorcised the ghosts of Jarrow, Wigan, and Merthyr Tydfil'.[3]

The government's industrial policy was also distinctive. An extensive programme of nationalisation, above all else, set Labour apart in this context. Public ownership was justified on two grounds: the desire to improve 'inefficient' pre-war industries; and the need to create a service sector of the great utilities. Neither argument impressed the opposition. In its early stages, nationalisation encountered little serious resistance. But once the Conservative party had recovered as a parliamentary force it put up far more than the token opposition often implied by historians of the period. In the case of the gas industry, for instance, the Tories tabled some 800 amendments in an effort to wreck the government's legislation. This pattern was repeated in the debates on road haulage, and especially in the heated exchanges over the steel industry — measures which the Conservatives sought to reverse after returning to power in the 1950s. The form of management adopted by nationalised industries, soon to be the subject of intense controversy in Labour ranks, was partly determined by the preferences of the trade union movement — another sign of the government's conciliatory industrial policy. Although strikes remained prohibited by law, relations between ministers and union leaders were, on the whole, harmonious. No restrictions were placed on collective wage bargaining, and, in a move of profound symbolic importance, the government quickly repealed the 1927 Trades Disputes Act. This was vital to the creation of a corporate economy. Henceforth, the 'contracting in' principle for the levy to Labour funds was removed, regulations on the closed shop were modified, and restrictions on picketing and secondary industrial action largely disappeared. Churchill, as we have seen, ruled out any such action during the war under pressure from Conservative back-benchers, whose attachment to the 1927 Act continued after the war. A new framework for union–government relations, consolidating the experience of wartime, was thus by no means inevitable in 1945.[4]

Labour's commitment to welfare reform, similarly, went beyond wartime orthodoxy in some, if not all, respects. National insurance was one area of policy where the parties had broadly overlapped in 1945, though, as we have seen, Churchill still believed the Beveridge scheme could be refined in a non-socialist direction. The Labour cabinet, by contrast, ensured the early passage into law of a comprehensive new system of social security. Although financial pressures ruled out the possibility of paying benefits at subsistence level standards, James Griffiths, in presenting the legislation, saw it as 'the beginning of the establishment of the principle of a National Minimum Standard'. Labour supporters, moreover, saw the reform in an altogether more positive light than did their opponents. For ministers, the inclusion of means-tested national assistance was necessary in order to provide a safety net for those unable to meet insurance payments. But for Conservative spokesmen, means-testing was defended on rather different grounds: as an essential safeguard against the threat of 'scrounging'.[5] In education, another area of broad agreement during the war, Labour ministers did come under criticism from the party for cautiously sticking to the terms of the 1944 Act. The tripartite structure of secondary schools, for instance, was soon felt to be socially divisive. The education department did, however, succeed in securing Treasury funds to improve conditions for teachers and to update delapidated school buildings; before her untimely death, in 1947, Ellen Wilkinson also pressed ahead with the raising of the school-leaving age, in spite of cabinet worries about the mounting cost of welfare reform.[6]

Other areas of social policy had a sharper ideological cutting edge. As Minister of Health, Aneurin Bevan has often been criticised for giving insufficient priority to the nation's housing needs. But, again, there were distinctive elements: in a conscious effort to favour working-class families, the government deliberately shifted attention from private house-building to the local authority sector. Rents for council tenants were heavily subsidised, and public sector housing received its first major advance since the Wheatley Act in the 1920s. At the same time, by following the Uthwatt Report as a guide to planning the physical environment, Bevan soon antagonised his opponents. Some parts of the Town and Country Planning Act passed in 1947, notably compensation terms and the betterment levy, were resisted by Conservatives in the Commons and eventually repealed when Churchill returned to power.[7] And if Labour did disappoint in the number of new properties built after 1945, then part of the reason for this, of course, was the importance attached to the centrepiece of the whole welfare programme, the National Health Service.

Medical reform, as we have seen, had been extensively discussed during the war, making it unlikely that Labour would produce an entirely new scheme. The new government, nevertheless, went much further than both the 1944 white paper and the revised plan favoured by Willink. Bevan's aim at the outset was to bring all voluntary hospitals into one state system, to establish group practice in the health centres and to encourage payment by salary where possible. Opposition to these proposals was spearheaded by the British Medical Association (BMA), who forced various concessions on the minister, but again Conservatives in parliament decided to mount a rearguard action. Tory back-benchers voted *en bloc* against the government, thus making it difficult to sustain the view that the National Health Service was the product of wartime consensus. The extent of partisan disagreement on this topic could be seen in the language used by Willink, who moved as an amendment that:

this House, while wishing to establish a comprehensive health service, declines to give a Second Reading to a Bill which prejudices the patient's right to an independent family doctor, which retards the development of the hospital services by destroying local ownership and gravely menaces all charitable foundations and which weakens the responsibilities of local authorities without planning the health services as a whole.[8]

The post-war settlement was, thus, to a much greater extent than has been recognised, *Labour's* settlement. 'Labour's post-war reforms', concludes one recent study, 'were set firmly in the party's own tradition of democratic socialism, whatever its anomalies and inconsistenices.'[9] In retrospect, we can see that the precise form in which the welfare state emerged owed much to progressive intellectual opinion during the war. But the decisive push in practical, legislative terms came only after 1945. Where the coalition could reach only ambiguous compromise, Attlee's administration forged a new economic and social order, and did so in the face of continued resistance from Conservative leaders. It follows that had there been a genuine wartime consensus, then much of Labour's domestic programme would have proved uncontentious, which was clearly not the case. Nor, on the available evidence, can it be assumed that the welfare state would have been established in the same way had Churchill remained in office as 'the man who won the war'. The Tory record in wartime, together with the plans of the caretaker government, pointed in a rather different direction: to an extension of state welfare only as and when the expansion of the free market economy permitted. Indeed, it is tempting to speculate that a post-war Conservative government might have followed the pattern of Lloyd George's coalition after the First World War. Such a comparison, as Kenneth Morgan points out, puts Labour's achievement clearly in perspective:

Both post-war governments, that of 1919 and of 1945, derived their momentum — indeed, their very existence — from the social radicalism of wartime. The Attlee government, unlike its predecessor, actually kept the momentum going ... rather than spearheading a reaction against it. A far higher priority was given to social expenditure than after 1918. A prime emphasis was placed on full employment.... Britain after 1945 was a less tension-ridden, more unified society than that which emerged in the Lloyd George era after 1918, overlain as the latter was by the aura of corruption and adventurism. This time, the vision of a 'land fit for heroes'... was not wantonly forgotten or betrayed.[10]

Why, then, did the existence of 'Butskellism', of much greater party co-operation, become such a commonplace assumption by the 1950s? The answer to this question, arguably, can be found not in the war years or the early stages of the Attlee government, but rather in developments after 1947. In the first place, the Labour cabinet began to lose its cohesion and radical sense of direction after being shaken by a series of economic crises. The severe winter of 1946–47, the convertibility crisis of August 1947 and the need for devaluation in 1949 — all shook the confidence of Labour ministers and led to a gradual redefinition of policies and priorities. Against the backdrop of the Cold War, physical planning of the economy became identified less with wartime efficiency and more with the totalitarian methods of the Eastern European states. By 1949 planning, which had been so central to Labour's programme at the end of the war, had largely given way to demand-management of the economy by fiscal means. As Chancellor after 1947, Stafford Cripps also insisted on new ceilings beng placed on public expenditure. Henceforth, Labour's cherished welfare reforms became the source of considerable internal wrangling, culminating in Bevan's damaging resignation over the decision to introduce charges for various medical services. And, at the same time, doubts about the value and purpose of nationalisation came rapidly to the fore. Many party activists pressed for the completion of the steel take-over as a sign of commitment to the further socialisation of the economy; others were concerned that the nationalised industries — already under attack for lack of profitability and poor industrial relations — were becoming a political liability. Labour, in short, made a 'retreat to consensus' after 1947. The mixed economy began to appear as a permanent achievement rather than as something that might be developed by further transfers of wealth and power; in the course of two close election contests in 1950 and 1951, 'consolidation' became the guiding theme.[11]

Important changes also took place on the Conservative side, again changes that really came about only after 1947. By this time, the shock of a humiliating electoral defeat, combined with further set-backs in by-elections, made inevitable some rethinking of domestic policy. Although Churchill insisted on maintaining a flexible, pragmatic approach, progressives led by Rab Butler managed to incorporate in the *Industrial Charter* of 1947 a broad commitment to the mixed economy, including an attachment to Keynesian-style demand-management. The 1951 election also served to strengthen the new convergence of political opinion. Churchill returned to Downing Street with only a small majority, and was conscious that Labour had actually polled more votes, piling up huge majorities in its industrial heartlands. As a result, progressive Tories found their position within the government strengthened. Rab Butler, for example, now went to the Treasury instead of Lyttelton, and, on the whole, the liberal free market tradition within the party was left on the sidelines. There was, moreover, a world of difference for Conservatives between opposing changes in opposition, and accepting the status quo in office, especially when reforms were of proven popularity. Nowhere was this borne out more clearly than in the case of the National Health Serivce, the central features of which were maintained by successive Tory administrations in the 1950s. 'The service established in 1948', concludes the official history, 'was regarded by both the Government and the profession as the best compromise that could be secured in the circumstances. Rather than risk destabilising the system the opposing sides came to accept the lines of truce as permanent boundaries. Gradually a spurious consensus grew up around the system as a whole, thereby granting permanence to many features that had been regarded as temporary expedients.' To threaten the essentials of the health service, Conservative MPs were agreed, would be to court electoral disaster.[12]

In terms of practicalities, therefore — of the options available to the opposing front-bench teams — 'consensus' became an appropriate label for British politics in the 1950s. Unlike the period before 1947, there had now emerged broad cross-party agreement: about the maintenance of the welfare state; about the working of the mixed economy; and about the need for fiscal management to maintain high levels of employment. It would be misleading, though, even at this juncture, to claim that policy agreement was complete. Labour spokesmen retained an attachment to elements of physical planning; whereas Butler at the Treasury deliberately ruled out deficit finance as a means of meeting economic recession, despite his party's earlier pledges.[13] What this implied, in a wider sense, was that the new dispensation could only be accurately defined in negative, as much as positive, terms. Labour had retreated to consensus because of external pressures, mainly economic and electoral; having implemented so much of its long-standing programme, the party became embroiled in the task of constructing a new vision of socialist politics, one building upon the acknowledged achievements of the Attlee years. The Conservative party, for its own reasons, had settled for a 'reassuring blanket of Churchillian tranquillity' — a term that might equally be applied to the subsequent premierships of Eden and Macmillan.[14] Neither side, in effect, knew how best to advance from the momentous changes introduced after the war. This did not mean that ideological differences had disappeared. Anthony Crosland's powerful polemic, *The Future of Socialism*, published in 1956, was written as an impassioned demand for greater social justice and equality. Two years later Ian MacLeod — speaking for the moderate wing of Conservatism — responded by attacking the 'Santa Claus' state, going on to identify the principal conflict of the day as 'Opportunity v. Equality'.[15] At Westminster and beyond, the clash of ideas thus continued unabated, sustaining an adversarial system of politics which continued to centre on what were, by any standard, profound disagreements: about the distribution of power and wealth; about public versus private provision; and about the type of society Britain would become in the longer term. 'Mr Attlee's consensus', we must conclude, was built upon shallow foundations. This was why, when inevitably confronted in time by fresh challenges, by changing economic and political pressures, it was certain to break down.

Notes

1 Addison, *Road to 1945*, pp. 14 and 271–8. Kavanagh and Morris, *Consensus Politics*, pp. 13–14, strongly reinforce this view, claiming that after the war ideological differences were 'merely the stuff of electioneering'.

2 A. Bullock, *Ernest Bevin: Foreign Secretary 1945–51*, London, 1983, esp. pp. 59–80.

3 Morgan, *Labour in Power*, pp. 180–4. See also A. Cairncross, *Years of Recovery: British Economic Policy 1945–51*, London, 1985.

4 Morgan, op. cit., pp. 94–127.
5 A. Deacon and J. Bradshaw, *Reserved for the Poor*, London, 1983, pp. 45 ff.
6 B. Hughes, 'In defence of Ellen Wilkinson', *History Workshop*, VII, 1979.
7 Michael Foot, *Aneurin Bevan*, Vol. II, *1945–60*, London, 1973, esp. pp. 80–5.
8 V. 422 H. C. Deb., 5s., c. 222, 1 May 1946.
9 S. Brooke, 'Labour's war: party, coalition and domestic reconstruction 1939–45', unpublished D.Phil thesis, University of Oxford, 1988, p. 273.
10 Morgan, op. cit., p. 499.
11 The theme of a 'retreat to consensus' is outlined in L. Minkin, 'Radicalism and reconstruction: the British experience', *Europa*, V, 2, 1982.
12 See the conclusion to Webster, *Health Services Since the War*.
13 Butler's policy at the Treasury is carefully examined in N. Rollings, 'British budgetary policy 1945–54: a "Keynesian Revolution"?', *Economic History Review*, XL, 4, 1987.
14 The term is taken from P. Addison, 'Churchill in British politics 1940–55', in Bean (ed.), *Political Culture of Modern Britain*.
15 Anthony Crosland, *The Future of Socialism*, London, 1956; Ian MacLeod, 'The political divide', in Conservative Political Centre, *Future of the Welfare State*, London, 1958.

Appendix I

Senior ministerial office holders, 1939–45

National government (re-formed September 1939)

War Cabinet

Prime Minister	Neville Chamberlain
Lord Privy Seal	Samuel Hoare
	Kingsley Wood (from 3 April 1940)
Chancellor of the Exchequer	Sir John Simon
Foreign Secretary	Viscount Halifax
First Lord of the Admiralty	Winston Churchill
Secretary of State for Air	Kingsley Wood
	Samuel Hoare (from 3 April 1940)
Minister for Co-ordination of Defence	Lord Chatfield
Minister without Portfolio	Lord Hankey
Secretary of State for War	Leslie Hore-Belisha

Outside War Cabinet

Home Secretary	Sir John Anderson
Dominions Office	Anthony Eden
Board of Education	Earl De La Warr
	Herwald Ramsbotham (from 3 April 1940)
Minister of Food	Lord Woolton
Minister of Health	Walter Elliot
Secretary of State for India	Marquis of Zetland
Minister of Information	Lord Macmillan
	Sir John Reith (from 5 January 1940)
Minister of Labour and National Service	Ernest Brown
Secretary of State for Scotland	John Colville
Minister for Shipping	Sir John Gilmour

	Robert Hudson (from 3 April 1940)
Minister of Supply	Leslie Burgin
President of the Board of Trade	Oliver Stanley
	Andrew Duncan (from 5 January 1940)
Minister for Transport	Euan Wallace
Secretary of State for War	Oliver Stanley (from 5 January 1940)

Coalition government (May 1940–May 1945)

War Cabinet

Prime Minister and Minister of Defence	Winston Churchill
Lord President of the Council	Neville Chamberlain
	Sir John Anderson (from 3 October 1940)
	*Clement Attlee (from 24 September 1943)
Lord Privy Seal	*Clement Attlee
	*Stafford Cripps (in cabinet 19 February–22 November 1942)
Chancellor of the Exchequer	Kingsley Wood (in cabinet 3 October 1940–19 February 1942)
	Sir John Anderson (from 24 September 1943)
Foreign Secretary	Viscount Halifax
	Anthony Eden (from 22 December 1940)
Minister of State	Lord Beaverbrook (office established 1 May 1941)
	Oliver Lyttelton (29 June 1941–12 March 1942; became Minister of Production)
Home Secretary and Minister of Home Security	*Herbert Morrison (in cabinet from 22 November 1942)
Minister of Aircraft Production	Lord Beaverbrook (in cabinet 2 August 1940–1 May 1941)
Secretary of State for the Dominions	*Clement Attlee (in cabinet 19 February 1942–24 September 1943)
Minister of Labour and National Service	*Ernest Bevin (in cabinet from 3 October 1940)
Minister without Portfolio	*Arthur Greenwood (until 22 February 1942)

Minister of Reconstruction	Lord Woolton (office established 11 November 1943)
Minister of Supply	Lord Beaverbrook (in cabinet 29 June 1941–4 February 1942)
Minister of Production	Lord Beaverbrook (office established 4 February 1942)
	Oliver Lyttelton (from 12 March 1942)

Outside War Cabinet

First Lord of the Admiralty	*A. V. Alexander
Secretary of State for Air	**Archibald Sinclair
Minister of Aircraft Production	John Moore-Brabazon (from 1 May 1941)
	Jay Llewellin (from 22 February 1942)
	*Stafford Cripps (from 22 November 1942)
Secretary of State for the Dominions	Viscount Caldecote
	Viscount Cranborne (3 October 1940–19 Februaryy 1942 and 24 September 1943–May 1945)
Minister of Economic Warfare	*Hugh Dalton
	Viscount Wolmer (from 22 February 1942)
Board of Education	Herwald Ramsbotham
	Rab Butler (from 20 July 1941)
Minister of Food	Lord Woolton
	Jay Llewellin (from 11 November 1943)
Minister of Health	Malcolm MacDonald
	Ernest Brown (from 8 February 1941)
	Henry Willink (from 11 November 1943)
Home Secretary and Minister of Home Security	Sir John Anderson
	*Herbert Morrison (from 3 October 1940)
Secretary of State for India	Leo Amery
Minister of Information	Duff Cooper
	Brendan Bracken (from 20 July 1941)
Minister without Portfolio	*Sir William Jowitt (30 December 1942–8 October 1944)
Secretary of State for Scotland	Ernest Brown
	*Tom Johnston (from 8 February 1941)

Minister of Shipping	Ronald Cross (until 1 May 1941; office becomes War Transport)
Minister for National Insurance	*Sir William Jowitt (office established 8 October 1944)
Minister of Supply	*Herbert Morrison Andrew Duncan (30 October 1940–29 June 1941 and 4 February 1942–May 1945)
Minister of Town and Country Planning	W. S. Morrison (office established 30 December 1942)
President of the Board of Trade	Andrew Duncan Oliver Lyttelton (from 3 October 1940) Andrew Duncan (from 29 June 1941) Jay Llewellin (from 4 February 1942) *Hugh Dalton (from 22 February 1942)
Secretary of State for War	Anthony Eden David Margesson (from 22 December 1940) P. J. Grigg (from 22 February 1942)
Minister for War Transport:	Lord Leathers (from 1 May 1941)

*   Denotes Labour Minister
**   Denotes Liberal minister; all others Conservative or National

Caretaker government (1945)

Cabinet Ministers

Prime Minister and Minister of Defence	Winston Churchill
Lord President of the Council	Lord Woolton
Lord Privy Seal	Lord Beaverbrook
Chancellor of the Exchequer	Sir John Anderson
Foreign Secretary	Anthony Eden
Home Secretary	Sir Donald Somervell
First Lord of the Admiralty	Brendan Bracken
Minister of Agriculture and Fisheries	Robert Hudson
Secretary of State for Air	Harold Macmillan
Colonial Secretary	Oliver Stanley
Dominions Secretary	Viscount Cranborne
Secretary of State for India	Leo Amery
Minister of Labour and National Service	Rab Butler

Minister of Production and   Oliver Lyttelton
  President of the Board of
  Trade
Secretary of State for War   P. J. Grigg

Source: D. Butler and J. Freeman, *British Political Facts 1900–1960*, London, 1963.

Appendix II

Contested by-elections, September 1939–May 1945

Date	Constituency	Result	*Swing to and from official nominee* (%)
1939			
13 October	Clackmannanshire and Stirling East	Labour hold	+ 51.6
8 December	Stretford	Con. hold	+ 15.3
1940			
10 February	Southwark Central	Labour hold	+ 11.0
19–23 February	Cambridge University	Ind. Con. gain from Con.	2 seats previously
22 February	Silvertown, West Ham	Labour hold	+ 11.8
6 March	Kettering	Con. hold	+ 20.9
13 March	Leeds North East	Con. hold	+ 32.3
10 April	Argyll	Con. hold	+ 9.2
30 April	Glasgow, Pollock	Con. hold	+ 16.0
9 May	Renfrewshire East	Con. hold	+ 25.1
22 May	Middleton and Prestwich	Con. hold	+ 37.6
7 June	Newcastle North	Ind. Con. gain from Con.	− 48.2
12 June	Poplar, Bow and Bromley	Labour hold	+ 18.8
19 June	Croydon North	Con. hold	+ 23.6
6 December	Northampton	Con. hold	+ 41.9
1941			
25 February	Dunbartonshire	Labour hold	+ 43.1

Date	Constituency	Result	Swing to and from official nominee (%)
8 May	Birmingham, King's Norton	Con. hold	+ 30.1
28 May	Hornsey	Con. hold	+ 7.9
24 September	Scarborough	Con. hold	+ 6.9
26 September	The Wrekin	Con. hold	– 4.8
15 October	Lancaster	Con. hold	+ 3.2
27 November	Hampstead	Con. hold	+ 5.8
11 December	Edinburgh Central	Con. hold	+ 17.0
1942			
25 March	Grantham	Ind. gain from Con.	– 8.9
13 April	Cardiff East	National hold	+ 21.7
28 April	Glasgow, Cathcart	Con. hold	– 2.4
29 April	Wallasey	Ind. gain from Con.	– 35.7
29 April	Rugby	Ind. gain from Con.	– 13.3
8 May	Wandsworth	Con. hold	+ 9.8
18 May	Chichester	Con. hold	– 20.2
10 June	Llandaff and Barry	Con. hold	+ 5.5
25 June	Maldon	Ind. gain from Con.	– 22.1
30 June	Windsor	Con. hold	1935 election unopposed
8 July	Salisbury	Con. hold	– 3.7
12 August	South Poplar	Labour hold	+ 13.0
17 October	Manchester, Clayton	Labour hold	+ 39.6
1943			
25–29 January	University of Wales	Liberal hold	– 9.0
29 January	Hamilton	Labour hold	+ 15.4
10 February	Ashford	Con. hold	+ 10.5
11 February	Midlothian and Peebleshire North	Con. hold	– 11.0
12 February	King's Lynn	Con. hold	+ 4.2
16 February	Portsmouth North	Con. hold	– 6.9
18 February	Bristol Central	Con. hold	– 0.4
23 February	Watford	Con. hold	– 11.5

Date	Constituency	Result	*Swing to and from official nominee* (%)
7 April	Eddisbury	CW gain from Nat. Lib.	1935 election unopposed
20 April	Daventry	Con. hold	− 17.8
1 June	The Hartlepools	Con. hold	+ 16.3
8 June	Newark	Con. hold	− 18.2
9 June	Birmingham, Aston	Con. hold	+ 3.7
24 August	Chippenham	Con. hold	− 2.7
15 October	Peterborough	Con. hold	− 4.2
10 November	Woolwich West	Con. hold	+ 6.5
14 December	Acton	Con. hold	+ 1.8
15 December	Darwen	Con. hold	+ 1.9
1944			
7 January	Skipton	CW gain from Con.	− 12.2
3 February	Brighton	Con. hold	2 seats previously
17 February	West Derbyshire	Ind. Labour gain from Con.	1935 election unopposed
17 February	Kirkcaldy Burghs	Labour hold	− 4.7
29 February	Bury St Edmunds	Con. hold	1935 election unopposed
30 March	Camberwell North	Labour hold	+ 15.1
14 April	Clay Cross	Labour hold	+ 1.7
8 July	Manchester, Rusholme	Con. hold	− 9.3
20 September	Wolverhampton, Bilston	Con. hold	− 0.3
17 October	Berwick-upon-Tweed	Liberal hold	+ 36.4
1945			
9–13 April	Combined Scottish Universities	Ind. gain from National Liberal	3 seats previously
12 April	Motherwell	SNP gain from Labour	− 2.1
26 April	Chelmsford	CW gain from Con.	− 28.3
26 April	Caernarvon Boroughs	Liberal hold	+ 8.6

Date	Constituency	Result	Swing to and from official nominee (%)
15 May	Neath	Labour hold	1935 election unopposed
17 May	Newport	Con. hold	+ 2.8

Source: F. W. S. Craig (ed.), *Chronology of British Parliamentary By-Elections 1833–1987*, Chichester, 1987.

Select bibliography

Manuscript sources

Private papers

A. V. Alexander papers (Churchill College, Cambridge)
Viscount and Lady Astor papers (Reading University Library)
Clement Attlee papers (Bodleian Library, Oxford)
Lord Beaverbrook papers (House of Lords Record Office)
Ernest Bevin papers (Churchill College, Cambridge)
R. A. Butler papers (Trinity College, Cambridge)
Neville Chamberlain diary and papers (Birmingham University Library)
Stafford Cripps papers (Nuffield College, Oxford)
H. F. Crookshank diary (Bodleian Library, Oxford)
Clement Davies papers (National Library of Wales, Aberystwyth)
James Chuter Ede diary (British Library)
Paul Emrys Evans diary and papers (British Library)
Arthur Greenwood papers (Bodleian Library, Oxford)
James Giffiths papers (National Library of Wales, Aberystwyth)
Lord Hankey papers (Churchill College, Cambridge)
Cuthbert Headlam diary (Durham Record Office)
Leslie Hore-Belisha diary (Churchill College, Cambridge)
David Lloyd George papers (House of Lords Record Office)
3rd Earl Selborne papers (Bodleian Library, Oxford)
Viscount Simon papers (Bodleian Library, Oxford)
Richard Stokes papers (Bodleian Library, Oxford)
Euan Wallace diary (Bodleian Library, Oxford)
Lord Woolton papers (Bodleian Library, Oxford)

Public Record Office, Kew

Cabinet papers	CAB 65 (War Cabinet minutes)
	CAB 66 (War Cabinet papers)
	CAB 71 (Lord President's Committee)
	CAB 87 (Committees on Reconstruction)
Board of Education	ED 136 (Departmental papers on 1944 Act)
Ministry of Health	MH 77 (Negotiations on Health Service)
Ministry of Information	INF 1 (Home Intelligence Weekly Reports)

Ministry of Labour   LAB 10 (Industrial Relations)
Prime Minister's Office: PREM 4 (Premier's papers, 1940–45)

Others (see also Party Political Records)

Mass-Observation archive, University of Sussex

Party political records

Conservative party archive, Bodleian Library, Oxford.
Local Conservative association records (care of Dr J. A. Ramsden, Queen
  Mary College, London)
NUCUA, *General Election 1945: Notes for Speakers and Workers*, 1945
Mr Churchill's Declaration of Policy to the Electorate, 1945
Labour party NEC *Minutes and Reports*, 1940–45
Reports of the Annual Conference of the Labour Party
Labour's Immediate Programme, 1937
Labour's Aims in War and Peace, 1940
The Old World and the New Society, 1942
Let Us Face the Future, 1945

Official publications

Hansard, *Parliamentary Debates*, fifth series, 1940–45.
House of Commons Select Committee on National Expenditure, *Reports
  and Minutes*, 1940–45.
Social Insurance and Allied Services, Cmd. 6404, 1942.
Educational Reconstruction, Cmd. 6458, 1943.
A National Health Service, Cmd. 6502, 1944.
Control of Land Use, Cmd. 6514, 1944.
Employment Policy, Cmd. 6527, 1944.
Social Insurance, Cmd. 6550–1, 1944.
*Local Government in England and Wales during the Period of
  Reconstruction*, Cmd. 6579, 1945.

Newspapers and periodicals

National

Daily Express
Daily Herald
Daily Mail
The Economist
Evening Standard
Manchester Guardian
News Chronicle

New Statesman
The Observer
Sunday Times
The Times

Regional and local

Barry Herald
Birmingham Post
Durham City Advertiser
Manchester Evening News
Norfolk News and Weekly Press
Peterborough Standard
South London Observer
Western Daily Press
Western Mail and South Wales News
Western Morning News
Yorkshire Observer

Memoirs, diaries and contemporary writing
(Place of publication hereafter London, unless otherwise stated)

L.S. Amery, *My Political Life*, Vol. III, *The Unforgiving Years 1929–1940*, 1955.
Clement Attlee, *As it Happened*, 1954.
Earl of Avon (Anthony Eden), *The Reckoning*, 1956.
J. Barnes and D. Nicholson (eds), *The Empire at Bay: the Leo Amery Diaries 1929–1945*, 1988.
Robert Boothby, *Boothby: Recollections of a Rebel*, 1978.
W. J. Brown, *So Far . . .* , 1943.
Lord Butler, *The Art of the Possible*, 1971.
Cassius (Michael Foot), *Brendan and Beverley: an Extravaganza*, 1944.
Cato (Michael Foot, Frank Owen and Philip Howard), *Guilty Men*, 1940.
Winston S. Churchill, *The Second World War*, Vol. I, *The Gathering Storm*, 1948.
——, Vol. II, *Their Finest Hour*, 1949.
——, Vol. IV, *The Hinge of Fate*, 1951.
John Colville, *The Fringes of Power: Downing Street Diaries 1939–1955*, 1985.
Duff Cooper, *Old Men Forget*, 1953.
C. Cross (ed.), *Life with Lloyd George: the Diary of A. J. Sylvester 1931–1945*, 1975.
A. S. Cunningham-Reid, *Besides Churchill — Who?*, 1942.
Hugh Dalton, *The Fateful Years: Memoirs 1931–1945*, 1957.
D. Dilks (ed.), *The Diaries of Sir Alexander Cadogan 1938–1945*, 1971.
Tom Driberg, *The Best of Both Worlds*, 1953.
Walter Elliot, *Long Distance*, 1943.

Paul Einzig, *In the Centre of Things*, 1960.
Viscount Findhorn (James Stuart), *Within the Fringe*, 1967.
James Griffiths, *Pages from Memory*, 1969.
Lord Hailsham, *The Door Wherein I Went*, 1975.
Tom Harrisson, 'Who'll win', *Political Quarterly*, XV, 1944.
G. S. Harvie-Watt, *Most of My Life*, 1980.
Lord Home (Alec Dunglass), *The Way the Wind Blows*, 1976.
K. Jefferys (ed.), *Labour and the Wartime Coalition: from the Diary of James Chuter Ede, 1941–1945*, 1987.
J. M. Keynes, *How to Pay for the War*, 1940 .
Oliver Lyttelton, *The Memoirs of Lord Chandos*, 1962.
Harold Macmillan, *The Blast of War 1939–1945*, 1967.
——, *Tides of Fortune 1945–1955*, 1979.
Ian Mikardo, *Back-Bencher*, 1988.
R. J. Minney, *The Private Papers of Hore-Belisha*, 1960.
Lord Moran, *Winston Churchill: the Struggle for Survival*, 1966.
J. H. Morris-Jones, *Doctor in the Whips' Room*, 1955.
Herbert Morrison, *An Autobiography*, 1960.
N. Nicolson (ed.), *Harold Nicolson: Diaries and Letters 1939–1945*, 1967.
John Parker, *Father of the House: Fifty Years in Politics*, 1982.
F. W. Pethick-Lawrence, *Fate Has Been Kind*, 1943.
Morgan Philips-Price, *My Three Revolutions*, 1969.
B. Pimlott (ed.), *The Second World War Diary of Hugh Dalton 1940–1945*, 1986.
—— (ed.), *The Political Diary of Hugh Dalton 1918–40, 1945–60*, 1986.
George Reakes, *Man of the Mersey*, 1956.
R. Rhodes James (ed.), *Chips: the Diaries of Sir Henry Channon*, 1967.
Emanuel Shinwell, *Conflict Without Malice*, 1955.
——, *I've Lived Through It All*, 1973.
A. J. P. Taylor (ed.), *Lloyd George: a Diary by Frances Stevenson*, 1971.
—— (ed.), *Off the Record: W. P. Crozier: Political Interviews 1933–1943*, 1973.
Viscount Templewood (Samuel Hoare), *Nine Troubled Years*, 1954.
F. Williams, *A Prime Minister Remembers*, 1961.
Earl Winterton, *Orders of the Day*, 1953.
Lord Woolton, *The Memoirs of the Rt. Hon. the Earl of Woolton*, 1959.

Biographies

Earl of Birkenhead, *Halifax: the Life of Lord Halifax*, 1965.
A. Bullock, *The Life and Times of Ernest Bevin*, Vol. II, *Minister of Labour 1940–1945*, 1967.
J. Campbell, *Nye Bevan and the Mirage of Socialism*, 1987.
D. Carlton, *Antony Eden: a Biography*, 1981.
J. Charmley, *Duff Cooper: the Authorised Biography*, 1986.
C. Cooke, *The Life of Richard Stafford Cripps*, 1957.

B. Donoughue and G. W. Jones, *Herbert Morrison: Portrait of a Politician*, 1973.
K. Feiling, *The Life of Neville Chamberlain*, 1947.
M. Foot, *Aneurin Bevan*, Vol. I, *1897–1945*, 1962.
M. Gilbert, *Winston S. Churchill*, Vol. VI, *Finest Hour 1939–1941*, 1983.
——, Vol. VII, *Road to Victory 1941–1945*, 1986.
——, Vol. VIII, *Never Despair 1945–1965*, 1988.
J. Harris, *William Beveridge*, Oxford, 1977.
K. Harris, *Attlee*, 1982.
A. Howard, *RAB: the Life of R. A. Butler*, 1987.
C. E. Lysaght, *Brendan Bracken*, 1979.
H. Pelling, *Winston Churchill*, 1974.
B. Pimlott, *Hugh Dalton*, 1985.
R. Rhodes James (ed.), *Victor Cazalet: a Portrait*, 1976.
——, *Antony Eden*, 1986.
S. Roskill, *Hankey: Man of Secrets*, Vol. III, *1939–1963*, 1974.
Mary Soames, *Clementine Churchill*, 1979.
A. J. P. Taylor, *Beverbrook*, 1972.
J. W. Wheeler-Bennett, *John Anderson, Viscount Waverley*, 1962.

Other secondary works

P. Addison, 'Lloyd George and compromise peace in the Second World War', in A. J. P. Taylor (ed.), *Lloyd George: Twelve Essays*, 1971.
——, 'By-elections of the Second World War', in C. Cook and J. Ramsden (eds), *By-Elections in British Politics*, 1973.
——, *The Road to 1945: British Politics and the Second World War*, 1975.
——, 'The road from 1945', in A. Seldon and P. Hennessy (eds), *Ruling Performance: British Governments from Attlee to Thatcher*, 1987.
H. Agar, *Britain Alone: June 1940–June 1941*, 1972.
R. S. Barker, *Education and Politics 1900–1951: a Study of the Labour Party*, Oxford, 1972.
C. Barnett, *The Audit of War: the Illusion and Reality of Britain as a Great Nation*, 1986.
T. D. Burridge, *British Labour and Hitler's War*, 1976.
Lord Butler (ed.), *The Conservatives*, 1977.
A. Cairncross and N. Watts, *The Economic Section 1939–1961*, 1989.
A. Calder, *The People's War: Britain 1939–45*, 1969.
J. Charmley, *Chamberlain and the Lost Peace*, 1989.
D. N. Chester (ed.), *Lessons of the British War Economy*, Cambridge, 1951.
R. B. Cockett, *Twilight of Truth: Chamberlain, Appeasement and the Manipulation of the Press*, 1989.
W. H. B. Court, *Coal* (Official History of Second World War), 1951.
M. Cowling, *The Impact of Hitler: British Politics and British Policy 1933–1940*, Cambridge, 1975.
A. Deacon and J. Bradshaw, *Reserved for the Poor*, 1983.

D. Dilks, 'The twilight war and the fall of France: Chamberlain and Churchill in 1940', in D. Dilks (ed.), *Retreat from Power*, Vol. II, *After 1939*, 1981.

P. Goodhart, *The 1922: the Story of the Conservative Backbenchers' Parliamentary Committee*, 1973.

P. H. J. H. Gosden, *Education in the Second World War: a Study in Policy and Administration*, 1976.

R. J. Hammond, *Food*, Vol. I, *The Growth of Policy* (Official History), 1951.

W. G. Hancock and M. Gowing, *British War Economy* (Official History), 1957.

E. L. Hargreaves and M. Gowing, *Civil Industry and Trade* (Official History), 1957.

J. Harris, 'Social planning in war-time: some aspects of the Beveridge Report', in J. Winter (ed.), *War and Economic Development*, Cambridge, 1975.

——, 'Some aspects of social policy in Britain during the Second World War', in W. J. Mommsen (ed.), *The Emergence of the Welfare State in Britain and Germany*, 1981.

——, 'Political ideas and the debate on State welfare', in H. L. Smith (ed.), *War and Social Change: British Society in the Second World War*, Manchester, 1986.

D. Howell, *British Social Democracy*, 1976.

D. Kavanagh and P. Morris, *Consensus Politics from Attlee to Thatcher*, Oxford, 1989.

J. M. Lee, *The Churchill Coalition 1940–1945*, 1980.

P. Lewis, *A People's War*, 1986.

R. B. McCallum and A. Readman, *The British General Election of 1945*, 1947.

I. MacLaine, *Ministry of Morale: Home Front Propaganda and the Ministry of Information in World War Two*, 1979.

J. MacNicol, *The Movement of Family Allowances 1918–1945*, 1980.

D. Marquand, *The Unprincipled Society: New Demands and Old Politics*, 1988.

K. Middlemas, *Power, Competition and the State*, Vol. I., *Britain in Search of Balance, 1940–1961*, 1986.

R. J. Moore, *Churchill, Cripps, and India, 1939–1945*, Oxford, 1979.

K. O. Morgan, *Labour in Power 1945–1951*, Oxford, 1984.

H. M. D. Parker, *Manpower: a Study in War-Time Policy and Administration* (Official History), 1957.

H. Pelling, *Britain and the Second World War*, 1970.

B. Pimlott, *Labour and the Left in the 1930s*, Cambridge, 1977.

——, 'The myth of consensus', in L. M. Smith (ed.), *The Making of Britain: Echoes of Greatness*, 1988.

J. A. Ramsden, *The Age of Balfour and Baldwin 1902–1940*, 1978.

D. Reynolds, 'Churchill and the British "decision" to fight on in 1940: right policy, wrong reasons', in R. Langhorne (ed.), *Diplomacy and*

Intelligence during the Second World War: Essays in Honour of F. H. Hinsley, Cambridge, 1985.

A. J. Robertson, 'Lord Beaverbrook and the supply of aircraft, 1940–1941', in A. Slaven and D. H. Aldcroft (eds), *Business, Banking and Urban History: Essays in Honour of S. G. Checkland*, Edinburgh, 1982.

R. S. Sayers, *Financial Policy, 1939–1945* (Official History), 1956.

——, '1941 — the first Keynesian budget', in C. Feinstein (ed.), *The Managed Economy: Essays in British Economic Policy and Performance Since 1929*, Oxford, 1983.

J. Schneer, 'The Labour left and the general election of 1945', in J. M. W. Bean (ed.), *The Political Culture of Modern Britain*, 1987.

G. M. Thomson, *Vote of Censure*, 1968.

C. Webster, *The Health Services Since the War*, Vol. I, *Problems of Health Care: the National Service before 1957* (Official History), 1988.

Journal articles

C. Barnett *et al.*, 'The wartime roots of Britain's industrial decline', *Contemporary Record*, I, 2, 1987.

A. Booth, 'The "Keynesian Revolution" in economic policy-making', *Economic History Review*, XXXVI, 1, 1983.

——, 'Economic advice at the centre of British government, 1939–1941', *The Historical Journal*, XXIX, 3, 1986.

——, 'Britain in the 1930s: a managed economy', *Economic History Review*, XL, 4, 1987.

S. Brooke, 'Revisionists and fundamentalists: the Labour party and economic policy during the Second World War', *The Historical Journal*, XXXII, 1, 1989.

D. W. Dean, 'Problems of the Conservative sub-committee on education', *Journal of Educational Administration and History*, III, 1, 1970.

C. Harvie, 'Labour in Scotland during the Second World War', *The Historical Journal*, XXVI, 4, 1983.

M. Harrison, 'Resource mobilisation for world war II: the U.S.A., U.K., U.S.S.R., and Germany, 1939–1945, *Economic History Review*, XLI, 2, 1988.

K. Jefferys, 'R. A. Butler, the Board of Education and the 1944 Education Act', *History*, LXIX, 227, 1984.

——, 'British politics and social policy during the Second World War', *The Historical Journal*, XXX, 1, 1987.

G. C. Peden, 'Sir Richard Hopkins and the "Keynesian Revolution" in employment policy 1929–45', *Economic History Review*, XXXVI, 2, 1983.

H. Pelling, 'The 1945 general election reconsidered', *The Historical Journal*, XXIII, 2, 1980.

J. S. Rasmussen, 'Party discipline in war-time: the downfall of the Chamberlain government', *Journal of Politics*, XXXII, 1970.

D. M. Roberts, 'Clement Davies and the fall of Neville Chamberlain, 1939–40', *Welsh History Review*, VIII, 2, 1976.
N. Rollings, 'British budgetary policy 1945–54: a "Keynesian revolution"?', *Economic History Review*, XL, 4, 1987.

Unpublished theses

P. Addison, 'Political change in Britain, September 1939 to December 1940', D.Phil., University of Oxford, 1971.
S. Brooke, 'Labour's war: party, coalition and domestic reconstruction 1939–45', D.Phil., University of Oxford, 1988.
A. Calder, 'The Common Wealth party 1942–1945', D.Phil. University of Sussex, 1967.
R. B. Cockett, 'The government, the press and politics in Britain 1937 to 1945', Ph.D., University of London, 1988.
R. J. Earwicker, 'The labour movement and the creation of the National Health Service 1906–1948', Ph.D., University of Birmingham, 1984.
R. Hastings, 'The labour movement in Birmingham 1927–45', M.A., University of Birmingham, 1959.
M. Kemp, 'The left and the debate over Labour party policy, 1943–50', Ph.D., University of Cambridge, 1985.
H. Kopsch, 'The approach of the Conservative party to social policy during World War Two', Ph.D., University of London, 1970.
R. MacLeod, 'The development of full employment policy 1938–1945', D.Phil., University of Oxford, 1978.
D. Ritschel, 'Non-socialist planning in the interwar period', D.Phil., University of Oxford, 1987.
I. H. Taylor, 'War and the development of Labour's domestic programme, 1939–45, Ph.D., University of London, 1978.

Recent publications

Since *The Churchill Coalition* was first published in 1991, several additions have been made to historiographical debates about wartime politics in Britain.

The two most important that relate to the consensus theme are: Stephen Brooke's D.Phil thesis, cited in the epilogue, published as *Labour's War: the Labour Party during the Second World War*, Oxford, 1992; and Paul Addison's revised edition of *The Road to 1945*, London, 1994.

On other aspects of the war years, Sheila Lawlor has re-examined the early months of the coalition in *Churchill and the Politics of War, 1940–1941*, Cambridge, 1994.

Fifty years on from the Labour triumph of 1945, attention has turned increasingly to the 'swing to the left' in public opinion. G. H. Bennett has analysed the best known wartime by-election in 'The wartime political truce and hopes for post-war coalition: the West Derbyshire by-election, 1944', *Midland History*, 17, 1992.

A revisionist perspective on the 1945 election, claiming that Labour's victory owed less to socialist idealism than usually claimed, has been developed in: Tony Mason and Peter Thompson, '"Reflections on a Revolution"? The political mood in wartime Britain', in Nick Tiratsoo (ed.), *The Attlee Years*, London, 1991; and Steven Fielding, 'What did "the people" want? The meaning of the 1945 general election', *The Historical Journal*, 35, 3, 1992. The same line of interpretation is found in the broader context of politics throughout the 1940s in *England Arise*, Manchester, 1995, by Steven Fielding, Peter Thompson and Nick Tiratsoo.

For two recent overviews of the period, see Brian Brivati and Harriet Jones (eds), *What Difference did the War Make?*, Leicester 1993, and Kevin Jefferys (ed.), *War and Reform: British Politics during the Second World War*, Manchester, 1994. The latter is part of the MUP series, 'Documents in Contemporary History', and contains a collection of documentary extracts taken from wartime newspapers, diaries, letters, memoirs and official government papers.

Index